Trevor Royle lives and works in Edinburgh. He is a regular contributor to the *Glasgow Herald* and the BBC World Service; his plays have been broadcast on BBC Radios 3 and 4 and he is the editor of the literary magazine, *Lines Review*. Amongst his recent publications are two highly praised military histories, *The Kitchener Enigma* and *The Best Years of Their Lives*, a social history of post-war National Service.

By the same author

The Kitchener Enigma
The Best Years of Their Lives

TREVOR ROYLE

War Report

The War Correspondent's View of Battle
from the Crimea to the Falklands

GRAFTON BOOKS

A Division of the Collins Publishing Group

LONDON GLASGOW
TORONTO SYDNEY AUCKLAND

Grafton Books
A Division of the Collins Publishing Group
8 Grafton Street, London W1X 3LA

Published by Grafton Books 1989

First published in Great Britain by
Mainstream Publishing 1987

Copyright © Trevor Royle 1987

ISBN 0-586-20290-0

Printed and bound in Great Britain by
Collins, Glasgow

Set in Baskerville

Contents

	Preface	7
1	The Newly Invented Curse to Armies	9
2	George Warrington Steevens and the Sudan	40
3	Edgar Wallace and The Great Boer War	78
4	Charles à Court Repington and the First World War	109
5	Claud Cockburn and the Spanish Civil War	145
6	Chester Wilmot and the Second World War	178
7	James Cameron and the Korean War	220
8	The Savage Wars of Peace	250
	Notes	288
	Select Bibliography	292
	Index	296

Preface

This is not a history of war reporting; rather it is a study of six leading war correspondents put into the context of modern war. All were different in their approach to their task, yet all faced similar problems: they covered wars which were fought far away from their home base, they had to deal with the vagaries of editorial control and they all had to face the uncertainties of military or political censorship. All of them, too, wrote books about their experiences, thereby making substantial contributions to the history of war literature. With the exception of Colonel Repington of *The Times*, all were front-line reporters, that is, war correspondents who accompanied British armies into combat and who then wrote first-hand accounts of battle. Repington was a military correspondent, a desk-bound commentator whose forte was analysis, but I have included him because his account of the Shells Crisis of 1915 was initiated during a visit to the front line.

I owe several debts of gratitude to those who have helped me to prepare this book. Mrs Patricia Cockburn kindly read the chapter on Claud Cockburn and the Spanish Civil War and made a number of helpful corrections and observations. The chapter on Chester Wilmot and the Second World War could not have been written but for the generous help given to me by Mrs Edith Wilmot, who not only made me an extended loan of her husband's papers but also commented on my findings. The chapter on James Cameron and the Korean War was read by the doyen of British journalists, Sir Tom Hopkinson, and Tony Carter of Thames Television added a number of suggestions about the Korean War. They all have my thanks.

I acknowledge with thanks permission to include in this volume quotations from: Claud Cockburn, *Cockburn Sums Up* (Quartet Books, London, 1981); Michael Herr, *Dispatches* (Pan Books), Copyright © Michael Herr, 1968, 1969, 1970, 1979; Phillip Knightley, *The First Casualty* (André Deutsch, 1975); Eric Linklater, *Our Men in Korea* (HMSO), 1952); George Orwell, 'Looking Back on the Spanish Civil War', (The Estate of the Late Sonia Brownwell Orwell and Secker and Warburg Ltd); Chester Wilmot, contributions to *War Report* (Reproduced from *War Report, D-Day to VE Day*, edited by Desmond Hawkins with the permission of BBC Enterprises Ltd). For any errors or omissions, I naturally and formally apologize.

I should like to thank the following for permission to reproduce illustrations: BBC Hulton Picture Library (1, 3, 4, 5, 8, 9, 10); The City of London School (2); Imperial War Museum (6, 11, 13); *Irish Times* (7).

1

The Newly Invented Curse to Armies

War has always exercised a hold on man's imagination and yet, until fairly recent times, it tended to be regarded as a distant and glorious affair conducted by small numbers of heroic men in faraway places. Once the fighting had come to a stop the battles could be romanticized and the soldiers immortalized as heroes. War was also a significant area of human development, difficult to ignore, and from the beginnings of recorded history writers have been fascinated by the exploits of men in armed combat. The Athenian historian Thucydides left a brilliant narrative of the disastrous war which Athens waged against Sparta; a serving soldier himself, he used his experience of battle together with eye-witness accounts to fashion compelling descriptions of war which have retained their freshness and originality many centuries later. Like his fellow historian Herodotus, who flourished earlier in the 5th century B.C., Thucydides understood the importance of collecting first-hand accounts, testing them for accuracy as far as was possible, and then arranging them into an agreeable narrative. Although pure historians have questioned his methods, Thucydides did at least face up to the problem of using contemporary reports, based largely on oral accounts, and of placing them in an historical perspective.

From the very beginning, then, literature has wanted to be in on the action, for war has not only been a fascinating subject, it has been – and remains – a popular one. In the preface to his translation of Homer's *Iliad* in 1715, Alexander Pope expressed the fancy that his readers would be

interested as much by the violent imagery as by the poetry
itself.

Nothing is so surprising as the description of Homer's battles,
which take up no less than half the *Iliad*, and are supplied with so
vast a variety of incidents that no one bears a likeness to another;
such different kinds of deaths, that no two heroes are wounded in
the same manner; and such a profusion of noble ideas, that every
battle rises above the last in greatness, horror and confusion.

On that level it is Homer's ability to describe violent death
in gory detail that interested Pope; certainly his own
translation, however loose it might be, did not attempt to
avoid the horrors of warfare and the bloody results of close-
quarter combat.

> Next Erymas was doomed his fate to feel:
> His opened mouth received the Cretan steel;
> Beneath the brain the point a passage tore,
> Crashed the thin bones, and drowned the teeth in gore.
> His mouth, his eyes, his nostrils, pour a flood;
> He sobs his soul out in the gush of blood.
> (XVI, 414–419)

Homer was writing within a tradition which regarded
warfare and killing as heroic activities: the hero was praised
for organizing death and destruction and combat was seen
as an essential component of organized society. Early poets,
or bards, were employed to record the exploits of the
winning side in a battle and many of the best lines in
Anglo-Saxon poetry are those concerned with descriptions
of fighting. Even when the result was hardly glorious, as in
The Battle of Maldon, the poet could moralize the causes of
defeat and pour scorn on those who failed to live up to the
ideal of the true warrior. Although the poem is concerned
more with the ancient Germanic heroic code, it also pro-

vides a dramatic account of the battle which took place at the River Blackwater (Pant) in Essex on 10 August 991 when an invading Danish army was opposed by Byrhtnoth, ealdorman of Essex. The audience would be familiar with the facts of the battle and would respond to the powerful statement of fidelity and determination shown by Byrhtnoth's supporters in their attempts to avenge his death.

In the Anglo-Saxon and Celtic traditions the heroic ideal of the reckless warrior became an important myth, capable of sustaining the leadership of the nation and its army – the Old English word *folc* means both, the idea being interchangeable in early times. The poets who were paid to write about the fighting prowess of their chiefs also saw battle and were able to bring to their accounts the kind of first-hand description demanded by their audiences. For those people war and free-booting were a natural mode of life, and the accounts of the heroic activities of the warrior caste were expressed in straightforward and functional stories which were passed on from one generation to the next. Thus the account of a battle created by the poet who had witnessed it would be kept alive in the collective consciousness of the clan or tribe and its freshness would not be lost by countless retellings.

In Gaelic Scotland the tradition survived into relatively modern times; for example, the poet Iain Lom's description of the Battle of Inverlochy, fought between the Clan Campbell and Montrose's Highland and Irish forces, on 2 February 1645, has all the economy and vigour of a piece of journalism.

> Alasdair of sharp, biting blades,
> if you had the heroes of Mull with you,
> you would have stopped those who got away,
> as the dulse-eating rabble took to their heels.

Alasdair, son of handsome Colla,
skilled hand at cleaving castles,
you put to flight the Lowland pale-face:
what kale they had taken came out again.

You remember the place called the Tawny Field?
It got a fine dose of manure;
not the dung of sheep or goats,
but Campbell blood well congealed.

Iain Lom was present at the battle, fighting in Montrose's
army, and his narrative is contained in a carefully phrased
long poem written with skill and learning. Elsewhere in the
poem Iain Lom, a fierce Royalist, takes the opportunity to
exult over the defeat of the hated Clan Campbell and to
indulge in some pro-Royalist boasting, but it is the sharp
imagery of his descriptions of battle and his controlled use
of language that give this piece of war literature its edge.
His directness of utterance, his urgency of expression and
his pointed comments on the cut and thrust of battle are all
necessary ingredients in any successful account of warfare.

The advent of modern weapons of war from the 15th
century onwards helped to make war less heroic and more
mechanical, reducing armed combat to an impersonal,
almost clinical, activity. Where there was honour in sword-
play, ran the argument of those who recorded war, there
was only horror and degradation in the bullet and the
cannon-ball. The new technology of warfare also helped to
change the face of war literature. Some writers reacted to
the new conditions with awe and presented realistic pictures of the violence of modern combat – into this category
falls Samuel Daniel's *The Civil Wars between the two Houses of
York and Lancaster* (1609) with its realistic description of
'artillerie, th' infernall instrument, new-brought from hell'.
Daniel was appalled by this modern engine of war and his

readers were doubtless as astonished by his descriptions of artillery fire as recent generations have been by photographs of nuclear explosions. Other 17th-century writers, like Samuel Butler, John Donne and John Milton, attacked the heroic tradition of personal combat but were also prepared to admit that war could be a necessary evil. Their belief that war was not a noble activity but a means to an end connects them to later thinking on the nature of warfare. From their time onwards war literature has become conspicuous by its subject matter and tone, exercising as peculiar a fascination on the consciousness as war itself.

For many people who have never come into contact with the battlefield, war literature has become one of their principal means of gauging the reality of armed combat. Men who fought in the First World War have admitted that many of their ideas of service and patriotism were furnished by writers like G. A. Henty and Rudyard Kipling. Poems as different in appeal as Tennyson's *Charge of the Light Brigade*, Newbolt's *Vitae Lampada* or Brooke's *Peace* have also helped to stiffen the backbones of men facing enemy fire for the first time in their lives. Even hideously graphic descriptions of battle and violent death find a place in the mythology of war and many soldiers have found them to be a helpful exorcism. Siegfried Sassoon's *Memoirs of an Infantry Officer* contains frightening descriptions of trench warfare; V. M. Yeates's *Winged Victory* is a grim account of the lot facing bomber pilots during the First World War; both leave the reader in little doubt that war is a hellish business, yet both are popular books, classics of their kind. Partly, their success can be traced to the vicarious interest man has always taken in war, partly too, they are well written and highly charged accounts; but, above all, they provide the reader with a credible image of what it is like to be at the sharp end of battle.

In recent times the photographer and the war artist have fulfilled a similar function. Traditionally, the war artist's painting could only be an illusory representation of battle, sanitized by time and distance – one thinks in this respect of Stanley Berkeley's evocative, though highly stylized, painting of the charge of the 21st Lancers at Omdurman, all carefully posed horses and elegantly butchered men. To the soldier, who witnessed battles subsequently immortalized in paintings, the artist's vision was often at odds with history. Was it really possible for the charging horses to have been so carefully orchestrated? Did men cut down by the Dervishes die so cleanly? Obviously in most cases the artist had to put his creative instincts before the demands of historical accuracy, a colourful and heroic picture being considered more admirable than the reality of smoke, screams and broken bodies.

Although photographs brought a new immediacy to the art of reporting battles, even this new means of communication created fresh problems. Photographs of heroic action or of stubborn resistance were one thing but pictures of the hideously maimed dead were quite another. Many photographs taken during the First World War, for example, were not published at the time for the good reason that they might have discouraged young men from volunteering for service in the armed forces. The photographers, too, tended to focus on dramatic events rather than on the detritus of battle, with the result that however hideous might be the subject matter, there is a terrible beauty in the final result. Robert Capa's famous photograph of the death of a Republican soldier is a realistic depiction of that moment when a bullet sunders the life of a human being, yet it is also rightly regarded as a work of supreme artistry captured under difficult conditions.* ('If your picture wasn't any good, you're not standing close enough,' Capa would claim. He also covered the Second World War and was killed in action during the war in Indo-China.) Similarly, the photograph of the frigate HMS *Antelope* exploding in San Carlos Water during the Falklands campaign of 1982 provided evidence of the efficacy of modern high explosives but there is, too, a beautiful symmetry to the explosion which helps to distance the viewer from the event itself. Photographs like that bring a dramatic intensity to our understanding of war, but, being vignettes, they can never tell the whole story. That can only come from the detached reporter at the seat of war, from the newspaper writers who came to be known as war correspondents.

The first known newspaper or newsletter to appear in English was a single-sheet publication known as the *Corrant out of Italy, Germany &c* which was printed in Amsterdam in 1620; the first English journal containing home news, *The Heads of Severall Proceedings In this Present Parliament*, did not appear until November 1641. It was followed by a proliferation of newspapers, broadsheets and journals which fed the public demand for news during the Royalist and parliamentary civil war of 1642–1649. By 1645, 14 newspapers were on sale in London. Four years later a printing law silenced all but two officially recognized publications, the *Mercurius Politicus* and *The Publick Intelligencer*, but by then the age of the modern newspaper had been ushered in with its reliance on features, political argument, reports

* *Life* magazine published the photograph on 12 July 1937 with the caption: 'Robert Capa's camera catches a Spanish soldier the instant he is dropped by a bullet through the head in front of Cordoba.' It has been established for some time now that Capa's photograph was of a soldier stumbling while training; nevertheless, this knowledge does not lessen the impact which the photograph made at the time.

from other parts of the country and human-interest stories.
(In Scotland the earliest recorded newspaper was the
Mercurius Scoticus of 1651.)

From the very outset the men who ran those early
publications had to be a phlegmatic breed. Marchamont
Nedham, the editor of *Mercurius Politicus*, had to flee to
Holland in 1660, having offended political opinion in
England, and his place was taken by Henry Muddiman
who went on to found the first real English newspaper as
we know it today, *The Oxford Gazette*. It was first published
in November 1665, the court then being at Oxford; a year
later it became the *London Gazette* and survives to this day
as a record of official appointments under the direction of
Her Majesty's Stationery Office. In an attempt to curb the
powers of men like Nedham and to encourage editors of
Muddiman's ideas, the new newspapers were subjected by
successive governments to a variety of restrictions. There
was a tax on paper, thus limiting most 18th-century
newspapers to four pages; a tax on advertisements, rapidly
emerging as a major source of income; and a Stamp Duty
which was not repealed until 1855. Nevertheless, by the
reign of Queen Ann and throughout the century the
newspapers continued to establish themselves as a powerful
means of mass communication. Much of the news might
have been 'meagre tidings of what had happened long
before, or never happened at all', but the very existence of
these early newspapers fed a hunger for news. Much was
copied from the foreign press or pirated from rivals and a
vogue grew for publishing travellers' letters. Advances in
technology also changed the face of the newspapers themselves: mechanical typesetting in 1838, the rotary press in
1846, photolithography in 1852, half-tone illustrations in
1871, the Linotype keyboard in 1884. By the mid-19th

century most London newspapers had steam presses and the age of mass circulation had begun.

By then, too, the first war correspondents – or 'specials' as they were known – had appeared on the scene. The man to claim the honour of being the first-ever war correspondent was a barrister called Henry Crabb Robinson who wrote for *The Times*, founded in 1785. A friend of the English poets Wordsworth, Coleridge, Hazlitt and Lamb, Robinson was also a German scholar and it was this latter interest which persuaded John Walter, the newspaper's proprietor, to send him to Germany in 1807 to cover Napoleon's campaign along the River Elbe.

Robinson's first report 'from the seat of war' came from Napoleon's victory over the Russians at the Battle of Friedland but he hardly proved himself to be an industrious journalist. His despatch took several weeks to reach London and he did not trouble himself to visit the scene of the battle, preferring instead to rely on information picked up in Altona near Hamburg where he was staying. Nevertheless, the novelty of providing news from a faraway war persuaded Walter to send Robinson to Europe again in the following year to record the arrival of Sir David Baird's troops sent to reinforce Sir John Moore's army at Corunna. Robinson duly reported the ensuing battle for *The Times* but once more he stayed away from the scene, content to use the accounts published in the local newspapers. His last despatch did not mention either the British victory or the death of Moore. Robinson was not asked to write any further despatches and he returned to London to lead a successful life as a man of letters and critic, dying in 1867 at the age of 92. Curiously, this first British war correspondent was distantly related to Lord Kitchener, who kept up a life-long hostility to the presence of journalists on the

battlefield: Robinson's brother Habbakuk married Elizabeth Kitchener, the future field marshal's great-aunt.

Kitchener was neither the first nor the last soldier to
bemoan the appearance of the war correspondent. *The
Times*'s experiment of appointing a writer to cover the
conflict in Europe had been copied by other publications
with the result that it did not take long for senior army
officers to question the presence of civilian correspondents
accompanying their men on the line of march. From the
very beginning there were strained relations between the
newspapermen and the military – witness this letter written
by Sir Arthur Wellesley, the army's commander in Spain,
to Lord Liverpool, the government's Secretary for War.

I beg to draw your Lordship's attention to the frequent paragraphs in the English Newspapers, describing the position, the
numbers, the objects, the means of attaining them possessed by
the armies in Spain and Portugal. In some instances the English
Newspapers have accurately stated, not only the regiments occu-
pying a position, but the number of men fit for duty of which each
regiment was composed; and this intelligence must have reached
the enemy at the same time as it did me, at a moment at which it
was most important that he should not receive it.

Quite how the information was helping the enemy in
France was unclear for all news took several days to reach
London by ship and coach, but Wellesley's admonition set
the seal on the problem which all future war correspondents
would have to face. As a privileged civilian the war
correspondent is in a position to watch the army at work
without having to do any of that work himself. Even in
battle, when the soldier and the reporter share many of the
same dangers and discomforts, that closeness is not a
guarantee of mutual sympathy. The soldier, after all, is a
professional, bound by his duty and loyalty to obey orders

and to take risks; the war correspondent is a spectator compelled to remain on the battlefield only to get a good story. To the army this can often look like a war correspondent cashing in on the soldier's experience; to the newspaper proprietor or editor that is precisely the reason for the correspondent's presence. This clash of interests leads to a further problem: in the army's eyes the information gleaned by the correspondent and then published in his newspaper can appear to be a threat to security. In that case the war correspondent not only seems to be writing voyeuristically about dangers suffered by others, in certain circumstances he could be regarded as adding to them.

Military censorship was not to be introduced until later in the 19th century but the dilemma of whether to withhold strategically important facts or to report them in the national interest existed from the very beginning. On the one hand military leaders were used to conducting their wars in foreign countries far from the gaze of the inquisitive British public: they regarded war correspondents as an unnecessary imposition and as a possible threat to security. On the other hand newspaper owners, encouraged by changes in production technology, new means of distribution and improvements in communication, knew that war reports helped to sell their products: they wanted their correspondents to gather in the latest and most controversial or exciting stories 'from the seat of war'. If these circumvented official obstructions, then so much the better.

The problem came into focus in 1854 when Britain went to war against Russia in the Crimea, the first European war the country had fought in nearly 40 years. By then, war correspondents had established themselves as a necessary adjunct to any military campaign and most of the intervening conflicts in Europe had been covered by the London press. Charles Lewis Guneison of the *Morning Post*

occupies an important place in the history of war reporting
for his front-line reports from the Spanish Civil War of
1835–1837: so comprehensive and up-to-date were his
despatches that when he was taken prisoner he faced
execution as a Carlist spy and only the intervention of Lord
Palmerston saved him from the firing squad. He claimed to
be the first real war correspondent in that he actually
reported from the scene of battle, whereas Robinson relied
on the accounts of others; but the father of the modern war
correspondent was William Howard Russell who covered
the Crimean War for *The Times*.

At the time of the war in the Crimea modern technology
was beginning to catch up with journalism; in particular,
the invention of the electric telegraph in the 1840s spelled
the end of the leisurely written despatch and introduced a
new urgency to news gathering. To facilitate communication between the battlefront and the British and French
capitals a telegraph line had been extended to Varna in
Bulgaria: at a stroke news of war was only hours away from
the newspaper readers of Europe. Its introduction also
meant that the most successful war correspondent was the
man who had not only uncovered the best stories but who
was then able to transmit them fastest back to home base.
Russell never accustomed himself to using the telegraph,
being unwilling to commit his stories to instant communication with London before he had time to check his facts.
'I cannot describe to you the paralysing effect of sitting
down to write a letter after you have sent off the bones of it
by lightning,' he once complained to John Thadeus Delane,
the editor of *The Times*. That reluctance did not interfere
with his sense of professionalism, though, and he used the
telegraph to good effect in September 1855 when he was
the first to report the long-awaited fall of Sevastopol after
its year-long siege.

Russell fell into journalism almost by accident. He was born on 28 March 1820 in Lily Vale, County Dublin, and was educated at Trinity College, Dublin, with the ambition of being called to the bar. Fate intervened in 1841 when a cousin, John Russell, arrived in Ireland to cover the elections for *The Times* and, finding himself overstretched, engaged his young relative to assist him. Knowing not a little about the impassioned and frequently violent nature of Irish electioneering, William Howard Russell made a good fist of the job and as a result he was asked by Delane to join his staff in the Press Gallery of the House of Commons in London. It was a good offer. *The Times* had outdistanced its rivals both in its circulation and in its editorial content; it sold twice as many copies a day as its competitors and it prided itself on the accuracy of its news coverage. More importantly, perhaps, it had at its helm a shrewd and capable editor in Delane. As his new boss had made it clear that working for *The Times* was akin to enjoying the membership of an exclusive club whose prestige outweighed any shortcomings in pay, Russell wisely kept up his legal studies while working as a part-time journalist. (The Lobby correspondents only worked while Parliament was in session.) In 1846 he married and, finding his income to be insufficient, switched his allegiance to the *Morning Chronicle*, an ill-judged move because the newspaper fell into financial difficulties a year later. Delane then persuaded Russell to return to *The Times* and for the next 20 or so years he was to be a regular contributor to its pages. In all, Russell was to cover five major campaigns for *The Times* and the *Daily Telegraph*, in so doing winning five campaign medals; and he was knighted for his services to journalism in 1895, 12 years before his death on 10 February 1907.

When Delane suggested to Russell that he accompany

the British Army to the Crimea in 1854 the prospect seemed
rosy enough. A very agreeable excursion with handsome
pay and allowances was how it was put to him in the
editor's office. In the event Russell was to remain in the
Crimea for the duration of the war – apart from one short
break – and by the time he had returned to London in 1856
he had secured himself a place in history. Not only had he
reported all the major battles with a clarity and accuracy
which brought the war into the homes of the British upper
classes, but his frank revelations of military incompetence
changed the face of the war and brought about radical
changes in the army's attitudes towards the treatment of
the men.

Russell gave early notice of his intentions in one of his
first despatches to Delane, describing the chaos which
awaited the British troops at their first stopping-off point in
Gallipoli.

The men suffered exceedingly from cold. Some of them, officers
and privates, had no beds to lie upon. None of the soldiers had
more than their single regulation blanket. They therefore reversed
the order of things and dressed to go to bed, putting on all their
spare clothing before they tried to sleep. The worst thing was the
continued want of comforts for the sick. Many of the men
labouring under diseases contracted at Malta were obliged to stay
in camp in the cold, with only one blanket under them, as there
was no provision for them at the temporary hospital.[1]

He campaigned for changes to be made in the men's
uniform to allow for the change in climate – hot in the
summer, bitterly cold in winter – and at home his strictures
were backed up by Delane. 'Continue as you have done, to
tell the truth, and as much of it as you can,' the editor told
his reporter, 'and leave such comment as may be dangerous
to us, who are out of danger.' As could be expected the

strength of feeling expressed in Russell's despatches did not win him many friends in the British high command. He was regarded with a good deal of contempt, as a mere parasite who got in the way and who contributed nothing to the war effort. Early in the campaign he was denied food and transport and it was only Delane's intervention which put Russell and his fellow correspondents on a regular footing in the British camp. (Russell was accompanied by Thomas Chenery, also of *The Times*, Nicholas Woods of the *Morning Herald* and J. A. Crowe of the *Illustrated London News*.)

Ostensibly the British were in the Crimea with their French and Turkish allies to prevent further Russian encroachment into central Europe and the near east but it was a task for which they were ill-equipped. The administration of the army had changed little since the time of the Napoleonic wars and the commander-in-chief, Lord Raglan, was an elderly administrator whose best years were behind him. From the very outset Russell was convinced that this mild-mannered man was the wrong choice of leader; while admitting his personal courage and his dignified bearing, Russell questioned whether this 'brave and gallant gentleman ever possessed the ability to conceive and execute large military plans'.

Following a fitful summer spent in Bulgaria the allies moved to the Crimea in September 1854. The move made little sense as the Turks had already cleared the Russians from their borders and the allies' immediate strategy of capturing the Crimean peninsula and its huge fortress of Sevastopol was highly questionable. To begin with, though, things went tolerably well. The Russians were repulsed at the Battle of the River Alma, where the war could have been won had not Raglan given way to French indecision. Instead of following up their advantage, the allies dithered,

allowing the Russians to slip into Sevastopol and to bring
up reinforcements. Initially, the allies thought to sit tight
and besiege the fortress but the Russians' strength of
numbers and their own inability to complete the investment
involved them in two bloody battles which saw some of the
fiercest fighting of the campaign – Balaclava and Inkerman.
The battles were also famous for the stand of the 93rd
Highlanders who faced unflinchingly the Russian heavy
cavalry, and for the equally heroic, though melancholy,
charge of the Light Brigade against the Russian guns. Of
the Highlanders' action, which occurred in the early stages
of Balaclava, Russell had nothing but praise.

The heavy brigade in advance is drawn up in two lines. The first
line consists of the Scots Grays [sic] and their old companions in
glory, the Enniskillens [sic]; the second of the 4th Royal Irish, of the
5th Dragoon Guards, and of the 1st Royal Dragoons. The Light
Cavalry Brigade is on their left, in two lines also. The silence is
oppressive; between the cannon bursts one can hear the champing
of bits and the clink of sabres in the valley below. The Russians on
their left drew breath for a moment, and then in one grand line
dashed at the Highlanders. The ground flies beneath their horses'
feet; gathering speed at every stride, they dash on towards that thin
red streak topped with a line of steel. The Turks fire a volley at
800 yards, and run. The Russians come within 600 yards, down
goes that line of steel in front, and out rings a thundering volley
of Minié musketry. The distance is too great; the Russians are not
checked, but still sweep onwards with the whole force of horse
and man, through the smoke, here and there knocked over by the
shot of our batteries above. With breathless suspense every one
awaits the bursting of the wave upon the line of Gaelic rock; but
ere they come within 150 yards, another deadly volley flashes
from the levelled rifle, and carries death and terror into the
Russians. They wheel about, open files right and left, and fly back
faster than they came. 'Bravo, Highlanders! well done,' shout the
excited spectators; but events thicken. The Highlanders and their
splendid front are soon forgotten, men scarcely have a moment to
think of this fact, that the 93rd never altered their formation to

receive that tide of horsemen. 'No,' said Sir Colin Campbell, 'I did not think it worthwhile to form them even four deep!' The ordinary British line, two deep, was quite sufficient to repel the attack of these Muscovite cavaliers.

The 'thin red streak' emerged again as the more felicitous 'thin red line' in Tennyson's lines about the action and established itself as a cliché of Victorian jingoism, but Russell's newspaper reports were already beginning to make a different kind of impact on the public at home. For the first time the newspaper reader was being brought face to face with the reality of war and, as Russell made clear, stark facts did not always make the prettiest of pictures.

A shell came right among the staff – it exploded in Captain Somerset's horse, ripping him open; it then struck down Captain Gordon's horse and killed him at once, and then blew away General Strangways' leg, so that it hung by a shred of flesh and bit of cloth from the skin. The poor old General never moved a muscle of his face. He said merely in a gentle voice, 'Will anyone be kind enough to lift me off my horse?' He was taken down and laid on the ground, while his life-blood ebbed fast, and at last he was carried to the rear.

Strangways was in command of the Royal Artillery detachments at Inkerman and was riding beside Raglan when he received his fatal wound; after being told by a surgeon that his case was hopeless, the old general said simply, 'Then let me die among my gunners.' The Russian casualties at Inkerman were five times those suffered by the allies but it was an indecisive battle and with winter fast approaching the long siege of Sevastopol entered its most disagreeable stage. With storms and blizzards raging round them, the British and French forces prepared to face up to a dreadful winter, woefully ill-equipped, lacking proper quarters and clothes, short of food and without the most elementary

medical facilities. Cholera, dysentery and malaria added to
the miseries of the cold and starving troops. Of the 56,000-
strong Anglo-French army which wintered in the Crimea in
1854–1855, nearly 14,000 spent time in hospital where they
languished in conditions of unimaginable horror. Russell
was by then in no mood to keep this information to himself.

Hundreds of men had to go into the trenches at night with no
covering but their greatcoats, and no protection for their feet but
their regimental shoes. The trenches were two and three feet deep
with mud, snow and half-frozen slush.

As to the town itself [Balaclava], words could not describe its
filth, its horrors, its hospitals, its burials, its dead and dying
Turks, its crowded lanes, its noisome sheds, its beastly purlieus,
or its decay. The dead, laid out as they died, were lying side by
side with the living, and the latter presented a spectacle beyond
all imagination. The commonest accessories of a hospital were
wanting; there was not the least attention paid to decency or
cleanliness – the stench was appalling – the foetid air could barely
struggle out to taint the atmosphere, save through the chinks in
the walls and roofs, and, for all I could observe, these men died
without the least effort to save them. They were laid just as they
were let gently down upon the ground by the poor fellows, their
comrades, who brought them on their backs from the camp with
the greatest tenderness, but who were not allowed to remain with
them. The sick appeared to be tended by the sick, and the dying
by the dying.

Descriptions of that kind were not calculated to win
Russell friends in political circles. The Prince Regent called
him a 'miserable scribbler', Sidney Herbert at the War
Office suggested that the army should lynch him and
several of London's leading gentlemen's clubs barred *The
Times* from their smoking rooms. Delane, though, was not
to be so easily dissuaded from what he considered to be his
natural duty. Having enjoined Russell to keep to the
straight and narrow in his reports and to tell the truth, he

backed up his reporter's stories with a series of thundering editorials aimed at destroying the government's complacency. At his instigation a *Times*' fund was set up to provide medical aid for the British troops and some £20,000 was contributed by a British public shocked by Russell's disclosures. It also led to the appointment of Florence Nightingale and her 38 fellow nurses who did wonders to improve the medical care of the suffering in the British military hospital at Scutari. The public conscience had been touched and offers of help came in from all quarters; the war in the distant Russian peninsula could not be ignored by fireside readers of *The Times* and other newspapers. Russell's reports had been amplified by Chenery's and between them the two men left their readers in little doubt that this war, hailed in the early stages as a glorious adventure, had turned into a brutal and bloody affair where soldiers died unnecessary deaths due to unbelievable military blunders.

If Russell had been 'honoured by a good deal of abuse for telling the truth' – as he later described the uproar which greeted his revelations – worse was to follow when it was suggested that his despatches were assisting the Russian war effort. Raglan, who had not been spared by Russell since the missed opportunity on the River Alma, caustically told his superiors that the enemy had no need of a secret service as all they had to do was to read *The Times*. In turn, representations were made to Delane to ensure that sensitive information was not published in his pages. Alarmed by the pressure, Russell offered to present his despatches to the Deputy Adjutant-General for comment but this promise of honourable self-censorship was never taken up by the military command in the Crimea. After the war, Tsar Nicholas I of Russia mischievously claimed that he discovered what was happening to his forces in the Crimea by reading *The Times*, but Russian officers at the front got nearer the truth of the matter when they pointed out that the British press revealed nothing they did not already know. To British troops under enemy fire, though, the whispered information that their positions had been given away by *The Times* was often accepted at face value and Russell had to bear the consequences. On more than one occasion his baggage was left behind and he had to live with the sullen stares and the blank hostility of the men whom, paradoxically, he was trying to help. Many of the officers simply regarded him as a *parvenu*, as a mad-dog Irishman bent only on discrediting the British Army in the eyes of the world.

Of those who accused him of disclosing secrets, of painting an over-vivid picture of British suffering or of letting down the side, Russell had this to say:

But I could not tell lies to 'make things pleasant'. There was not a single man in the camp who could put his hand upon his heart and declare he believed that one single casualty had been caused to us by information communicated to the enemy by me or any other newspaper correspondent. The only things the partisans of misrule could allege was, that I did not 'make things pleasant' to the authorities, and that, amid the filth and starvation, and deadly stagnation of the camp, I did not go about 'babbling of green fields', of present abundance, and of prospects of victory.

By the beginning of 1855 Russell's refusal 'to make things pleasant' had begun to bite. Aberdeen's ministry fell and was replaced by a new administration under Lord Palmerston. Worn out by his failure to complete the investment of Sevastopol, Raglan resigned in the summer and died of fever a few days later; he was replaced by General Sir James Simpson and the war spluttered on until the spring of 1856. By then the allies were tired of the stalemate and the war had become so unpopular in France that Napoleon III threatened to withdraw his troops unilaterally.

As a result of the ensuing Treaty of Paris some cosmetic changes were made to remove the immediate territorial difficulties but they did little to solve the problem known as the 'Eastern Question' whose imponderables were to rumble on for many years to come. Russia surrendered her grip on the mouth of the Danube, the Dardanelles were closed to foreign ships in time of peace and Turkey's independence was guaranteed in return for the tongue-in-cheek promise that there would be a programme of reforms in her Ottoman Empire. The real winner turned out to be the ordinary soldier. Partly as a result of Florence Nightingale's work, the Red Cross organization was founded in 1864 and it was due to Russell's and Chenery's vivid reports that more attention was given to the medical care of the British armed forces. Many years later, Field Marshal Sir Evelyn Wood, who had served in the Crimea as a young officer, was happy enough to give the credit to the man who had once been the army's public enemy number one.

He [Russell] incurred much enmity, but few unprejudiced men who were in the Crimea will now attempt to call in question the fact that by awakening the conscience of the British nation to the suffering of its troops, he saved the remnants of those grand battalions we landed in September.[2]

By 19th-century European standards, the Crimean War was not a major conflict, neither was it especially brutal – many of the mistakes and hardships endured by the British Army had been experienced in Wellington's time, and the ordinary British soldier was no stranger to misfortune – yet in British military mythology it continues to occupy a pre-eminent position. That it does so is due in no small measure to Russell's efforts. He exposed the army's shortcomings and reported back to an audience who got to know what the soldiers were experiencing and who cared. As a war correspondent he also established a style which was to be imitated by many other journalists who followed him – vivid pictures of the army in the field, imposing accounts of battle and interviews with the senior officers. He also underlined the confusion of battle, even to the trained eye, and many years later in his book *The Great War With Russia* (1895) he was to claim that in the beginning the strain of war reporting was well-nigh insupportable.

How was I to describe what I had not seen? Where learn the facts for which they were waiting at home? My eyes swam as I tried to make notes of what I had heard. I was worn out with excitement, fatigue, and want of food. I had been more than ten hours in the saddle; my wretched horse, bleeding badly from a cut in the leg, was unable to carry me. My head throbbed, my heart beat as though it would burst. I suppose I was unnerved by want of food and rest, but I was so much overcome by what I saw that I could not remain where the fight had been closest and deadliest. I longed to get away from it – from the exultation of others in which thought for the dead was forgotten or unexpressed. It was now that the weight of the task I had accepted fell on my soul like lead.

Many soldiers, even battle-hardened veterans, have expressed similar views after being in combat. Only a few ever manage to get an over-view of the whole battle; the majority only remember the fighting itself, the confusion and the noise of men and weapons. On some sectors there might be no fighting at all: many soldiers fighting on the Western Front in the First World War have commented on the loneliness and the emptiness of the battle area. They had no clearer view than the men involved in the thick of the fighting. From the evidence of Russell's accounts, the fighting in the Crimea was more localized, consisting of close-quarter affairs which tended to focus the observer's attention on the horrors of violent death by bullet, shellfire or the bayonet. This kind of combat, though, did not make the battles any easier for Russell to comprehend. To be able to file detached and accurate reports Russell had to speak to the main protagonists. A word with an infantry colonel would give him a clue as to whether the men had behaved well under fire and whether or not an objective had been secured; interviews with survivors of an engagement would yield a personal point of view, whereas staff officers could give an off-the-record account of strategic gains and losses.

The British officers in the Crimea took an ambivalent attitude to Russell's requests. Some dismissed them out of hand, others thought it better to speak to him for fear that he would otherwise print an inaccurate story which could be harmful to their prospects. To this love-hate relationship Russell brought a good deal of bluff Irish charm which usually disarmed his critics and made them ready to confide in him. He also took good care to talk to the men, discovering the important lesson that while a soldier might be reticent or tongue-tied out of the front line, in the heat of battle he was often prepared to talk and to give some idea of what he was going through. By the campaign's end Russell had become an experienced observer who could understand the ebbs and flows of battle and report them in a thoroughly professional and trustworthy manner.

Because he was the first successful war correspondent, Russell established a code of practice and behaviour by which all future reporters were to be judged. He commands a place in history for uncovering maladministration and indifference, but his success as a campaigning journalist has tended to obscure the fact that he was a first-class reporter. To that task he brought energy, an open mind, an eye for detail and a compassion for the fighting soldier. He also carried with him the not inconsiderable weight of *The Times* and in that respect he owed much to Delane, his editor, who always stood four-square behind him. Russell repaid that debt by adding to the newspaper's political influence at home – it was widely thought that his despatches from the Crimea had helped to topple the government – and on his death *The Times* hailed him as the greatest war correspondent of his day.

To all who knew him he was the cheeriest, brightest, most likeable of companions . . . All newspaper work is of its nature ephemeral. Mr Russell, however, could have said truly that he had accomplished ⸮ feat unparalleled in the annals of journalism, that he had written newspaper articles which would be remembered as long as Englishmen interest themselves in the records of English valour, English heroism, English disasters and English victories.

The Crimean War was only the beginning of Russell's career as a war correspondent. Within a year of its conclusion he was in India to cover the mutiny of 1857; he was in America in 1861 to report the American Civil War for *The Times* and he served Delane again during the Franco-Prussian War of 1870. That proved to be his final wartime assignment for the newspaper which had given him his start in life: the rapid movements of the Prussian army had exposed his dislike of the telegraph and many of his reports were stale news by the time they were published. During the Zulu War of 1879 he wrote for the *Daily Telegraph* and that was destined to be his last campaign. During the course of covering those wars, though, Russell never lost sight of the lessons he had learned in the Crimea. His despatches were models of their kind, well balanced, accurate and fair; he also remembered Delane's exhortation to tell the truth and to leave the political battles to him. In India Russell was sharply critical of the punitive reprisals meted out to the mutineers, while in America he was virtually hounded out of the country because he chose to tell the truth when Union soldiers turned tail and fled from the battlefield during the Battle of Bull Run.

When the *Daily Mail* claimed in 1897 that 'the Victorian era is destined to go down in history as emphatically the period of small wars', it was not making an idle boast. The British might only have fought one major international war in the Crimea, but elsewhere the empire was far from peaceful. Most of the conflicts were little more than skirmishes, police actions against native opposition (the Boer War of 1880 being an exception) but the one-sided nature of the fighting did not make them any less attractive. Newspaper readers could thrill to the exploits of British soldiers against Afghanistan tribesmen, Ashanti warriors, Dervishes, Maori rebels and the like; even defeats or hardships like Majuba Hill or the Siege of Lucknow could be made memorable when transformed into stories of British stoicism and resolution. The British soldier, previously a despised species, became a glamorous figure, a red-coated hero confronting native opposition with disciplined calm in the remote areas of Empire. Roberts's march from Kabul to Kandahar, Napier with his elephants in Abyssinia, the Gordons at Dargai, ten Victoria Crosses at Rorke's Drift, the charge of the Lancers at Omdurman: these became treasured ikons of Victorian martial heroism, revered by the British newspaper-reading public.

The images appeared under many different guises – in the plots of novels, as the theme of poetry or as the subject of countless paintings – but the main substance, in the later years of the century at least, came from journalists. Stories

of blood-soaked sand, wily or simply comic native opposition and British pluck against the odds helped to create the
myth that Britain was an invincible power, that the Empire
was a magnificent playground created for adventure and
that outside it there existed only alien savagery and misrule.
Many of the popular writers who extolled British prowess
of arms had in fact started life as war correspondents. G. A.
Henty, a contributor to the *Boy's Own Paper*, who wrote
massively popular tales of derring-do, accompanied Napier
to Abyssinia, Wolseley to the Ashanti War and covered
every European conflict from the Franco-Prussian War to
the Turko-Serbian conflict of 1912. The novelist and poet
George Meredith covered the Austro-Italian war for the
Morning Post and Alfred Austin, who was appointed Poet
Laureate in 1896, started his literary life as a journalist
reporting the Franco-Prussian War. He was very much the
imperial poet, and an execrable one at that; on taking up
his appointment he immediately wrote a ghastly poem
about the Jameson Raid for *The Times* in words which
typified the hysterical self-confidence of the later Victorian
imperialists.

> There are girls in the gold-reef city,
> There are mothers and children too!
> And they cry, 'Hurry up! for pity!'
> For what can a brave man do?
> If ever we win they'll blame us;
> If we fail, they will howl and hiss.
> But there's many a man lives famous
> For daring a wrong like this.

Other Victorian writers who also had experience as war
correspondents included the American-born novelist Richard Harding Davis; the creator of Sherlock Holmes, Arthur
Conan Doyle; Rudyard Kipling who took an almost mysti-

cal delight in the Empire; Winwood Reade, the author of the controversial novel *The Martyrdom of Man*; and Stephen Crane, the author of *The Red Badge of Courage*, who originally made his name reporting the American Civil War for the *New York World*.

The public appetite for news of war was fed largely by the press and in turn the newspapers had to keep up with technological developments to meet the demand. Telegraph cables began to criss-cross the world, Reuters' news service arrived in London in 1858, fast steamships shortened journey times and the ever-expanding railway network made distribution easier and helped to speed up the collection of news. The successful newspapers were those which published the hottest news first and the rapid gathering and transmission of their stories became a pre-requisite for the journalists in the field. The most successful Victorian war correspondent in this respect was Archibald Forbes, an uneven-tempered Scot who was acknowledged by his rivals to be a master of the telegraphic despatch. During the Franco-Prussian War he demonstrated his dexterity by not only sending first-class reports, intelligently written, accurate and colourful, but by scooping his fellow journalists on more than one occasion. Forbes often claimed that his success owed as much to his ability to 'read' a battle as it did to his personal strength. These were characteristics noted by his protégé Frederick Villiers, who later became no mean war correspondent himself.

Moreover he [Forbes] was by nature an ideal war correspondent, for he could do more work, both mentally and physically, on a small amount of food, than any man I have ever met. Amid the noise and battle and in close proximity to bursting shells, whose dust would sometimes fall upon the paper, I have seen him calmly writing his description of the fight – not taking notes to be worked up afterwards, but actually writing a vivid account that was to be transmitted by wire. His one great aim was to get off the first and best news of the fighting; and he never spared himself till that was done.[3]

According to Forbes, the ideal war correspondent should always involve himself in a battle, expose himself to the same risks faced by the soldiers and then have the strength and capacity to send off his despatches even when he was dog-tired, hungry and in strange surroundings. The coming of the telegraph and improved means of transport might have made the lot of the reporter easier, but in the field, whether it was in the war-torn Metz or the wilds of Afghanistan, the good war correspondent had to be resourceful and patient. Despatches had to be sent by runner or rider to the nearest telegraph office and very often this task had to be undertaken by the journalist himself. Native opposition or warring European armies did not always differentiate between enemy soldiers and civilian war correspondents and in the hardest-fought campaigns the gentlemen of the press had to share the soldiers' dangers and discomforts. They also had to learn to live with the censor.

During the American Civil War, General Sherman banished war correspondents from the front and threatened to shoot those who attempted to transmit information which could be useful to the enemy. Even in the remote little wars of Empire correspondents had to submit their despatches to a military censor who had the power to edit and alter copy which he felt might prejudice the army's safety. Correspondents who evaded the censor did not remain long in their positions of trust: even the gifted Forbes was banished to the rear during the Afghanistan War for disobeying Roberts's instructions. In his widely read manual, *The Soldier's Pocket Book* (1869), Sir Garnet

Wolseley spoke for his generation when he described war correspondents as 'those newly invented curse to armies who eat the rations of the fighting man and do not work at all'.

Gradually a pattern was beginning to emerge. Victorian commanders could see little reason for the presence of reporters during battles, regarding them at best as liabilities who might get in the way, and at worst as possible spies. Many generals thought it intolerable that unqualified civilians could comment on military matters; to them the needs of the war correspondent were the least consideration during a campaign. Others, the more forward-looking types, came to believe that the war correspondent was a simple fact of military life. That being so, it made sense to take him into the army's confidence so that the war correspondent would feel duty-bound to impose his own form of self-censorship. After all, they reasoned, if a journalist was given all the facts and then told the likely consequences of any action he was less likely to betray sensitive information which could cost lives. Swanning around the battlefield and picking up rumours, he could come across half-digested stories which would be damaging if published. Roberts was a good example of a Victorian soldier who cared about his relations with the press, arguing that if treated in an adult way, war correspondents could be useful allies. During the Boer War he instituted a policy of producing regular and reliable communiqués, and in India and Afghanistan he had gone out of his way to be helpful, even to men like Forbes who occasionally broke his trust. On taking up command in North Africa in 1942, General Sir Harold Alexander, later to become Field Marshal Earl Alexander of Tunis, took a similar view of his own relationship to the accompanying press corps.

My own opinion is that the press correspondent is just as good a
fellow as any military officer or man who knows a great many
secrets, and he will never let you down – not on purpose – but he
may let you down if he is not in the picture, merely because his
duty to his paper forces him to write something, and that
something may be most dangerous. Therefore he must be kept in
the picture.[4]

Sometimes, though, that 'something' could be uncompli-
mentary or critical, and even the most liberal commander
could feel threatened by the press if he believed his trust to
have been 'betrayed'.

The war correspondent himself was in a difficult position.
He knew that he was an expensive commodity, that it cost
a good deal of money to keep him in the field and that in
consequence his editor demanded results. He had to learn
to dig behind the bland assurances of official communiqués
and, when necessary, to quiz men who might not regard
him as a friend or ally. In time of war he was the public's
only watch-dog, providing a link between the forces and
the public and producing a realistic view of the conflict.
Like every public activity reported by the press, it was
essential that war should not be ignored. The main actions
had to be described, commented upon or criticized; the
protagonists had to be interviewed and their views sought.
Soldiers, too, liked to feel that they were being appreciated
– this sensation could range from a commander's satisfaction that his actions were being treated sympathetically, to
the simple pleasure of a soldier reading about his unit in a
newspaper report. By the same token, not all stories could
be reported – either in the interests of security or in the
vaguer realms of preserving good taste – and a consensus
had to be achieved between telling the whole story and
reserving information which might be useful to an enemy.
That balance was never going to be easy to achieve: good

journalists are inquisitive, frank and intelligent writers who want to get to the heart of a story. Their needs could often be at odds with the military point of view. From the very beginning, the relationship between the military and the press was to be blighted by misunderstandings caused largely by ignorance of the other's position.

Until the First World War transformed forever hitherto familiar modes of warfare, most conflicts were small, easily managed and relatively simple to comprehend. War correspondents 'at the seat of war' had reasonable freedom of action and, despite the presence of the military censor who controlled telegraphic despatches, they could still write more leisurely and more realistic background stories which went back to home base uncensored by post. It was a time which came to be known in later years as the golden age of the war correspondent.

2

George Warrington Steevens and the Sudan

In no other 19th-century campaign is the golden age of the war correspondent better expressed than in Kitchener's reconquest of the Sudan. It was far away, romantic and glamorous and like many other Victorian adventures it had a strange beginning. Indeed, Britain would probably not have bothered herself with that barren country had it not been for involvement in Sudan's neighbour, Egypt.

To the late-Victorian mind, Egypt was something of an obsession. Through its territory ran the waters of the Suez Canal, the great trade route to India and the East, and it was this imperial jugular that aroused Britain's greatest interest. By arranging for the purchase of British shares in the Suez Canal Company in 1875, Prime Minister Disraeli had given Britain a stake in Egypt's economy and it was this financial participation which drew her eventually into the Sudan. Within four years of the British purchase Egypt was bankrupt and an international debt commission had been established to regulate the country's exchequer; this necessary move fired nationalist sympathies and in 1882 Britain was forced to take action against an Arab revolt, thereby drawing herself deeper into Egypt's affairs. Egypt might have remained a vassal state of the Sultan of Turkey, her finances in the control of the international commission, but to all intents and purposes the British action brought the country within her sphere of influence under the British Agent, Sir Evelyn Baring, later to become Lord Cromer.

To complicate matters, however, intervention in Egypt

meant that Britain also had to contend with the Sudan – a vast country one-third the size of the United States – which formed part of the realm of the Khedive of Egypt and which, by 1883, was in the grip of a Pan-Islamic revolt led by the Mahdi. This powerful personality, born Mohammed Ibn Al-Sayd Abdullah, claimed to be the Mahdi, the 'expected one', descendant of the prophet Mohammed, and it was his intention to guide his people towards freedom by ridding the country of the hated infidel Egyptians and their British overlords. The raising of a Holy War was his chosen instrument and news began to filter out of the Sudan of the fall of Egyptian garrisons and the slaughter of communities opposed to Mahdist ideals. To the jingoists in Britain this information was anathema; they demanded that some sort of action be taken to save or secure the Sudan and as so often happened when the Empire faced an extremity, the public called for a hero, in this case, General Charles Gordon.

The story of Gordon's last stand at Khartoum, of the blundering efforts to save him, and of his eventual death in January 1885 at the hands of the Mahdists, is well enough known, but it was the immediate aftermath which was to leave the lasting impression. London was swept by a mood of hysteria which lasted several weeks and which drew crowds to Downing Street to hoot and jeer at the Prime Minister; Queen Victoria wrote to Gordon's sister expressing her 'grief inexpressible' and the initials of Gladstone's nickname (Grand Old Man) were reversed to read 'Murderer of Gordon'.

Gladstone, though, was not the man to be drawn off course by name-calling or by public hysteria. The Sudan was evacuated and the border sealed off to leave the inhabitants to their Dervish devices; it was not to be until the following decade that concern over the control of the

head-waters of the Nile made the reconquest of the Sudan
a strategic necessity. In 1892 the command of the Egyptian
Army fell to Major-General Sir Horatio Kitchener, an
engineer whose early career had been spent as an intelligence officer in Palestine and the Sudan and who had been
the last British soldier to remain in contact with Gordon.
Thorough, capable, ambitious, yet lacking the emotional
intuition which marks the great battlefield commander,
Kitchener was the ideal man for the long and painstaking
task of reconquest. A series of successful skirmishes against
Dervish opposition had convinced him that his Egyptian
troops were up to the mark as soldiers but it was his
intention that the campaign should be governed more by
careful forward planning than by any display of *élan* in
battle.

In 1896 he made his first move by engaging in a limited
demonstration along the Nile to ease the pressure on an
Italian force which was being attacked by the Dervishes in
neighbouring Abyssinia. This was ordered by Prime Minister Salisbury in the interests of shoring up the Triple
Alliance (Italy's alliance of 1882 with Germany and Aus-
tria-Hungary), but it also gave Kitchener the excuse to
achieve his ambition of leading an Egyptian army into the
Sudan to smash Mahdist rule and to avenge the hapless
Gordon. That same year, in September, the northern
province of Dongola was captured, a move which allowed
cautious plans to be laid for further campaigns within the
coming years. Kitchener was impatient to push ahead but
before he could do so he had to win the unqualified support
of the politicians at Westminster and to build up his army
and its lines of communication along the Nile. The following year was spent consolidating his position and by the
beginning of 1898 Kitchener had won Government

approval to strike back at the Sudan with an army 25,000 strong.

Throughout the early spring of that year the town of Wadi Halfa on the Egyptian-Sudanese border had been a hive of activity. Trains clanked regularly along the lines laid through its dusty streets, taking men and equipment deep into the Sudan to reinforce the Anglo-Egyptian army which was slowly taking shape in the wastes of the Nubian desert at Berber. The locomotive sheds, boiler-houses and fitting sheds worked round the clock to service the seem-ingly endless stream of trains and in their shanty-town buildings off the side-streets, Greek and Egyptian mer-chants were doing brisk business providing both necessities and luxuries for those who followed in the wake of the advance south – men anxious to witness the ringing down of the final curtain in Kitchener's invasion of the Sudan and his smashing of Mahdist rule. Amongst those passing through Wadi Halfa were British officers seeking second-ment to Kitchener's army; representatives of the travel firm of Thomas Cook and Sons whose river steamers had helped to make possible the military advance down the Nile; an assortment of Victorian adventurers drawn to the Sudan by the scent of a glorious imperial victory and 16 war correspondents whose task it was to cover the final stages of the campaign.

They were a mixed bunch. Some, like Bennet Burleigh of the *Daily Telegraph*, Frederick Villiers of the *Illustrated London News*, and Frank Scudamore of the *Daily News*, were experienced journalists, veterans of previous imperial cam-paigns who presented their stories and opinions in meas-ured and thoughtful bulletins; others were amateurs, like Ernest Bennett, a self-important Oxford don who repre-sented the *Westminster Gazette*, or his friend, Henry Cross of the *Manchester Guardian*, whose only qualification was that he was a schoolmaster and a rowing Blue. A few, like Frank Rhodes of *The Times*, brother of Cecil Rhodes, and Winston Churchill of the *Morning Post*, had previous military experience. Qualified or not, none met with the approval of Kitchener, the Sirdar (commanding officer) of the Anglo-Egyptian army, who had done his best to confine them far from the front at Wadi Halfa. Only two of their number had been granted any special favours – Hubert Howard, another correspondent of *The Times*, and George Warrington Steevens, whose charm and youthful high spirits had eased his way to a unique personal interview with the famous warlord.

Major-General Sir Horatio Herbert Kitchener is forty-eight years old by the book; but that is irrelevant. He stands several inches over six feet, straight as a lance, and looks out imperiously above most men's heads; his motions are deliberate and strong; slender but firmly knit, he seems built for tireless, steel-wire endurance rather than for power or agility: that also is irrelevant. Steady, passionless eyes shaded by decisive brows, brick-red rather full cheeks, a long moustache beneath which you divine an immovable mouth; his face is harsh, and neither appeals for affection nor stirs dislike. All this is irrelevant too: neither age, nor figure, nor face, nor any accident of person, has any bearing on the essential Sirdar. You could imagine the character just the same as if all the externals were different. He has no age but the prime of life, no body but one to carry his mind, no face but one to keep his brain behind. The brain and the will are the essence and the whole of the man – a brain and a will so perfect in their workings that, in the face of extremest difficulty, they never seem to know what struggle is. You cannot imagine the Sirdar otherwise than as seeing the right thing to do and doing it. His precision is so inhumanly unerring, he is more like a machine than a man. You feel that he ought to be patented and shown with pride at the Paris International Exhibition. British Empire: Exhibit No. 1, *hors concours*, the Sudan Machine.[1]

Coming from a member of the species which Kitchener so despised, Steevens's words were a remarkable tribute.

Ernest Bennett had described a meeting with Kitchener as being 'as barren of results as it was humiliating. The only parallel to it which I can think of is that of a row of curates before a brusque and autocratic bishop.'

Like many other leading soldiers of his generation, Kitchener had an ambivalent attitude towards the press. As a young man, when he was making his way in the Egyptian Army in the rank of major, or bimbashi, his discreetly leaked information to the press during the Gordon relief expedition had brought his name to the attention of readers of *The Times*. Then, in 1888, as governor of Suakin, the eastern seaport of the Sudan, a series of hard-hitting letters to that same newspaper had confirmed him in the public mind as a coming man in Egyptian affairs; but when, in 1892, he was appointed Sirdar of the Egyptian Army, discretion became his invariable rule. His feelings were shared by more than one of his fellow officers: a young cavalry captain called Douglas Haig, who was attached to the Egyptian cavalry, wrote to his sister that the accompanying press corps were. '. . . most degrading. They can't tell the whole truth even if they want to. The British public likes to read sensational news, and the best war correspondent is he who can tell the most thrilling lies.'

Early in the campaign Kitchener had shown his dislike of war correspondents by keeping them waiting in the hot sun outside his tent before sweeping past them with an imperious command: 'Get out of my way, you drunken swabs!' Particular antipathy was reserved for Winston Churchill who went into battle seconded to the 21st Lancers. He owed his unique position – part serving officer, part employed war correspondent – to family connections and to the machinations of his mother who had put considerable pressure upon Kitchener to accept her son into his army. Eventually Kitchener had relented, but he continued to regard Churchill with suspicion, believing that he was nothing less than a spoiled, medal-bagging young puppy who owed everything to political influence and nothing to personal ability. In that estimation he was mistaken as Churchill displayed great courage at Omdurman and he repaid his debt to those who had helped him by writing *The River War*, one of the best accounts of the campaign, which was published in 1899. Not that Churchill was enamoured of the Sirdar. 'Kitchener may be a general,' he told his mother, 'but never a gentleman.'

Kitchener's distrust of the press corps was not confined to personal loathing. To protect his own interests at home he did not want the final stages of the campaign to be reported until victory was certain: that was one reason why he had ordered the correspondents to remain at Wadi Halfa where they would be fed information by his Director of Intelligence, the remarkable Arabist, Major Reginald Wingate. It was only after representations had been made by the editor of *The Times*, G. E. Buckle, that Kitchener was forced to accede to the request that correspondents be allowed to accompany his army to its expected place of battle with the Dervishes at Khartoum. Even then, as Steevens discovered, Kitchener did not make the going easy for the accompanying gentlemen of the press.

I sat on a box of tinned beef, whisky, and other delicacies, dumped down on a slope of loose sand. Round me lay another similar case, a tent, bed, and bath, all collapsible and duly collapsed into a brown canvas jacket, two brown canvas bags containing saddlery, towels, and table-linen, a chair and a table lashed together, a wash-hand basin with shaving tackle concealed inside its green canvas cover, a brown bag with some clothes in it, a shining tin canteen, a cracking lunch-basket, a driving-coat, and a hunting-crop. On one side of me rose the embankment of the main line to Berber; fifty yards on it ended suddenly in the sand, and a swarm of Arabs were shovelling up more of it for their lives. On the other side of me, detached, empty, quite alone, stood the saloon which brought me from Halfa. It was going back again tonight, and then I should be quite loose and outcast in the smiling Sudan.

I sat and meditated on the full significance of the simple military phrase, 'line of communications'. It is the great discovery of the Sirdar that he has recognized that in the Sudan the communications are the essence and heart of the whole problem. And now I recognized it too.

Steevens had taken his kit – six cases full of clothes, food, 'a thousand cigarettes, champagne, whisky, port, sauternes, punsch and likor' (*sic*) – and two servant boys by steamer to Aswan where he had bought camels and horses for the long journey south. At Wadi Halfa he thought to transport the beasts by train or steamer only to discover that Kitchener's brother Walter, the army's Director of Transport, had put a stop to all such luxuries. The only solution seemed to be to buy a camel locally and travel lightly, but even that was not to be.

Now came the time to take my chance. And here, sure enough, comes a chocolate Arab, with the information that he has any number of camels to let. The chance has turned out a good one, after all. But then comes along a fair Englishman, on a shaggy grey pony; I was told he was the Director of Transport. That's all right; I'll ask his advice. Only, before I could speak, he suavely drew the attention of correspondents to the rule that any Arab hiring camels already hired by the army was liable to two years' imprisonment. The news was not encouraging; and of course the Arabs swore that the army had not hired the best camels at all. I believed it at the time, but came to know the Arabs better afterwards. Anyhow here I sat, amid the dregs of my vanishing household, seventy miles from Berber – no rail, no steamer, no horse, no camel. Only donkeys, not to be thought of – and, by George, legs! I never thought of them, but I've got 'em, and why not use 'em. I'll walk.

Perhaps it was that sense of 'get up and go' which Steevens so cheerfully put in his *Daily Mail* report that commended him to Kitchener. Men who trembled in his company or who dithered when in difficulty he could do without; like many powerful or overbearing men he could be charmed or even deflated by men who were prepared to stand up to him.

Steevens was the youngest of the journalists attached to the Khartoum expedition – he was only 28 – but his career had already attracted a good deal of attention in London's literary and political circles. Born on 10 December 1869, he had been educated at the City of London School where he topped a distinguished academic and sporting career by winning a Classics scholarship to Balliol. The school magazine said of his achievements: 'The mere quantity of his knowledge was astonishing; his command over it still more so. He had a Napoleonic faculty for instantaneous and complete concentration of his intellectual forces.' But it was not just academic ability that furthered his star; he also possessed a quicksilver mind and a gift for making the English language his servant. A First in Classics was followed by a Fellowship at Pembroke, but by 1894 his heart had turned to journalism. That same year he married and took up an appointment with the *Pall Mall Gazette* which had recently been taken over by William Waldorf Astor; by the time Steevens joined the staff the *Pall Mall* had lost many of the literary inclinations of its founder, Frederick Greenwood, and had espoused the politics of the ruling Conservative Party, especially those of its 'New Imperialist' wing. Although fellow *Pall Mall* writers like W. E. Henley doubted his high Toryism and thought that he often wrote only to please the Government, Steevens quickly became the newspaper's star turn with an uncanny ability to capture the heightened and popular emotions of those who espoused the New Imperialism.

When Alfred Harmsworth, the self-made Dublin-born

newspaper proprietor, started the *Daily Mail* in 1896,
Steevens was at the top of his shopping list for writers who
would provide stories echoing the newspaper's boast that it
was 'the embodiment and mouthpiece of the imperial idea'.
On coming down from Oxford, Henley had described
Steevens as being 'in the soft-hat-and-scarlet-tie stage of
youthful manhood: a rather shy, a rather sulky, or (so it
seemed) a rather junior don'. Under Harmsworth's tutelage
all such traces were to disappear and Steevens was to
become the mouthpiece of those who believed that Britain
possessed 'the mightiest and most beneficial Empire ever
known in the annals of mankind'.

Initially, the quality of his new reporter's mind suggested
to Harmsworth that he should be employed as a leader
writer, but after a handful of indifferent articles Steevens
was sent out on assignment. He wrote a series of entertaining articles about the streets of London, revealing a talent
for evocative description and meticulous observation which
greatly appealed to the *Mail*'s growing readership. In an
age when there were few cameras to assist 'colour' reporting, Steevens's ability to record and describe the passing
scene was a godsend to his paper and Harmsworth knew it.
The following year, 1897, he was sent to Germany to write
16 articles under the revealing title, 'Under the Iron Heel'.
What followed was a series of 'Hun-bashing' essays – the
Germans' love of obeying orders, the subservience of the
ordinary soldier to the officer corps, excessive warmonger-
ing, being only a few of the topics he covered – but
underneath the patriotic phrases and the slick suggestions
of British superiority, lay highly readable descriptions of
the German way of life. Prejudiced and even jingoistic he
might have been, but to his fellow professionals in Fleet
Street, Steevens had emerged as one of the best descriptive
feature writers of his day: when the chance came to follow

Kitchener to Khartoum he had all the qualifications
required in the good war correspondent.

The year 1897 also saw the 60th anniversary of the
accession to the throne of Queen Victoria and when the
Mail started publication plans were well in hand to celebrate her Diamond Jubilee in style. It was a slightly
hysterical year, one which saw British self-congratulation
reach its apotheosis: at sea, the Royal Navy ruled the
waves, and on land, making his inexorable and victorious
progress down the Nile, was the impressive figure of
Kitchener. The press, especially the *Mail*, quickened the
pulse of popular opinion by concentrating on the heroic
deeds of Empire, and at home in the suburbs the British
people pondered Kitchener's every move and thrilled to the
possibility of another chunk of red being added to the map
of Africa.

It was in that mood that the 16 members of the press
corps had assembled at Wadi Halfa to finalize their prep-
arations and to begin the journey south to Berber where
they would join the bulk of Kitchener's army. The youthful
Steevens made it mainly on foot, relying on the odd lift
from army transports, Burleigh and Scudamore rode on
Arab horses, but the strangest form of transport was
reserved for the eccentric Fred Villiers who rode to Khartoum on a green bicycle which survived the campaign
unpunctured in spite of the harshness of the terrain it had
to cover. At last they were on their way. True, they had to
submit their despatches to Wingate who acted as
Kitchener's censor and, true, they all had to share the same
military telegraph for their communications but each man
was confident not only in his own skills but in the different
entrepreneurial skills of his editor. Rhodes and Howard
were to furnish cautious yet authoritative reports for publi-

cation in *The Times*. Bennet Burleigh's *Telegraph* pieces were models of their kind – precise about military details and with enough colour to bring the events alive for his readers thousands of miles away. He was to scoop his colleagues by correctly forecasting the Battle of Omdurman: the *Telegraph* carried a report on the impending battle in its edition of 2 September, the day the battle actually occurred. (The death of Howard after the battle forced *The Times* to use Burleigh's reports too.) Unbeknownst to each journalist, four of the journalists – Bennett, Burleigh, Churchill and Steevens – were also writing 'instant books' on the campaign. In this minor journalistic skirmish Steevens was to emerge as victor, his book, *With Kitchener to Khartoum*, being published by William Blackwood within weeks of the campaign's end.

Something of Steevens's style and of his grasp of military matters can be caught in his description of the Sudanese troops who fought in Kitchener's army under the command of white NCOs and officers.

They love their soldiering, do the blacks, and take it very seriously. When they stood at attention they might have been rows of black marble statues, all alike as in the ancient temples, filling up the little square of crumbling mud walls with a hole in its corner, so typical of the Berber landscape. Then the English colonel snapped out something in Turkish: in an instant the lines of each company had become fours; all turned with a click; the band crashed out a march – barbaric Ethiopian, darky American, or English music-hall, it is all the same to the blacks – and out swung the regiment. They moved off by companies through a narrow alley, and there lay four new-killed goats, the sand lapping their blood. Every officer rode, every man stepped, over the luck token; they would never go out to fight without it. Then out into the main street, every man stepping like a conqueror, the band blaring war at their head; with each company a little flag – blue, black, white, amber, or green, or vermilion – on a spear, and half way down the column the colour the Camerons gave them when they shared the glory of Ginnis. Boys trailed behind them, and their women, running to keep up, shot after them the thin screams that kindle Sudanese to victory. A black has been known to kill himself because his wife called him a coward. To me the sight of that magnificent regiment was a revelation. One has got accustomed to associate black skin with something either slavish or comical. From their faces these men might have been loafing darkies in South Carolina or minstrels in St James's Hall. But in the smartness of every movement, in the pride of every private's bearing, what a wonderful difference! This was quite a new kind of black – every man a warrior from his youth up. 'Lu-u-u, lu-u-u,' piped the women; the men held up their hands and made no sound, but you could see the answer to that appeal quivering all down the column. For 'we', they say, 'are like the English; we are not afraid.'

Today the liberal mind might shrink from Steevens's condescending words but his military intuition was right. Throughout the campaign the black Sudanese soldiers – many of them deserters from the ranks of the Mahdi's army – had proved to be fine soldiers: Steevens's shrewdness in recognizing their martial prowess was to pay dividends when he came to report the Battle of Omdurman and the part played by them in gaining eventual victory. He also got it right about the crucial role played by their commanding officers, experienced campaigners like General Archibald Hunter and his brigade commanders, Colonels Macdonald, Maxwell, Lewis and Collinson. Like the other journalists, Steevens was particularly intrigued by Hector Macdonald who was known throughout the army as 'Fighting Mac' and who was one of its most colourful personalities. Three years younger than Kitchener, Macdonald was a Gordon Highlander who had risen through the ranks – unusual in Victorian times – and he was an experienced soldier with eighteen years of active service behind him. As an ex-Colour-Sergeant who believed in the solid virtues of drilling as a means of instilling discipline, he was ideally suited to train the unruly, though brave, Sudanese troops and he had become an important cog in Kitchener's plans for victory.

Unlike his chief, though, Macdonald took a tolerant attitude towards the press and regularly offered them entertainment in his quarters. 'Never mind all that,' he told Steevens and Burleigh when they arrived to interview him. 'What are you going to have to drink?' If it is part of a war correspondent's success to forecast events and to pinpoint key personalities, then Steevens had made an early start in recognizing the potential of the Sudanese battalions and of their easy-going and experienced commander, Hector Macdonald.

The war correspondents were given their first taste of action on 8 April when, after a forced night march, Kitchener's 14,000-strong army attacked a Mahdist force led by the Emir Mahmud at the strategically important position of Atbara, the confluence of the Blue and White Niles. The battle itself was hardly an edifying spectacle: after a furious bombardment of the *zeriba* (fortified stockade) containing the Mahdist forces, Kitchener's men swept in along a broad front to crush the enemy by dint of superior numbers and firepower. At the forefront of the charge were the men of the 1st Bn Cameron Highlanders, Kitchener's favourite regiment, and in their wake, at a safe distance, Steevens and his fellow journalists. Kitchener had given a general order that all correspondents were to dismount when under Dervish fire – only the diminutive Villiers was permitted to remain on his horse on the argument that he could not otherwise see what was happening – but so fierce had become the Anglo-Egyptian firepower that Steevens and his colleagues had been able to ride into the *zeriba* unscathed.

For now began the killing. Bullet and bayonet and butt, the whirlwind of Highlanders swept over. And by this time the Lincolns were in on the right, and the Maxims, galloping right up to the stockade, had withered the left, and the Warwicks, the enemy's cavalry definitely gone, were volleying off the blacks as your beard comes off under a keen razor. Farther and farther they cleared the ground – cleared it of everything like a living man, for it was left carpeted thick enough with dead. Here was a trench; bayonet that man. Here a little straw tukl; warily round to the door, and then a volley. Now in column through this opening in the bushes; then into line, and drop those few desperately firing shadows among the dry stems beyond. For the running blacks – poor heroes – still fired, though every second they fired less and ran more. And on, on the British stumbled and slew, till suddenly there was unbroken blue overhead, and a clear drop underfoot. The river! And across the trickle of water the quarter-mile of dry sand-bed was a fly-paper with scrambling spots of black. The pursuers thronged the bank in double line, and in two minutes the paper was still black-spotted, only the spots scrambled no more. 'Now that,' panted the most pessimistic senior captain in the brigade – 'now I call that a very good fight.'

After the battle Kitchener allowed himself a moment's relaxation, Steevens and others marvelling to see him smile and speak gently to the men of the Camerons as they buried their dead. But that display of generosity could not hide the fact that the Atbara had been won at a terrible cost – 600 casualties, mainly borne by the Camerons and the Seaforth Highlanders. At home in Britain, though, the victory was met by a trenchant display of public excitement which had been whipped up largely by Steevens's account of the battle and its aftermath.

Back swung the blacks from battle. The band of the Twelfth specializes on Mr Gus Elen: it had not been allowed to play him during the attack – only the regimental march till the bandsmen were tired of it, and then each instrument what it liked – but now the air quoted came in especially apposite.

They had caught 'em alive O. Hardly one but had slung behind him a sword or a spine-headed spear, a curly knife, or a spiky club, or some other quaint captured murdering-iron. Some had supplemented their Martini with a Remington, an inch calibre elephant-gun with spherical iron bullets or conical shells, a regulation Italian magazine rifle, a musket of Mahomet Ali's first expedition, a Martini of '85, or a Tower rifle of '56 with a handful of the cartridges the sepoys declined to bite. Some had suits of armour tucked inside them; one or two, Saracen helmets slung to their belts. Over one tarbush waved a diadem of black ostrich plumes. The whole regiment danced with spear-headed banners blue and white, with golden letters thereupon promising victory to the faithful. And behind half-a-dozen men tugged at one of Mahmud's ten captured guns; they meant to ask the Sirdar if they might keep it.

The band stopped, and a hoarse gust of song flung out. From references to Allah you might presume it a song of thanksgiving. Then, tramp, tramp, a little silence, and the song came again with an abrupt exultant roar. The thin-legged, poker-backed shadows jerked longer and longer over the rough desert shingle. They had been going from six the bitter night before, and nothing to eat since, and Nakheila has been 111° in the shade, with the few spots of shade preoccupied by corpses. That being so, and remembering that the British and wounded had to follow, the Second Brigade condescended to a mere four miles an hour. And 'By George! you know,' said the Bey, 'they're lovely; they're rippers. I've seen Sikhs and I've seen Gurkhas, and these are good enough for me. This has been the happiest day of my life. I wasn't happier the day I got the DSO than I've been today.'

The vast new readership of the *Daily Mail* – by 1898 its readership was around half a million – thrilled to stuff of that kind, artless descriptions of British pluck and derring-do against savage opposition. It was Harmsworth's intention that the newspaper should concentrate less on news and more on topics which would provide a popular talking point. Thus the editorial emphasis was on such easily grasped ideas as the superiority of the British soldier, the dastardly nature of Mahdist rule or the personalities of the men leading the Anglo-Egyptian army. Harmsworth likened the technique to throwing a stone into a pond and watching the resultant ripples excite public opinion and thereby gain more sales.

Steevens was not slow to master the technique and to turn it to his own, and Harmsworth's, advantage. After the Battle of Atbara the Liberal *Manchester Guardian* was critical of Kitchener because it was rumoured that not only had no prisoners been taken but that wounded Dervishes had been shot out of hand. Steevens retorted by arguing that there would always be casualties in any war and that, in any case, British troops often had to kill or be killed when wounded Dervishes opened fire on them once the battle was over. More to the point of the Liberals' argument, perhaps, was the news that the captured Emir Mahmud had been put in chains and led in triumph behind Kitchener during the victory parade in Berber on 14 April, in a scene which could have come out of the Victorian history book – the Romans leading their slaves in triumph before the Capitol. This is precisely how Steevens portrayed it to his excited readership.

It was more like a Roman triumph than anything you have ever seen – like in its colour, its barbarism, its intoxicating arrogance. The Sirdar reached Berber an hour or so after sunrise; the garrison – Macdonald's brigade – had bivouacked outside. The Sirdar rode up to the once more enfranchised town, and was there received by a guard of honour of the 1st Egyptians, who had held the town during the campaign. The guns thundered a salute. Then slowly he started to ride down the wide main street – tall, straight, and masterful in his saddle. Hunter Pasha at his side, his staff and his flag behind him, then Lewis Bey and some of his officers from Fort Atbara, then a clanking escort of cavalry. At the gate he passed under a triumphal arch, and all the street was Venetian masts and bunting and coloured paper, and soldiers of the 1st presenting arms, and men and women and children shrieking shrill delight.

Well might they; for they have tried both rules, and they prefer that of Egypt. So they pressed forward and screamed 'Lu, lu,' as they saw returning the Sirdar and their Excellencies, these men of fair face and iron hand, just to the weak and swiftly merciless to the proud. And when these had passed they pressed forward still more eagerly. Farther behind, in a clear space, came one man alone, his hands tied behind his back. Mahmud! Mahmud, holding his head up and swinging his thighs in a swaggering stride – but Mahmud a prisoner, beaten, powerless. When the people of Berber saw that, they were convinced. It was not a lie, then: the white men had conquered indeed. And many a dark-skinned woman pressed forward to call Mahmud 'Dog' to his face: it was Mahmud, last year, who massacred the Jaalin at Metemmeh.

By this time the Sirdar had come almost to the bazaar, at the north end of the town; and there was a small platform with an awning. He dismounted, and so did the officers; then took his stand, and in came the troops. At their head the brigadier – 'old Mac', the bronzed and grizzled, who has lived in camp and desert and battlefield these twenty years on end. Then the blacks, straight as the spears they looted at Nakheila, quivering with pride in their officers and their own manhood – yet not a whit prouder than when they marched out a month before. Then the cavalry and the guns and the camel-corps – every arm of the victorious force. And Berber stood by and wondered and exulted. The band crashed and the people yelled. 'Lu-u-u, lu-u-u-u' piped the black women, and you could see the brave, savage, simple hearts of the black men bounding to the appeal. And the Sirdar and General Hunter and the others stood above all, calm and commanding; below Bey and Bimbashi led battalions or squadrons or battery, in undisturbed self-reliance. You may call the show barbaric if you like: it was meant for barbarians.

There is no irony in Steevens's words. He was writing for that part of a generation which believed itself to be superior and which spent its daily ½d in the expectation of the *Daily Mail* confirming that supremacy. It was a self-satisfied age and Steevens's journalism echoed the arrogance, smugness and shared esteem which characterized much of British society in the aftermath of Victoria's Diamond Jubilee.

Seen in that light, Steevens emerges as one of the
prophets of Empire, even though he was never quite able
to express his theories to his readership in a coherent
manner. That is not to say that he was an uncritical
journalist or that, as many suggested, he had sublimated
his Balliol mind to Harmsworth's sensationalism. During
the campaign it had become painfully obvious that the
boots issued to the British soldiers were not of a quality to
withstand the severity of the terrain in which they were to
be used. Steevens believed the *Mail*'s readership had to be
informed.

All these are inevitable accompaniments of a forced march; what
might have been avoided, and should have been, was the scandal
that the men's boots gave out. True, the brigade had done a lot of
marching since it came up-country, some of it – not much – over
rock and loose sand. True, also, that the Sudan climate, destructive of all things, is particularly destructive of all things stitched.
But the brigade had only been up-river about a month, after all,
and no military boot ought to wear out in a month. We have been
campaigning in the Sudan, off and on, for over fourteen years; we
might have discovered the little peculiarities of its climate by now.
The Egyptian army uses a riveted boot; the boots our British boys
were expected to march in had not even a toe-cap. So that when
the three battalions and a battery arrived in Berber hundreds of
men were all but barefoot: the soles peeled off, and instead of a
solid double sole, revealed a layer of shoddy packing sandwiched
between two thin slices of leather. Not one man fell out sick; those
who dropped asleep went on as soon as they came to, and
overtook their regiments. But every available camel was burdened
with a man who lacked nothing of strength or courage to march
on – only boots. General Gatacre had half-a-dozen charges; every
one was carrying a barefoot soldier, while the general trudged
with his men. All the mounted officers did the same.
    It is always the same story – knavery and slackness clogging
and strangling the best efforts of the British soldier. To save some
contractor a few pence on a boot, or to save some War Office
clerk a few hours of the work he is paid for not doing, you stand
to lose a good rifle and bayonet in a decisive battle, and to break

a good man's heart into the bargain. Is it worth it? But it is always happening; the history of the Army is a string of such disgraces. And each time we arise and bawl, 'Somebody ought to be hanged.' So says everybody. But nobody ever is hanged.

Steevens's report was published in the *Mail* in the wake of the Battle of Atbara and its appearance caused questions to be asked in the House of Commons. The War Office's retort that the boots were high-quality footwear but that the work done by the British troops had tried them too severely brought an immediate response from Steevens. 'It is a strange sort of answer,' he wrote, 'to say that a military boot is a very good boot, only you mustn't march in it.' After further campaigning by the *Mail* the War Office conceded that they would have to 'invent a boot which even General Gatacre [commanding the British Division] and the desert sand would not be able to wear out'. Boot problems have never entirely deserted the British Army. During the Falklands war of 1982, a campaign which had many similarities to the Khartoum expedition of 1898, British boots were again found to be wanting for the terrain over which the main battles were fought.

The Battle of Atbara marked the end of the first part of the campaign and allowed Kitchener's forces to be consolidated while he, his senior officers and the entire press corps hurried off north to spend the hot season in the relative comfort of Cairo and elsewhere. During the lull Steevens kept his readers entertained with descriptions of Cairo life out of season – most wealthy Cairenes and the entire British community fled to the cool of the Mediterranean during the stuffy heat of July.

By daylight Cairo looked like a ball-room the morning after. One hotel was shamelessly making up a rather battered face against next season. The verandah of Shepheard's, where six months ago you could not move for tea-tables, nor hear the band for the buzz of talk, was quite empty and lifeless; only one perspiring waiter hinted that this was a hotel. The Continental, the centre of Cairene fashion, had a whole wing shuttered up; the mirrors in the great hall were blind with whiting, and naked suites of bedroom furniture camped out in the great dining-room. Some shops were shut; the rest wore demi-toilettes of shutter and blind; the dozing shopkeepers seemed half resentful that anybody should wish to buy in such weather. As for scarabs and necklaces and curiosities of Egypt, they no longer pretended to think that any sane man could give money for such things. As you looked out from the Citadel, Cairo seemed dazed under the sun; the very Pyramids looked as if they were taking a holiday.

Steevens spent most of his spare time in Cairo picking up useful pieces of information from those officers unlucky enough to have been posted to training duties in the huge barracks of Kasr-el-Nil and he also made good use of the interlude by preparing for what everyone guessed would be the campaign's culmination. Having lost most of his kit during the first march south, Steevens decided to travel lightly and to ensure that most of his journey would be completed by steamer and rail as far as Atbara where horses would be waiting for him. And then it was the beginning of August with the officers returning to Cairo 'like schoolboys, wild to get back'. The war was on again and Steevens hurried south to observe Kitchener's army assembling at Wadi Hamed for the assault on Khartoum where the Mahdist forces were gathering in strength in the neighbouring fort of Omdurman. It was an imposing spectacle – just as Kitchener intended it to be – and when the march began on 21 August the army stretched three miles across the desert, the final touch of grandeur being the appearance at its head of Kitchener mounted on a white charger.

Two days later, from the top of a hill called Jebel Royan,

Major W. S. Gordon, nephew of the murdered martyr, gazed through his telescope and through the haze of the desert heat, forty miles away, he caught the army's first glimpse of Omdurman with the white dome of the Mahdi's tomb clearly visible above the houses of the town. Armed by Wingate's intelligence reports, Kitchener had learned that the Khalifa had withdrawn all his forces into the walls of Omdurman and that it was his intention to lure the Anglo-Egyptian army into a wasteful attack on its defences. Absolute faith told the Khalifa that he was only required to wait there and to allow the infidels to exhaust themselves beneath the hot sun before his army rushed forth to deliver the blow of the divinely just. But that reasoning took no account of the power of lyddite or the range of the British howitzers.

An ultimatum was sent to the Khalifa calling on him to surrender or at least to evacuate women and children from Omdurman before the expected artillery barrage began. This was refused and on 1 September the howitzers and the guns of the accompanying gunboats opened fire on the Dervish positions. To Steevens and his fellow journalists assembled with the army on the Kerreri ridge above the town it was a terrible sound as the five-inch shells roared through the air with the fury of an express train. Although they could not see the destruction it was clear to the journalists that the pounding would drive the Mahdist forces out of Omdurman to meet Kitchener's army which had taken up position by a bend in the River Nile below the amphitheatre of the Kerreri hills to the north, and the hills of Jebel Surgam to the south.

Kitchener had drawn up his troops in a wide arc with the river behind him. On the right, to the north, was Macdonald's brigade covering Maxwell's 2nd Egyptian Brigade in the centre. Gatacre's British Division took up

the left of the line of battle, backed by Maxims and three
batteries of artillery. They were to bear the first brunt of
the attack which began at 6.30 A.M. on 2 September when
the main Dervish force under Osman Azrak launched a
full-scale frontal attack on the British lines. To the waiting
troops this presented an awe-inspiring spectacle: line after
seemingly irresistible line of Dervishes making their way
forward in tight battle order, a wave of humanity pressing
forward to break on the concentrated fire of the British
infantry. And through the cool early morning air came the
chants of the devout. '*La llaha illa llah wa Muhammad rasul
ullah*' – 'There is but one God and Muhammad is the
messenger of God.'

The noise of something began to creep in upon us; it cleared and
divided into the tap of drums and the far-away surf of raucous
war-cries. A shiver of expectancy thrilled along our army, and
then a sigh of content. They were coming on. Allah help them!
they were coming on.

It was now half-past six. The flags seemed still very distant, the
roar very faint, and the thud of our first gun was almost startling.
It may have swung forward, and a mass of white flying linen
swung forward with it too. They came very fast, and they came
very straight; and then presently they came no farther. With a
crash the bullets leaped out of the British rifles. It began with
the Guards and Warwicks – section volleys at 2000 yards; then,
as the Dervishes edged rightward, it ran along to the Highlanders, the Lincolns, and to Maxwell's Brigade. The British stood
up in double rank behind their zariba; the blacks lay down in
their shelter-trench; both poured out death as fast as they could
load and press trigger. Shrapnel whistled and Maxims growled
savagely. From all the line came perpetual fire, fire, fire, and
shrieked forth in great gusts of destruction.

And the enemy? No white troops would have faced that torrent
of death for five minutes, but the Bagarra and the blacks came on.
The torrent swept into them and hurled them down in whole
companies. You saw a rigid line gather itself up and rush on
evenly; then before a shrapnel shell or a Maxim the line suddenly

quivered and stopped. The line was yet unbroken, but it was quite still. But other lines gathered up again, again, and yet again; they went down, and yet others rushed on. Sometimes they came near enough to see single figures quite plainly. One old man with a white flag started with five comrades; all dropped, but he alone came bounding forward to within 200 yards of the 14th Sudanese. Then he folded his arms across his face, and his limbs loosened, and he dropped sprawling to earth beside his flag.

It was the last day of Mahdism, and the greatest. They could never get near, and they refused to hold back. By now the ground before us was all white with dead men's drapery. Rifles grew red-hot; the soldiers seized them by the slings and dragged them back to the reserve to change for cool ones. It was not a battle, but an execution.

By 8.30 A.M. the first massacre was almost over. Pounded by howitzer shells, riddled by machine-guns and scythed down by a hail of dum-dum bullets, 2,000 Dervishes had been urged on by their emirs to certain death. Even the normally stoical British soldiers in Kitchener's army, many of them veterans of past imperial skirmishes, were shocked by what they had witnessed and privately echoed Steevens's conclusion that it had been less of a battle and more of a full-scale slaughter. 'The valour of those poor half-starved Dervishes in their patched jibbahs would have graced Thermopylae,' wrote Lt-Col Charles Townsend of the XIIth Sudanese – later to win fame during the First World War as 'Townsend of Kut' – and few present at the battle disagreed with his sentiments.

However, it was not all over yet. Steevens missed the famous charge of the 21st Lancers who attacked a Dervish position while reconnoitring the ground between Kerreri and Omdurman, winning three Victoria Crosses in the process; but he was on hand to give an eye-witness account of the action upon which final victory depended. Having repulsed the first Dervish attack, Kitchener decided to push

south to Omdurman to take the town quickly and cheaply
but he had misread the Dervish intentions: far from being
crushed, they had regrouped to the north of the Kerreri
ridge in a new army under Yakub, the Khalifa's son. As
the Anglo-Egyptian army swung south Macdonald's brigade on the right was left to bring up the rear without any
cover and soon an expanse of territory opened up between
it and the main force. It was an ideal position for Yakub to
exploit but Macdonald was alive to the danger facing his
brigade. A galloper – his ADC, Lieutenant Pritchard – was
sent to Kitchener asking for instructions: the Sirdar's reply
ordered Macdonald not to engage but to continue his
march. No sooner were the words out of his mouth than
the sound of gunfire could be heard across the plain as the
first shots were fired against Yakub's attack. Riding beside
Kitchener was Steevens who immediately understood the
military implications of Pritchard's request. With Burleigh
in attendance he swung his horse round and made for the
army's rearguard where the two correspondents found
Macdonald 'very gleeful in his usual grim way' preparing
for immediate battle. 'Gentlemen,' he addressed them
solemnly, 'I am delighted to welcome you and I think I can
show you some good sport.' Steevens's intuition about
Fighting Mac and the qualities of his Sudanese brigade
were about to pay off.

The sight of the approaching Dervishes had worked up
the Sudanese into a frenzy and they were blasting off their
rifles without thought of aim or, more importantly, of
ammunition. Confusion reigned as the air became loud
with rapid gunfire, screams and curses, as the Sudanese
fired for all they were worth. Realizing that his men could
quickly run out of ammunition if they continued to fire in
such a wasteful way, Macdonald walked out in front of his

men and knocked up their rifles with his swagger stick. The ploy worked and as the Dervishes approached Macdonald's lines they met a withering curtain of fire that sent them reeling. It was a brilliant example of controlled discipline, carried out under the most dangerous and terrifying circumstances; but no sooner had they repelled Yakub's men than a fresh danger confronted the Sudanese. A Camel Corps officer arrived with the news that a new and formidable force, numbering perhaps 20,000, was about to strike and that on Hunter's instructions he was to withdraw. Macdonald's response – reported by Burleigh – was simple enough: 'I'll no do it,' he said. 'I'll see them damned first. We maun just fight.'

What happened next was the wonder of all who saw it. Macdonald called his battalion commanders together and hurriedly sketched out in the sand a new plan of defence – they were to move their men, battalion by battalion, beginning with the XIth. To accomplish such a complicated manoeuvre on a parade ground would have tried even the hardest veterans, but to execute it under a barrage of heavy fire was a demonstration of leadership and controlled discipline at their strongest.

But the cockpit of the fight was Macdonald's. The British might avenge his brigade; it was his to keep it and to kill off the attack. To meet it he turned his front through a complete half-circle, facing successively south, west and north. Every tactician in the army was delirious in his praise: the ignorant correspondent was content to watch the man and his blacks. 'Cool as on parade,' is an old phrase; Macdonald Bey was very much cooler. Beneath the strong, square-hewn face you could tell that the brain was working as if packed in ice. He sat solid on his horse, and bent his black brows towards the green flag and the Remingtons. Then he turned to a galloper with an order, and cantered easily up to a battalion commander. Magically the rifles hushed, the stinging powder smoke wisped away, and the companies were rapidly

threading back and forward, round and round, in and out, as if it
were a figure of a dance. In two minutes the brigade was together
again in a new place. The field in front was hastening towards us
in a whitey-brown cloud of Dervishes. An order. Macdonald's
jaws gripped and hardened as the flame spurted out again, and
the whitey-brown cloud quivered and stood still. He saw everything; knew what to do; knew how to do it. At the fire he was ever
brooding watchfully behind his firing-line; at the cease fire he was
instantly in front of it: all saw him, and knew that they were being
nursed to triumph.

Having wheeled his brigade Macdonald then had the
task of meeting that last fanatical charge, and at one point,
as wave after wave of Dervishes charged, it seemed as if
their suicidal tactics might win the day. On some parts of
the front the Sudanese were engaged in fierce hand-to-hand
fighting, their ammunition having finally been exhausted,
and the Xth were already taking the brunt of the onslaught
with fixed bayonets. At that point the pressure began to
slacken as, on Kitchener's orders, General Wauchope's 1st
British Brigade attacked the remnants of Yakub's force and
the Lincolnshire Regiment arrived to strengthen Macdonald's right. The combined fire of the two brigades soon
dispersed this final onslaught and the enemy began to retire
to the safety of the Kerreri ridge with Macdonald's
Sudanese troops in hot pursuit. To Steevens, caught up in
the heat of the fighting, it was an awesome sight.

And the Dervishes? The honour of the fight must still go with the
men who died. Our men were perfect, but the Dervishes were
superb – beyond perfection. It was their largest, best, and bravest
army that ever fought against us for Mahdism, and it died
worthily of the huge empire that Mahdism won and kept so long.
Their riflemen, mangled by every kind of death and torment that
man can devise, clung round the black flag and the green,
emptying their poor, rotten, home-made cartridges dauntlessly.
Their spearmen charged death at every minute hopelessly. Their

horsemen led each attack, riding into the bullets till nothing was left but three horses trotting up to our line, heads down, saying, 'For goodness' sake, let us in out of this.' Not one rush, or two, or ten – but rush on rush, company on company, never stopping, though all their view that was not unshaken enemy was the bodies of the men who had rushed before them. A dusky line got up and stormed forward: it bent, broke up, fell apart, and disappeared. Before the smoke had cleared, another line was bending and storming forward in the same track.

It was over. The avenging squadrons of the Egyptian cavalry swept over the field. The Khalifa and the Sheikh-ed-Din had galloped back to Omdurman. Ali Wad Helu was borne away on an angareb with a bullet through his thigh-bone. Yakub lay dead under his brother's banner. From the green army there now came only death-enamoured desperadoes, strolling one by one towards the rifles, pausing to shake a spear, turning aside to recognize a corpse, then, caught by a sudden jet of fury, bounding forward, checking, sinking limply to the ground. Now under the black flag in a ring of bodies stood only three men, facing the three thousand of the Third Brigade. They folded their arms about the staff and gazed steadily forward. Two fell. The last Dervish stood up and filled his chest; he shouted the name of his God and hurled his spear. Then he stood quite still, waiting. It took him full; he quivered, gave at the knees, and toppled with his head on his arms and his face towards the legions of his conquerors.

Although Steevens, like others who had witnessed the slaughter, was rightly conscious of the Dervishes' bravery, he was stretching a point by over emphasizing the prowess of the Khalifa's men. Courageous and contemptuous of death they might have been, but their mettle had been no substitute for the superior firepower – the Lee Metford rifles, Maxim guns and howitzers – used by the Anglo-Egyptian army. Where Steevens's report did score was his realization that Kitchener's lack of tactical foresight had almost lost the day and that possible Defeat and a huge casualty list had only been avoided by Macdonald's prompt action in defending the army's rearguard. Steevens's – and

Burleigh's – description of the part played by Macdonald enhanced Fighting Mac's prestige but both correspondents were careful to remind their readers of Kitchener's role. Steevens was especially enthusiastic.

When the Sirdar moved his brigades southward he knew what he was doing. He was giving his right to an unbeaten enemy; with his usual daring he made it so. His game now was to get between the Dervishes and Omdurman. Perhaps he did not guess what a bellyful of beating the unbeaten enemy would take; but he trusted to his generals and his star, and, as always, they bore him to victory.

As a piece of straight reporting, Steevens's account of the Battle of Omdurman is first class. He stood behind the British positions when the Dervishes made their first assault at dawn and was able to give a first-hand account of the initial massacre; then, in the confusion of the army's march on Omdurman, he was able to read the significance of Macdonald's position and the part it was to play in gaining eventual victory. His post-battle analysis was also sound. He was critical of the rash charge of the 21st Lancers, describing their attack against armed infantry over unknown ground 'as grave a tactical crime as cavalry could possibly commit': yet he was also aware that its commanding officer, Colonel R. M. Martin, could hardly be censured by the War Office because 'the populace has glorified the charge of the 21st for its indisputable heroism'. With less reason, perhaps, he criticized Kitchener's decision not to dig a trench around his positions but conceded that disciplined firepower had made it superfluous. And, of course, he had already criticized the lack of tactical awareness which had endangered Macdonald's brigade.

Of the casualties – which numbered some 11,000 Dervishes dead – Steevens had this to say:

How the figures of wounded were arrived at I do not know. The wounded of a Dervish army ought not really to be counted at all, since the badly wounded die and the slightly wounded are just as dangerous as if they were whole. It is conceivable that some of the wounded may have been counted twice over – either as dead, when they were certain to perish of their wounds or of thirst, or else as prisoners when they gave themselves up. Yet, with all the deductions that moderation can suggest, it was a most appalling slaughter. The Dervish army was killed out as hardly an army has been killed out in the history of war.

It will shock you, but it was simply unavoidable. Not a man was killed except resisting – very few except attacking. Many wounded were killed, it is true, but that again was absolutely unavoidable. At the very end of the battle, when Macdonald's brigade was advancing after its long fight, the leading files of the 9th Sudanese passed by a young Bagarra who was not quite dead. In a second he was up and at the nearest mounted white officer. The first spear flew like a streak, but just missed. The officer assailed put a man-stopping revolver bullet into him, but it did not stop him. He whipped up another spear, and only a swerve in the saddle saved the Englishman's body at the expense of a wounded right hand. This happened not once but a hundred times, and all over the field. It was impossible not to kill the Dervishes: they refused to go back alive.

The losses in Kitchener's army amounted to forty-eight dead and 343 wounded, a sum which Steevens described as being 'so small as to be almost ridiculous'. At home in Britain, radicals treated the news of the victory with derision and expressions of outrage. In their view it had not been a battle but a massacre, the triumph of modern weaponry over the chainmail, swords and muskets of a bygone age; but Steevens remained loyal to the *Mail*'s editorial standpoint, that Omdurman was a glorious victory, fully vindicating the steadfastness and professionalism of the British soldier and his 'native' Egyptian and Sudanese comrades.

The battle over, Kitchener and his men swept into the mean streets of Omdurman, the soldiers regarding with amazement the collection of sprawling shacks and their poor wide-eyed inhabitants staring back at them as if they had come from another planet. Their immediate target was the domed tomb of the Mahdi and it was there that the final act in Kitchener's victory was played out. A stray British shell screamed overhead and burst amongst a group of nearby inhabitants, killing them instantly. Three other shells followed and although Kitchener and his party were well clear of the explosion, a piece of shrapnel killed Hubert Howard of *The Times*. Frank Rhodes, his colleague, had been injured in the shoulder, leaving *The Times* without a correspondent – and Scudamore's pony was another casualty. Nor were these the only losses to the press corps. Henry Cross of the *Manchester Guardian* succumbed a few days later to enteric fever. 'Years ago he had rowed in the Oxford Eight,' remembered Steevens, 'but enteric delights in seizing the most powerful frames.'

Later that night Kitchener held an impromptu press conference, dictating his despatch to Wingate by candle-light; then the correspondents took it in turn to send their own reports back to London via Cairo by courtesy of the military telegram system. Two days later, on Sunday 4 September, the final duty was completed with a service of remembrance in the gardens of Gordon's palace in Khartoum on the other bank of the Nile. Five hundred selected troops attended the ceremony – which was conducted on an ecumenical basis, at Kitchener's insistence – and they made an impressive sight. Amongst their number were kilted Highlanders, yeomen of the English counties, stately guardees and riflemen, men of the Camel Corps, fellahin soldiers of Egypt and native troops of the Sudan, resplendent under white fezzes topped by red hackles. Britain's imperial might had come to pay its last respects to the memory of a Victorian hero: in the centre of the serried ranks, head and shoulders above his brother officers, stood the erect figure of the Sirdar. Steevens's colourful description was geared to make his readers thrill to the dignity of the occasion:

Here were men that fought for Gordon's life while he lived – Kitchener, who went disguised and alone among furious enemies to get news of him; Wauchope, who poured out his blood like water at Tamai and Kirbekan; Stuart-Wortley, who missed by but two days the chance of dying at Gordon's side. And here, too, were boys who could hardly lisp when their mothers told them that Gordon was dead, grown up now and appearing in the fullness of time to exact eleven thousand lives for one. Gordon may die – other Gordons may die in the future – but the same clean-limbed brood will grow up and avenge them.

The boats stopped plugging and there was silence. We were tying up opposite a grove of tall palms; on the bank was a crowd of natives curiously like the backsheesh-hunters who gather to greet the Nile steamers. They stared at us; but we looked beyond them to a large building rising from a crumbling quay. You could see that it had once been a handsome edifice of the type you know in Cairo or Alexandria – all stone and stucco, two-storeyed, faced with tall regular windows. Now the upper storey was clean gone; the blind windows were filled up with bricks; the stucco was all scars, and you could walk up to the roof on rubble. In front was an acacia, such as grow in Ismailia or the Gezireh at Cairo, only unpruned – deep luscious green, only drooping like a weeping willow. At that most ordinary sight everybody grew very solemn. For it was a piece of a new world, or rather of an old world, utterly different from the squalid mud, the baking barrenness of Omdurman. A façade battered and blind, the tree drooping to earth – there was no need to tell us we were at a grave. In that forlorn ruin, and that disconsolate acacia, the bones of murdered civilization lay before us.

On the roof above the spot where Gordon had fallen the Union Jack sprang free from its pole, to be followed by the Egyptian flag, in recognition of the fact that the Sudan had been accepted into the Empire as an Anglo-Egyptian condominium, an arrangement whereby it would be ruled by Britain in Egypt's name. Then followed a simple yet moving service: the playing of the 'Dead March' and Gordon's favourite hymn, 'Abide With Me', followed by prayers, the 'Last Post' and a lament played by a piper of the Camerons. For many of the soldiers present it was a moving experience, and most surprisingly of all, even the Sirdar seemed to be affected. Unable to control his tears, Kitchener turned to General Hunter and asked him to dismiss the parade. Had a mountain of ice appeared in their midst the sight would have been no less surprising than the sight of Kitchener giving vent to his emotions: that he should have wept in public was the wonder of all who witnessed it. Before the gunboats returned to Omdurman with their passengers, half-an-hour was allowed for the men to wander through the gardens and to take stock of their achievement.

The reconquest of the Sudan and the victory at Omdurman made Kitchener's name. (He was awarded a peerage and received a public reward of £30,000.) It also established Steevens as a leading war correspondent and a journalist to be reckoned with in Fleet Street. His despatches from the front, published under the title of 'With Kitchener to Khartoum', had also added considerably to the *Mail*'s sales and when his book of the campaign was published under the same title a few weeks later it quickly went through eight editions. The Edinburgh publishing firm of William Blackwood had been setting it from the copy in the *Mail* and once the final despatches had arrived the book was quickly put to bed.

Its success was largely due to the fact that Steevens gave his readers a story which they had come to expect: the triumph of British arms, the patient strength of General

Kitchener, a thrilling account of the great battle at Omdurman, ending with the sobering thought that British peace and prosperity would now be the happy lot of the Sudanese people. And in the best spirit of the New Imperialism, Steevens insisted that it was British pluck which had achieved that happy state of affairs.

Surely enough, 'When Allah made the Sudan,' say the Arabs, 'he laughed.' You can almost hear the fiendish echo of it crackling over the fiery sand. And yet – and yet there never was an Englishman who had been there, but was ready and eager to go again. 'Drink of Nile water,' say the same Arabs, 'and you will return to drink it again.' Nile water is either very brown or very green, according to the season; yet you do go back and drink it again. Perhaps to Englishmen – half-savage still on the pinnacle of their civilization – the very charm of the land lies in its empty barbarism. There is space in the Sudan. There is the fine, purified desert air, and the long stretching gallops over its sand. There are the things at the very back of life, and no other to posture in front of them – hunger and thirst to assuage, distance to win through, pain to bear, life to defend, and death to face. You have gone back to the spring water of your infancy. You are a savage again – a savage with Rosbach water, if there is any left, and a Mauser repeating pistol-carbine, if the sand has not jammed it, but still at the last word a savage. You are unprejudiced, simple, free. You are a naked man, facing naked nature.

I do not believe that any of us who come home whole will think, from our easy-chairs, unkindly of the Sudan.

Above all, Steevens made his armchair readers feel that they themselves had been present in Kitchener's army during the campaign. In his articles he conveyed colourful descriptions of the Sudan as a land of heat and dust, a wilderness scorched by a desert sun: the reader could almost feel the parched throat and impatient thirst which accompanied the first long drink of the evening when the day's march was done. Certainly no other journalist of the campaign managed to describe so well the sense of relief

and satisfaction felt by those who drank long and deep in
the cool of the evening.

Now comes the sweet revenge for all the torments of the day. It is
quite dark by now, unless the moon be up, leaning to you out of a
tender blue immensity, silver, caressing, cool. Or else the sprightly
candles beckon from your dinner-table, spread outside the tent, a
halo of light and white in the blackness, alert, inviting, cool. You,
too, by now are clean and cool. You quite forget whether the day
was more than warm or no.

But you remember the thirst. You are cool, but within you are
still dry, very dry and shrunken. Take a long mug and think well
what you will have poured into it; for this is the moment of the
day, the moment that pays for the Sudan. You are very thirsty,
and you are about to slake your thirst. Let it be alcoholic, for you
have exuded much life in the day; let it above all be long. Whisky-
and-soda is a friend that never fails you, but better still something
tonic. Gin and soda? Gin and lime-juice and soda? Gin and bitter
and lime-juice and soda? or else that triumphant blend of all
whetting flavours, an Abu Hamed – gin, vermouth, Angostura,
lime-juice, soda?

Mix it in due proportions; put in especially plenty of soda – and
then drink. For this is to drink indeed. The others were only
flushing your body with liquid as you might flush a drain. But
this! This splashes round your throat, slides softly down your
gullet till you feel it run out into your stomach. It spreads blessedly
through body and spirit – not swirling through, like the Atbara,
but irrigating, like the Nile. It is soil in the sand, substance in the
wind, life in death. Your sap runs again, your biltong muscles
take on elasticity, your tummy bones toughen. Your self has
sprung up alive, and you almost think you know how it feels to
rise from the dead.

But on other counts, Steevens made mistakes. His impatience to get back to London once the battle was over
meant that he missed the historic meeting between
Kitchener and Marchand at Fashoda, a confrontation over
territorial rights which almost plunged Britain and France
into war. He ignored, too, the allegations that Kitchener's

soldiers had killed wounded Dervishes on the battlefield. Only Bennett – thoroughly disgruntled by Kitchener's attitude towards him – took up the story in the *Contemporary Review*. Neither did Steevens have anything to say about Kitchener's treatment of the Mahdi's tomb which was blown up and the Mahdi's embalmed corpse tossed into the Nile. The action caused a good deal of offence – even to Queen Victoria who described the Mahdi as 'a *man* of *certain* importance' – and Kitchener's newly-won popularity was put in jeopardy when questions were asked about his conduct in the House of Commons. Further outrage was occasioned by the story that Kitchener had kept the Mahdi's skull as a keepsake but on this Steevens and the *Mail* remained silent, an indication, no doubt, of the importance they attached to presenting Omdurman as a glorious victory.

Omdurman was the last of the imperial battles to be fought by a British army against inferior native opposition. Within fourteen months of the victory British troops were to be in action in another part of Africa as Britain began her long-drawn-out war against the Boers in South Africa. Once again war correspondents were to be sent to the battlefield by London editors now convinced more than ever before that war stories sold newspapers, and once again Steevens found himself in the front-line sending telegraphic despatches back to Carmelite House, the *Mail*'s Fleet Street headquarters. He witnessed the inglorious defeats of 'Black Week' – 16 December 1899 – which saw heavy British losses at Magersfontein, Stormberg and Colenso, and by Christmas he was holed up with a besieged British force in Ladysmith. Apart from a few messages flashed out by heliograph or despatched by the occasional native runner through the Boer lines, the war correspondents with Steevens had to keep their silence and turn to their diaries for future publication. To while away the time and to keep up the spirits of the besieged force, Steevens turned his energies to editing a news-sheet called – in deference to the absence of hard news – the *Ladysmith Lyre*. At the outset of the siege he was jaunty enough but by Christmas he was finding the inactivity 'weary, stale, flat, unprofitable'. 'Relieve us, in Heaven's name, good country-men,' he implored his readers, 'or we die of dullness.' Poor Steevens did not die of boredom: typhoid, the dreaded enteric fever, carried him off soon after Christmas on 15 January 1900.

Shortly before he died, his friend and colleague, W. T. Maude of the *Graphic*, was advised by a military doctor to tell Steevens that his end was near. Initially, Steevens expressed disbelief because he thought he was beginning to feel better, but as the news sank in he gave his last messages to Maude and then, having composed himself, he is sup-posed to have said: 'Well, Maude, we have been very good chums, and if I am going to die, let's have our final drink together. Get that last bottle of champagne that I have reserved for the relief of Ladysmith.' Three hours later Steevens was dead and with his passing went the self-parodying *Ladysmith Lyre*, the only newspaper he ever edited. Due to the danger of infection his body was buried that same night, shortly after midnight: the poignant scent was captured in his diary for posterity by H. S. Nevinson of the *Daily Chronicle*.

All the London correspondents came, and a few officers, Colonel Stoneman and Major Henderson, of the Intelligence Department, representing the staff. Many more would have come, but nearly the whole garrison was warned for duty. About twenty-five of us, all mounted, followed the little glass hearse with its black and white embellishments. The few soldiers and sentries whom we passed, halted and gave the last salute. There was a full moon, covered with clouds, that let the light through at their misty edges. A soft rain fell as we lowered the coffin by the ropes into the grave. The Boer searchlight on Bulwan was sweeping the half circle of the English defences from end to end, and now and then it opened its full white eye upon us, as though the enemy wondered what we were doing there. We were laying to rest a man of assured, though unaccomplished genius, whose heart had still been full of hopes and generosity. One who had not lost the affections and charm of youth, nor been dulled either by success or disappointment.[2]

Harmsworth was devastated by the news of the death and rushed off to Steevens's home in Clapham to prostrate himself in front of Mrs Steevens, crying in a loud voice that he had killed George by 'sending him to Ladysmith'. Kitchener, too, by then Chief of Staff to Lord Roberts in South Africa, was also upset by the news. In a rare communiqué he added his condolences to the many tributes which followed Steevens's early death: 'He was a model correspondent, the best I have ever known, and I should like to say how greatly grieved I am at his death.' Coming from a soldier who despised the press and who had come to dislike the whole 'newspaper business' (as he called it), it was no bad encomium.

But there was, too, a touch of irony in the mutual admiration the two men had for each other. Steevens's creation of Kitchener as 'the Sudan machine', a man of ambition and purpose whose icy personality brooked no opposition, helped to make the general's name with the British public and to turn him into one of the great imperial ikons. There were others, though, like Edgar Wallace, another correspondent of the *Daily Mail*, who insisted that so powerfully ingrained in the public imagination was Steevens's description, that Kitchener had to spend the rest of his life living up to it.

3

Edgar Wallace and The Great Boer War

Ever since their first confrontation at the end of the Napoleonic Wars, the British and the Boer communities in South Africa had lived in an uneasy co-existence which had all too frequently broken out into armed conflict. Descended from the 17th-century Dutch immigrants who had settled in Cape Colony, the Boers were more a tribe than a people, a tightly knit, hard-fisted race who put great trust in the providence of their fundamentalist Calvinistic religion. They disdained change, regarded the native black population as slaves and resented the presence of the British in a country they were determined to hold as their own. For their part, the British, who had come to South Africa through treaty and purchase, looked on the Boers as a nuisance, for the Cape was a vital pivot in their imperial trade routes. In 1837 the Boers made the first positive move when a series of mass emigrations, or 'treks', had taken the more intransigent of their people north to establish the Transvaal and the Orange Free State; while the British and the 'Cape Dutch' largely remained in the southern colonies of Natal, Rhodesia and Cape Colony.

Each side viewed the other with ill-disguised hostility and the unrest had broken out into open war in 1880 over a Boer refusal to pay taxes. During the limited engagement the British public had been treated to the undignified spectacle of well-trained British troops being defeated at Majuba Hill by apparently ignorant peasant farmers. Peace was eventually restored by Gladstone's Liberal Government and further bloodshed avoided; the Boers were given self-government under British suzerainty but a feeling grew within the British Army and in imperialist circles that the peace was without honour, that a military solution was possible and that, sooner or later, Majuba would have to be avenged.

It was an unsatisfactory arrangement, a powder-keg that was capable of exploding into open war; the fuse was provided by the discovery of seemingly endless supplies of gold in 1886 in Witwatersrand – the 'Rand' – south of Pretoria. The new wealth, or at least the promise of it, attracted speculators from Britain as well as from other countries and quite soon the Boers were outnumbered by these foreigners, or *uitlanders*. Distrust of British motives, fear of foreign involvement and a belief that the *uitlanders* would change the pastoral tenor of the Boer way of life led the Transvaalers under President Kruger to pass laws excluding non-Boers from involvement in affairs of state while retaining the right to tax them. Soon the cry of 'no taxation without representation' was being heard in the land, a plea which no self-respecting British government could ignore. Kruger had told his fellow countrymen that if they loved their country they would rue the day that gold was discovered and he had good reason to be so pessimistic. Johannesburg, the capital of the Transvaal, soon became a boom town.

Amongst the many adventurers who had made their fortunes in South Africa was Cecil Rhodes who believed that British imperial influence should one day extend from the Cape to Cairo. The intransigence of Kruger and the vainglory of Rhodes were to provide the first grounds for war between the two peoples. Encouraged by noises of *uitlander* discontent in the Transvaal, Rhodes allowed his associate Starr Jameson to ride over the border in 1895 in an ill-advised raid in support of an uprising which was

never likely to take place. Jameson was captured and
returned to London for trial, Rhodes was disgraced and
Britain made a laughing stock. More importantly, the
botched raid outraged Boer feelings throughout South
Africa. Kruger's stock rose to new heights and he was able
to persuade his neighbours, the Orange Free State, to enter
into a treaty of mutual defence.

In 1897 the British responded by appointing Lord Milner
Governor-General of Cape Colony and High Commissioner
to South Africa. One of the most brilliant of the New
Imperialists, he found little difficulty in adhering to the
belief that British rule should be pre-eminent in South
Africa and that it was morally indefensible for Britons to
be under the governance of such a backward race as the
Boers. That belief was shared by his immediate chief, the
Colonial Secretary Joseph Chamberlain, and was echoed
by many others; gradually they moved to the opinion that
such an unwelcome situation threatened the security of the
Empire and could only be retrieved by going to war.

Protracted negotiations took place between Kruger and
Milner during which neither side showed much adroitness:
each new concession was met by further impossible
demands until a showdown became inevitable. Ten thousand British troops were despatched to South Africa under
the command of Sir George White and the Boer parliament
in the Transvaal made plans for mobilization. Boer and
Briton finally went to war on 12 October 1899 after
Kruger's demands that Britain remove her troops from the
frontier had been contemptuously ignored in London. 'Mr
Kruger has asked for war, and war he must have,' thundered the *Daily Telegraph*, and other leader writers took
equally bellicose views as the London press began to beat
the patriotic drum. Amazement, derision and delight were
displayed in equal measure: amazement that the petty Boer

republics had challenged the might of the British Empire;
derision over the pathetic nature of their challenge; and
delight at the prospect of another easy victory over a distant
native people. If anything was more important to the
British press and its readership that October week it was
only Scintillant's narrow victory over Ercildoune in the
Cesarewitch, run that Wednesday.

By the weekend General Sir Redvers Buller, VC, one of
the country's foremost soldiers, was en route to South
Africa to take command of the imperial forces in what
everyone was agreed would be a short sharp war. He was
given a hero's send-off when he boarded the RMS *Dunottar
Castle* at Southampton and the slightly hysterical mood of
his departure was caught in a cartoon which appeared in
Punch that week. It showed two London street-urchins
discussing the forthcoming conflict. 'The Boers will cop it
now,' one is telling the other. 'Farfer's gone to South Africa,
an' looken 'is strap!'

To most people in Britain, Buller's task was simple
enough and if past form were anything to go by the Boers
would be slapped down before Christmas. After all, they
reasoned, was not the British Army the most professional,
the best drilled and the hardiest army in the world? The
tactics which had triumphed from Peiwar Kotal to Omdurman would surely tell on the veldt against a Boer force
which was little more than a makeshift citizens' militia. In
the event, though, the fighting was to last three years, the
Boers were to gain some notable successes and Britain's
eventual victory was to require rather more effort than the
simple wielding of Farfer's strap.

Sailing with Buller on the *Dunottar Castle* was an army of
war correspondents who had been despatched by their
editors to cover the war in South Africa. Some were
American like William Dinwiddie of *Harper's* and J. O.

Knight of the *Chicago Times and Herald*, but for the most part
they were British, the most renowned of their number being
Winston Churchill whom we last met in the Sudan. Once
again Churchill was going to war in an anomalous position.
He had persuaded Buller to grant him a commission in the
South African Light Horse – just as he had manoeuvred
Kitchener into allowing him to ride with the 21st Lancers
at Omdurman – yet he was still employed by the *Morning
Post*. The deal that he had struck with his editor is also
worth mentioning: he was to be paid £1,000 for four
months' work and £200 per month plus expenses for any
longer period. (In the event he remained in South Africa
until October 1900.) At the end of his tour Churchill
reckoned that he had made a profit of £10,000 from his
journalism and lecture tours and from the publication of
his best-selling book, *London to Ladysmith via Pretoria* (1900).
Churchill also believed in covering a war in style – with
him to South Africa aboard the *Dunottar Castle* went two
dozen bottles of wine, six bottles of port and eighteen
bottles of malt whisky.

The duality of Churchill's position almost cost him his
life when he was captured on board an armoured train near
Colenso in November and then imprisoned in Pretoria. The
Boer General Joubert was of a mind to execute him because
he was in uniform and carrying arms, but Churchill
managed to elude his captors and the story of his escape by
train to the safety of Lourenço Marques became one of the
more colourful incidents of the early part of the war.

The truck in which I ensconced myself was laden with great sacks
of some soft merchandise, and I found among them holes and
crevices by means of which I managed to work my way to the
inmost recess. The hard floor was littered with gritty coal dust,
and made a most uncomfortable bed. The heat was almost stifling.
I was resolved, however, that nothing should lure or compel me

from my hiding place until I reached Portuguese territory. I expected the journey to take thirty-six hours; it dragged out into two and a half days. I hardly dared sleep for fear of snoring. I dreaded lest the trucks should be searched at Komati Poort, and my anxiety as the train approached this neighbourhood was very great. To prolong it we were shunted on to a siding for eighteen hours either at Komati Poort or the station beyond it. Once again they began to search my truck, and I heard the tarpaulin rustle as they pulled at it, but luckily they did not search deep enough, so that, providentially protected, I reached Delagoa Bay at last, and crawled forth from my place of refuge and of punishment, weary, dirty, hungry, but free once more.[1]

The incident added lustre to Churchill's name; even a music-hall song was composed about him and his exploit, extolling him as the 'latest and the greatest correspondent of the day'.

From the very outset of the voyage Buller resented the presence of the journalists on board the *Dunottar Castle* and he issued an order forbidding his officers to speak to the press – the majority of his forces were travelling separately on a variety of troopships and civilian liners hastily pressed into service by the Admiralty. To a certain extent Buller's antagonism did not hamper the press corps who were still caught up in the jingoistic fervour of their departure. At that point in the war their newspapers only wanted good-natured stories which spoke of British pluck and of the certainty of eventual victory. Because they had to use the ship's telegraph Buller's staff was able to censor the correspondents' reports, but such was their buoyancy of mood – and a lack of any hard news – that no one cared to send anything other than cheerful anecdotes about life on board. Typical of these was the day the *Dunottar Castle* overhauled an elderly troopship, the *Ninevah*. After asking if Buller were on board the men on the *Ninevah* gave 'three lusty cheers' to which the stately liner replied with a hoot on its siren.

The two ships pulled apart, but from the masts of the troopship came one last message: 'Who won the Cesarewitch?' With easy confidence like that, recorded one journalist, Booth of *Pearson's War News*, surely the outcome of the war was a foregone conclusion.

The war in South Africa turned out to be one of the most widely reported of modern wars. At one point *The Times* had 20 correspondents in the field, led by Leo Amery who went on to edit the seven-volumed *Times History of the War in South Africa*. Bennet Burleigh led the *Telegraph*'s team, Frederick Villiers was there with his green roadster bicycle and amongst the many seasoned veterans were Melton Prior of the *Illustrated London News*, Richard Harding Davis of the *New York World*, René Bull of the *Black and White*, Emerson Neilly of the *Pall Mall Gazette* and Vere Stint of Reuters. A feature of this war was the extent to which it was covered by press photographers, most of whom were freelance. The *Black and White* led the field with its comprehensive and carefully chosen photographic account of the war, and newspapers like the *Daily Mail* published fortnightly illustrated supplements – in the *Mail*'s case this was called *With the Flag to Pretoria* – which could be bound up and made into volumes. The war also introduced the British public to its first experience of moving pictures of war. Cameras from the Biograph Company of London had recorded Buller's departure from Southampton and the Warwick Trading Company was established to film the events of the war with moving-picture cameras. There was tremendous excitement when those early newsreels captured a dramatic incident in which a British Red Cross team came under Boer fire while attending wounded soldiers on the veldt. Later, though, it transpired that this was merely a propaganda film shot in the early morning on London's Hampstead Heath and using actors to play the brave British doctors and their dastardly Boer assailants. Other 'war films' were later discovered to have been shot at Blackburn in Lancashire.

With so many correspondents in South Africa – at one point there were almost 300, representing British, European and American publications – fresh news stories were at a premium in the early stages of the war. The country was big, too, and the war a war of movement, thus forcing journalists to follow their hunches or to pick up information as best they could. Burleigh advised the tenderfoots in his team to be 'out and about' and a good pony became the most important item in a correspondent's equipment; the experienced Steevens tagged on to General Sir George White's staff and witnessed the victory at Elandslaagte where the British cavalry exacted a bloody toll of their Boer opponents. 'A Triumph for British arms,' he told his readers. 'Majuba in reverse . . . squadrons of Lancers and Dragoon Guards storming in among them, shouting, spearing, stamping them into the ground.' That was his last bit of luck. By November he was ensconced in Ladysmith along with a handful of choice correspondents including Prior, H. W. Nevinson of the *Daily Chronicle* and Frank Rhodes of *The Times*. Mafeking, too, had been invested, taking Neilly, Stint and Angus Hamilton of *The Times* into a 216-day siege with Baden-Powell and his forces. Less fortunate were the journalists holed up in Kimberley with Cecil Rhodes: although their reports were censored by Colonel Kekewich, the military commander, the gold magnate continued to send uncoded messages to his friends and political supporters in London. At the height of the siege an absurd confrontation took place between the two men when Kimberley's newspaper, *The Diamond Fields Advertiser*, owned by Rhodes, accused the military authorities of unnecessarily prolonging the siege. Kekewich ordered the

editor to be arrested for breaking his censorship, only to be
informed by Rhodes that he had hidden the offending
newspaperman down one of his mines. Such was the
strength of Rhodes's influence that he was able to arrange
the dismissal of Kekewich after the siege was lifted on 15
February 1900.

For the war correspondents in South Africa a major
irritant in their day-to-day work was censorship. Although
Roberts had introduced a system of regular communiqués,
the British military authorities operated a strict censorship
of all telegraphed despatches. Against native tribes in
distant parts of the world, news of British movements could
be safely published in the London press without fear of it
reaching the enemy. During the Boer War, though, secrecy
had to be the order of the day. With telegraphed despatches
reaching London and the European capitals within a
matter of hours, useful information about British plans
could be wired back to the Boers by those unfriendly to
Britain – and it has to be remembered that some European
governments, the French and the Germans in particular,
were hostile to the British war effort in South Africa.
(Kruger's emissary in Brussels, Dr Leyds, passed on sensational stories about so-called British atrocities to the
European press. Mostly these were believed.)

The usual practice was for correspondents to wire brief
despatches to head office and to follow them up with longer
background stories which went by mail. Much depended
on the newspaper's resources. The *Mail*'s correspondents
had an unlimited telegraph account whereas the *Manchester
Guardian*'s correspondents, J. B. Atkins and Filson Young,
had to work within a restricted budget and most of their
reports were posted back to England. These were not
generally subjected to military censorship because they
were several weeks in transit and, therefore, did not reflect

the latest military situation; but all cables had to be passed by the military authorities before they could be despatched.

Censorship not only required journalists to occasionally withhold the truth; in some cases it was employed to tell the world a story the military authorities wanted to make public for reasons of their own. This was the case in the reporting of the siege of Mafeking, a story which was to become the epitome of British courage in adversity and endurance in the face of great odds. The reality was somewhat different. Baden-Powell, the town's military commander, was a virtual dictator and for all the potty inventiveness and improvisation he brought to the task of protecting his charges from the investing Boer force, he was also deeply aware of the symbolic nature of his command. His first despatch set the tone for the subsequent siege: 'October 21st. All well. Four hours bombardment. One dog killed.' When it was published in London the British public took Mafeking to its heart and the siege became one of the great stories of the war. *The Times* considered that the defending garrison represented 'the true grit of the breed' and B-P – as he was known – became a valuable property, his features appearing on buttons, tea-caddies, postcards, wherever there was marketable space. The press lionized him, too, even though the correspondents knew that there was another story to tell.

Shortly after the siege began it was still possible to get in and out of Mafeking with impunity. Reuters' American correspondent was able to ride into Mafeking to report on the situation but when the British correspondents asked permission to leave, Baden-Powell put his foot down. 'I consider it best,' he recorded, 'that they should not thus evade censorship by a staff officer, and spread all the gossip of the place in "interviews" on reaching Cape Town.' He had good reason to feel alarmed at what the journalists

might say. Courageous, admirable, even quirky, his efforts
to raise morale might have been, but they were directed
mainly at Mafeking's white population. His prodigious
ability to expand the available food supplies over a six-
month period of siege, for example, was achieved at the
expense of the black population. Their rations were cut
back to starvation levels and Baden-Powell gave them the
choice of either going hungry or leaving the garrison,
thereby running the gauntlet of the Boers. It was not much
of an option, for Baden-Powell knew full well that the
native Baralongs and Fingoes could expect little mercy
from their natural enemy, the Boer.

Mafeking's white population was prepared to accept
Baden-Powell's food policies but to Hamilton of *The Times*
the sight of the starving blacks was too disturbing to be
ignored. A report of the hardships facing the inhabitants of
Mafeking was smuggled out by native runner but *The Times*
refused to publish it. Quite simply, the myth of Mafeking
and its heroic stand had taken such a grip on the public
imagination that no paper dared to question it by printing
the truth. In his record of the siege, *Besieged with B.P.: A
Full and Complete Record of the Siege*, Neilly got near the heart
of the matter when he described the piteous existence of the
native population.

I will only say now that I saw several actually die of hunger, and
will quote one instance. I was returning to my hotel one afternoon
in the first week of May, and saw outside my room several white
men looking at something on the ground. When I arrived I saw
that the 'something' was a little Kafir boy of about twelve years
who lay on the ground, a living skeleton in the agonies of death.
The commissariat officer was among those who watched him, and
fate threw open the miserable rag that covered the child's chest
and displayed his little bones protruding, as though to say to the
official, 'The lad dies of hunger.' Anything more depressing than
the sight of these struggling remains of humanity it would be

impossible to imagine. Hunger weakened us: it killed the wretched natives.

Neilly neither underestimated the strategic importance of holding on to Mafeking, nor did he ever under-rate the energy and commitment Baden-Powell brought to its defence. But like the other war correspondents in the town he did realize that the introduction of food rationing favoured the whites at the expense of the black population: this information no newspaper would publish and Neilly had to wait until the end of the siege before his diary could be published in book form.

The siege of Mafeking was notable, too, for the murder of E. G. Parslow of the *Daily Chronicle* who helped to run the local newspaper, the *Mafeking Mail*. Following a night of hard drinking he got into an argument with a half-mad artillery officer called Murchison. When Parslow questioned his tormentor's claim to be a gentleman Murchison drew a pistol and shot him. (He was sentenced to death by Baden-Powell, but later reprieved on account of his military services during the siege.) Altogether, fifteen journalists lost their lives in South Africa, either in combat or through illness, amongst their number J. I. Calder of Reuters and, of course, Steevens in Ladysmith.

At the end of the Boer War the *Daily Mail*'s leading correspondent in South Africa, Edgar Wallace, had this to say about military censorship:

Lord Kitchener says that he does not hold himself responsible for the accuracy of news cabled from this country, but in spite of his repudiation one cannot refuse to accept responsibility for items that pass through the hands of a censor appointed by him, and duly instructed in regard to the nature of the news that may pass through unchallenged. If I wanted to cable from here that the situation was unusually optimistic, do you think the censor here would offer any objection to it going? But if I wished to send the truth, that the country around is full of Boers, and rebels are joining the commandos daily, would the censor pass that without being called to book by Kitchener in three weeks' time? And yet it would be true; and yet it would not inform the enemy of our intentions. So much for censorship.[2]

This is a fair summary of the problems facing the war correspondent who wants to write accurate reports without breaching military security, yet of all the journalists who covered the war in South Africa, Edgar Wallace was one of the least likely members of the press corps. It was not that he was one of the few to become a literary man – Arthur Conan Doyle served as a volunteer in the field hospital at Bloemfontein and went on to write one of the best accounts of the war in *The Great Boer War*, and Rudyard Kipling edited the bilingual newspaper, *The Friend*, in the same city – or that he was largely self-taught. So too was Bennet Burleigh. What marks out Wallace as a different type of correspondent is that he did little actual war reporting and that at the very end of the war in 1902 he managed to by-pass the strict code of censorship imposed by Kitchener, then the army's commander in succession to Roberts (who in turn had replaced Buller in January 1900), thereby to gain one of the greatest scoops of the war. Before that happy day he was to win a less agreeable reputation amongst his colleagues for his diatribes about Boer atrocities – largely of his invention – which caused a furore in London when they stole the headlines in the *Daily Mail*.

He was born Richard Horatio Edgar Wallace in Greenwich on 1 April 1875, the illegitimate son of an actress called Polly Richards, and his early years had been spent with the family of a Billingsgate fish porter and his wife. Following an elementary education he left school when he was only twelve, to become successively newsboy, errand boy, milk roundsman and labourer. At the age of eighteen he left home to enlist as a private in the Queen's Own Royal West Kent Regiment whose records give his statistics as standing 5 feet 4¾ inches, his weight 8 stones 3 pounds and his chest a mere 33 inches. Later he transferred to the Medical Staff Corps to train as a medical orderly and in 1896 he was sent to South Africa where he served in the military hospital at Simonstown. Encouraged by the wife of the Wesleyan chaplain, he began reading widely and was soon writing his own poetry, pale imitations of the patriotic doggerel verses made popular by Kipling. (In the years of his fame he was to marry the chaplain's daughter, Ivy Caldecott.) The *Cape Times* published one of his offerings in January 1898 – written to celebrate Kipling's arrival in South Africa – and within a month he had met the great man himself at a literary dinner in Cape Town.

Like many other self-made men Wallace had a good conceit of himself, and his early literary success – he was only twenty-three – encouraged him to seek other avenues of publication. From his pen came a stream of articles and poems for the local newspapers and magazines and if one piece were rejected it would be followed by a dozen more submissions. By 1899 he had persuaded himself that his future lay with journalism and he bought himself out of the army that same year. The outbreak of the Boer War in October gave Wallace his first real chance when Reuters appointed him their correspondent to accompany General Methuen's Kimberley Relief Force along the Modder River. Most of his reports were necessarily short – Reuters' cables cost one shilling a word – but his longer written reports were picked up in London and copied by the *Daily News* and the *Daily Mail*, the paper that was to make his name.

From the very outset of the war, the *Daily Mail*, under its editor Tom Marlowe, had been decidedly patriotic and

supportive of the government's efforts in South Africa to
bring the war to a successful and speedy conclusion. It had
passed from the jingoism of October 1899, through the
sombre horrors of Black Week which saw British morale
fall to its lowest ebb, to the heady days of Roberts's summer
triumphs of 1900 following the reliefs of Kimberley, Ladysmith and Mafeking. At the end of 1900 the war was
entering its long-drawn-out guerrilla phase, with Kitchener
in command of the imperial forces, and public interest was
beginning to wane. It was then that Wallace was appointed
the *Mail*'s principal war correspondent in succession to the
dashing American, Julian Ralph. From the very outset,
Wallace nailed his colours to the *Mail*'s mast.

The hate the Dutch colonist bears towards England is a product
of today. It is a hatred born of loathing. It is a hatred born of the
worse than lies that are today being circulated throughout the
length and breadth of this colony by Boer emissaries, by Bond
politicians, and by ministers of religion. And who is the villain,
who is the foul brute against whom every Dutch colonist's hand is
to be turned? Who, but brave, good-hearted, kindly Tommy – the
man who would gladly lay down his life to protect any woman in
the world, whether she were Dutch or English or Japanese.

This was written early in 1901 in reply to stories of British
atrocities which had been given a wide currency in the
European press on the evidence of Dr Leyds, and its homely
patriotism was soon to become the hallmark of Wallace's
journalism. Decidedly anti-Boer, he not only saw the
conflict in terms of British rights and Boer wrongs, he also
considered it his duty to express those opinions for the
benefit of the British public. Usually, these 'colour' pieces
were exceptionally well written, especially so when he dealt
with the dangers and difficulties the ordinary soldiers had
to endure in the war of nerves against the Boer guerrillas.

But all too often Wallace could not resist ending his articles with a tear-jerking sentimentality that smacked more of literary neatness than any verisimilitude – as in this account of the lot of the Australian scouts of the Victorian Mounted Infantry:

Out he goes to the dark unknown, with a lighted pipe between his teeth and his sooty billy clattering at his saddle, and when he comes back he will know more about the farms within a ten-mile radius, their values, their possibilities as forage providers, and the loyalty of their owners than the smartest Intelligence Officer that ever wore a yachting cap, and he will certainly have a better idea of the topography of the country than the government surveyor who prepares the maps we march by. Sometimes he stays out all night – the gay dog – and turns up in the morning after a night's debauch on rain-sodden biscuit and doubtful bully beef. Sometimes he doesn't turn up at all, and then Crook-Lawless sends an ambulance out for him – and under the driver's seat is a spade.

By 1901 reports in that vein were starting to go against the tide of national opinion as the public began to tire of the war and its casualties. Newspapers started to question the need to continue the fighting, arguing that peace could be achieved by negotiation, and some journalists expressed views which were considered to be pro-Boer. H. W. Massingham, the editor of the *Daily Chronicle*, was forced to resign when his anti-war sympathies led to a decline in the newspaper's circulation and the distinguished Anglo-American journalist Richard Harding Davis was expelled from his London club because he wrote his reports from Pretoria within the Boer camp. Other newspapers which attacked the government's war aims included the *Manchester Guardian*, whose correspondents were arrested after criticizing British treatment of the Cape Dutch, and the *Morning Leader* and the *Star*. Prominent amongst those homebased journalists who took an anti-war line was W. T. Stead,

formerly of the *Westminster Gazette*, who published the
famous pacifist pamphlet entitled *Shall I Kill My Brother
Boer?*

Edgar Wallace, though, had little interest in those liberal
protests and throughout the war he maintained a pro-
nounced anti-Boer line. Opinionated, though never dull,
colourful yet authoritative, his reports nevertheless con-
formed to the patriotic editorial line which the *Mail* knew
sold copies. His description of the trial of a party of Cape
Dutch who had blown up a train and murdered its crew
was typical of his approach.

They have had a trial, where they stood white and anxious, or
sullen and glowering, between two Guardsmen with fixed bayonets. They had seen their comrade who had turned King's
evidence slip in and out of the door – a little, pasty-faced man
with a fringe of whiskers – a man who kept his eyes averted from
the faces of the men he had destroyed, and mouthed hideous
grimaces in his nervousness. They had waited for the decision of
the court, and it had come; death for three, penal servitude for
two, freedom for the informer.

They had made a mistake, and they were to suffer. They had
thought it was a part of the game of war.

There is a symmetry to Wallace's journalism which is
redolent of the simple short story. His reports have a
beginning, a middle and an end, fleshed out with some
colourful description, a clever turn of phrase and a useful
moral at the conclusion. Some correspondents, jealous
perhaps of his sudden fame – the *Mail* hailed his journalism
as deserving the 'careful attention of every patriotic Englishman' – suggested that Wallace's reports were in fact
nothing but fiction. In one instance they were right and
Wallace's tendency to go to extremes in his writing almost
saw the *Mail* being cut off from the government-controlled
supply of official military information.

Wallace had already been in trouble with the military censor in the Orange Free State after sending coded messages back to London and his success had encouraged him to regard the art of outwitting the censor as something of a sport. Burleigh was another who delighted in tricking the censor but, hardly surprisingly, those antics enraged Kitchener. Not only did he despise the press corps and regard them as an unwanted liability, he remembered that Methuen's march to relieve Kimberley had been jeopardized because the Boers had picked up sensitive information from the British press reports. From the outset of his command in October 1900 Kitchener had tightened up military censorship and had made it an offence for soldiers to discuss the war with the accompanying correspondents. He also believed that there was little to report and that therefore information should be kept to a minimum. Roberts's victories in the field may have brought the war in the field to an end by the summer of 1900 but the Boers' decision to continue the struggle underground had turned it into a counter-insurgency war devoid of reportable pitched battles. To combat the Boer tactics Kitchener had introduced a system of sweeps and drives using cavalry and mounted infantry to seek out the Boer columns, and the country had been criss-crossed by a barbed-wire grid system with block-houses, or miniature forts, at key points. Kitchener's seeming inability to bring the war to a conclusion, the lack of newsworthy stories and the strict censorship exasperated the war correspondents who in turn were under orders from their editors to keep South Africa on the front page. Given such pressures, errors of judgement became inevitable.

In June 1901 Wallace came across a story which seemed to him to sum up the drudgery of war for the British soldier and the dangers he had to face from a brutal guerrilla enemy. From his sources in the South African railway system he heard news of a successful Boer attack in the south-west Transvaal on a British mounted column under the command of Brigadier-General H. G. Dixon. Hurrying north to Vlakfontein, the scene of the battle, Wallace picked up snippets of information about a massacre from the passing railwaymen and from a group of wounded soldiers awaiting evacuation. From them he concocted a fantastic story, one which broke the first rule of journalism – that a man should check his sources before rushing into print.

Abandoning the old methods of dropping the butt end of a rifle on the wounded soldier's face, when there was none to see the villainy, the Boer has done his bloody work in the light of day, within sight of a dozen eye-witnesses, and the stories we have hardly dared to hint, lest you thought we had grown hysterical, we can now tell without fear of ridicule. The Boers murder wounded men. Yes, the gentle, bucolic Boer, who was forced to take up the rifle, purchased for him a dozen years before by a paternal government, to guard the independence of his country, may be placed in the same category as the Matabele, the Mashona, the Dervish, the Afridi, and with every other savage race with which Britain has waged war. And the soldier who is stricken down on the field is no more certain that his life will be spared by brother Boer than he was that brother Fuzzy would pass him by.

Written as a letter – to escape the censor – Wallace's article caused a furore when it was published. The War Office accused the *Mail* of lying and threatened to exclude it from their regular supply of information about the war's progress. Harmsworth then retaliated by branding the politicians as suppressors of the truth, and the row dragged on into the autumn, culminating in a parliamentary debate. Fearing that the *Mail*'s attacks on War Minister Brodrick might be a breach of privilege a vote was taken at Westminster to decide whether or not to call Marlowe to the Bar of the House: this was narrowly defeated and by the year's end the matter was quietly forgotten. It had been a close-run thing for the *Mail* and for the reputation of its principal war correspondent in South Africa.

Kitchener, though, never forgave. He had Wallace arrested and sent down to Cape Town under an armed escort. Censorship was stepped up and for a week or two Wallace had to endure the calumny of his colleagues. Some questioned his motives and denounced him as a self-seeking scandalmonger. Others, like the experienced Alfred Kinnear of the Central News Agency, doubted the veracity of the story: their fears were not groundless. Although the facts were kept from the public and only became known long after the war's end, there had been no slaughter at Vlakfontein and the rumours of Boer atrocities were just that. Rumours. Dixon had lost forty-nine men killed and 130 wounded and the Boer casualties were forty-one dead and many more wounded; indeed, the Boer force, commanded by General Kemp, had to flee from the scene of the battle as British reinforcements rushed into the area.

There was, though, a tactical significance to the engagement at Vlakfontein which, had he been more experienced in military matters, would have given Wallace a clue to Kitchener's direction of the war in its final stages. The Boers' ability to continue fighting, thereby prolonging the war, convinced Kitchener that Britain would have to step up a gear and defeat the Boers at their own game. Dixon's drive on Vlakfontein and his timely rescue by reinforcements of mounted infantry was a typical example of the revised British tactics which meant more men, more patience, more time and the introduction of more units of mounted infantry. However ponderous and time-consuming those methods might have appeared on paper,

in practice they helped to bring the war to a satisfactory
conclusion early in the following year, 1902.

Wallace did not see things that way. Snubbed by
Kitchener and impatient of his sweeps and drives, he
engaged in a flurry of criticism against the army's commander, suggesting that what was required was the introduction of the 'mailed fist' to hammer the recalcitrant Boers
into defeat. Almost alone amongst the war correspondents
Wallace thought that Kitchener was too weak for the good
of his position and when a Boer newspaper editor in
Worcester was imprisoned for one year for disseminating
atrocity stories Wallace lost his patience. To his readers he
grumpily suggested that the man should have been shot
and the 'blame' for this omission be laid at the feet of Lord
Kitchener.

The iron hand of Kitchener was a myth, and fear gave place to
contempt. They had been afforded the spectacle of an editor who
attempted to fire their blood with stories of atrocities committed
on women and children charged at the Supreme Court, not with
spreading sedition whereby the safety of His Majesty's subjects
was endangered, but with having committed a libel whereby a
famous general's feelings had been hurt!

To generations reared on the idea that Kitchener was a
vindictive and cruel military leader, more a machine than
a man, Wallace's words may come as a surprise; yet for all
the wrong reasons there is some truth in his comment that
Kitchener showed overmuch caution in his direction of the
latter stages of the war. Throughout 1900 Kitchener had
maintained a policy of burning farms suspected of harbour-
ing guerrillas, with the result that he found his army facing
large marauding gangs of farmers, plus their women and
children, who swarmed over the blackened remains of a
ruined countryside. His solution to the problem was that

the dispossessed and the families of the Boers who had surrendered should be housed in protected camps alongside the main railway lines until the hostilities came to an end. The camps would be run on military lines, basic rations and accommodation would be provided and, as a consequence, the civilians would be kept clear of the main war zones. Brodrick was alarmed by the appearance of these internment, or concentration, camps but Kitchener paid little heed to the proper provision of the camps; people were herded together in crowded conditions and rations and medical comforts were always in short supply.

So confident was Kitchener that the Boers would not stand for his methods that he issued a proclamation saying that all Boer leaders would be banished and their land confiscated unless they surrendered by a certain date. By way of reply the guerrillas stepped up their campaign and even took their struggle into the Cape Colony. Clearly some other tactics had to be tried. Frustrated British soldiers began to turn a blind eye to the rules of war and at Brodrick's suggestion Kitchener introduced a policy of executing Cape rebels who had thrown in their lot with the guerrillas. Other captured Boers were imprisoned; and the Atlantic island of St Helena was used as a giant prisoner-of-war camp. At one point in the war Kitchener even suggested that the policy should be extended and that all captured Boers should be deported to the Dutch East Indies, Fiji or Madagascar.

By the beginning of 1901, though, he was tired of the war and frustrated by the failure of his draconian policies. Finding the Boers impossible to defeat, he came round to the view that the struggle could only be settled by negotiation. Kitchener's earliest attempt to force a breakthrough had been made at Middelburg in February 1901 but the talks foundered on Milner's insistence on unconditional

surrender. For the remainder of the year and beyond,
Kitchener kept up the pressure to open peace talks – in this
demand he was not entirely disinterested for he wanted the
war to end quickly so that he could take up the imposing
post of Commander-in-Chief in India under Lord Curzon.
It was not to be until April 1902 that he and Milner entered
into their final negotiations with the Boers; before then, in
an attempt to lower the political temperature, Kitchener
put a stop to the brutalities of the previous year, and it was
that easing up which so irritated Wallace.

In demanding harsher measures to be used against the
Boers Wallace was merely sticking to the editorial conventions which had made the *Mail* so successful. If the British
Empire were to remain strong, ran the argument, then it
had to demonstrate its strength of purpose to the rest of a
jealous world. However, in getting it right about the 'myth'
of Kitchener's 'iron hand', Wallace was also woefully off-
net. Just as he had misunderstood the import of the
skirmish at Vlakfontein, and had chosen instead to draw a
lurid picture of Boer atrocities, so too did he miss the point
of Kitchener's manoeuvres towards peace during the latter
half of 1901. Instead, he kept up a barrage of criticism,
expanding his belief that the war would have been in vain
if Britain did not insist on unconditional surrender and the
creation of a new Crown Colony in South Africa. (This was
Milner's line, whereas Kitchener favoured a negotiated
peace with concessions on both sides.) In keeping with the
expectations of his readers, Wallace would fall back on the
human consequences of British dithering whenever there
was little else to report.

Three miles to the right of the Boers' central position is a little
kloof – a narrow bush-grown opening between two kopjes falling
sheer. In such a place a man might be easily sniped, and no one

be any the wiser, especially if he was not missed except by a widow, who would fall to speculating why a letter did not come.

Here, where the grasses are thickest and the bushes more entangled, lies a man. His face is to the ground and cannot be seen, which is as well, for it is not good to look upon.

A little lizard basking on one sun-bathed patch of rock, twisting its head, looks curiously; a herd of buck, pattering timorously past, stops and gazes fearfully. Be curious, little lizard, this boy will throw no more stones; fear nothing, you round-eyed graceful creatures, the master's gun is resting in Kent, and that which he holds in shrunken, grey fingers, he cannot use.

Although Wallace was antipathetic to the kid-glove treatment and did not fully understand Kitchener's motives, he could not fail to miss the import of the preliminary peace negotiations which began in Pretoria in April 1902. Fearing that any precocious announcement might prejudice the talks Kitchener threw a security blanket over the town and forbade any correspondent to transmit information back to London. This order plunged the press corps into a frenzy of frustration, for here they were in Pretoria sitting on the doorstep of a story all Britain wanted to read, yet every channel of communication was closed to them. Wallace tried to send an innocuous despatch cautiously stating that a meeting had taken place between Kitchener and the Boer leaders Steyn and Burger but this was curtly rejected by the censor. Clearly, other means of contacting London would have to be found.

In a situation where secrecy becomes an obsession rumour comes into its own. Some said that peace was assured; others knew for certain that the Boers would fight on, that Germany was preparing for war; other stories had it that Kitchener had arrested the Boer leaders. Another rumour played with the idea that the Boers had gone back to their people to discuss the proposals and that the two sides would meet again at a place called Vereeniging, on

the banks of the Vaal, where the British had built a fortified
'peace camp'. This was the story that stuck, but when the
journalists decamped from Pretoria they found that there
was no way into the camp and that Kitchener had little
intention of giving anything away until after the treaty had
been signed and the negotiations brought to a satisfactory
conclusion.

The picture that began to emerge in the first meetings
was far from conclusive. While many of the Boers were
dispirited, hungry, ill-equipped and bereft of transport and
other comforts, a hard core of militants believed that the
guerrilla war could, and should, be continued. Many felt
that the war should be ended for the sake of the women
and the children in the concentration camps; the hardliners
argued that it was because of the future welfare of their
families that the victory should be sought in the field and
not around the negotiating table. Eventually, after much
heated and passionate discussion, it was the spectre of a
ruined homeland and of a people divided by civil war that
tipped the balance. By 21 May all Boer opposition to the
peace had evaporated and the following day the British
Cabinet agreed the main points of the proposed treaty: that
the Boers would acknowledge the King as their lawful
ruler; that self-government would follow in due course; and
that Britain would pay a grant of £3 million to help the
Boer states recover from the war. A further week was spent
in fine-tuning the details in Pretoria and the Boer commission returned to Vereeniging on 28 May to seek the
agreement of their delegates. Three days later it was all
over and on Sunday 31 May the negotiators travelled to
Pretoria where the treaty was signed in Kitchener's headquarters shortly before midnight.

During the period of the final negotiations Fleet Street
had been flooded by speculation and rumour. Only the

Daily Mail felt able to prophesy a successful outcome with any confidence and such was the certainty of their reports that their rivals suspected that it must be bluff. To the correspondents in South Africa, harried by their editors to do better, Wallace's despatches were a source of considerable annoyance. Clearly he must know something, they said in the bars of Pretoria's hotels, yet there remained in their minds the suspicion of the Vlakfontein atrocity stories. To add to their bewilderment, Wallace seemed at that point to be more concerned with speculating on the Stock Exchange than with covering the events at Vereeniging: during the course of each working day he was in the habit of travelling by train to Johannesburg to do business with a wealthy Jewish financier, Harry Freeman Cohen. And thereby hung a tale.

Aware that the censor would pass nothing but the most innocent message, Wallace had dreamt up a system whereby coded messages could be sent back to Cohen's brother in London and then passed on to Carmelite House. The agreed cipher was based on the purchase of shares, backed up by a broker's note should the censor question the validity of the message. Getting the information proved to be more difficult, but Wallace – who had been an ordinary soldier only three years previously – had kept up his contacts within the Army. A former colleague was a member of the headquarters staff at Vereeniging and he was paid to pass out clandestine messages on the progress of the talks. The method was simplicity itself. Instead of alighting at Johannesburg, Wallace would continue his journey to Vaal River, knowing full well that the train would pass the camp at Vereeniging; as it steamed by, Wallace's chum would be standing at the perimeter fence ostentatiously blowing his nose. A red handkerchief would mean stalemate, blue progress and white a successful conclusion.

It was the appearance of the red and the blue handkerchiefs and not leaked information – as the other correspondents suspected – that gave a confident ring to the *Mail*'s speculations in the period before the signing of the treaty. And as surely as night follows day, Wallace scooped the rest of the world on 31 May when the sentry's white handkerchief signalled the successful outcome of the talks. From Pretoria Wallace flashed the news back to London where, on Harmsworth's orders, the entire staff of the *Mail* was locked up overnight in Carmelite House to prevent any leakage of information. The following day, Monday 1 June, the *Mail* shrieked the PEACE headlines to a flabbergasted London. It was not until a day later that the details of the treaty were announced in the House of Commons.

The confirmation that the *Mail* had indeed scooped them was a bitter pill for Harmsworth's Fleet Street rivals. Only the *Daily Telegraph* had any inkling that a peace treaty was about to be signed and their information, too, depended on a coded message. On hearing the news that peace was in the offing, Burleigh had sent the *Telegraph* a simple – and innocent-sounding – two-worded message: 'Whitsuntide greetings!' At first the editorial staff was perplexed by the arrival of such a polite greeting, 'at the full rate from the seat of war'. But a little Christian reflection gave them the clue. Turning to the Prayer Book they found that the Whit Sunday text provided the answer: 'Peace I leave with you; my peace I give unto you; not as the world giveth, give I unto you. Let not your heart be troubled, neither let it be afraid.' Burleigh's second message – addressed to his brother – that he was coming home, confirmed the interpretation, but by then Wallace had scooped the rest of Fleet Street.

To defend its reputation against charges of buying information from corrupt clerks in the War Office, the *Mail* followed up its scoop by publishing the story of how Wallace had tricked the authorities. Far from appeasing Kitchener this only added salt to his wounds and after brooding on the matter for a month he ordered the military censor to remove Wallace's accreditation as a war correspondent.

I have been instructed to write and inform you [he told Wallace on 1 July] that in consequence of your having evaded the rules of censorship subsequent to the warning you received, you will not in future be allowed to act as war correspondent; and further, that you will not be recommended for the medal.

Nothing daunted, Wallace gave the story to the press when he arrived back in London that summer to bask in the glory of his sudden fame. In private, though, he resolved to take his revenge on Kitchener and at some later date to expose him as 'a man of ice and blood' – a curious line to take when only three months earlier he had accused the British Commander-in-Chief of being too soft with the Boers.*

The Boer War made Wallace's name and helped to point him in the direction of a literary career. From being a private soldier with ambitions at the outset of the war, he had emerged three years later with a reputation which hailed him as Britain's most astute and forthright war correspondent. Resolved to consolidate his position as a man of authority, he accepted Cohen's offer to establish him as the editor of an independent newspaper and in 1902 he returned to Johannesburg to become the founding editor

* The ban lasted Kitchener's lifetime. In 1914 Wallace was refused accreditation and wrote instead a daily column on military matters for the *Birmingham Daily Post*.

of the *Rand Daily Mail*. It was not a happy experience. The
sudden fame had gone to his head and a penchant for high
living and gambling left him in debt and in acrimonious
disagreement with his patron and mentor. By 1903 he was
back in London again, a penniless reporter with his mar-
riage on the rocks, working for the *Daily Mail*. Faced by
overwhelming financial problems, he turned to writing
fiction and in 1905 he published his first novel, *The Four
Just Men*. This simple crime thriller achieved a substantial
popular success, mainly due to an ingenious advertising
campaign which asked the public to provide a solution to
the method used by four just men to dispose of the Foreign
Secretary in the story.

Despite the favourable response, though, Wallace's
harum-scarum business methods lost him money and he
was plunged deeper into debt when he was sacked by
Harmsworth in 1907 after involving the *Mail* in two expensive libel suits. Although he was to return to journalism –
he was for a while racing editor of the *Evening Times* and
became President of the Press Club in 1923 – it was at this
point in his life that Wallace pinned his hopes on writing
fiction. First came his West African stories, the most
successful being *Sanders of the River* (1911), and then, after
the First World War, he turned to writing the mass
circulation adventure and crime fiction for which he
became famous. Well meriting the nickname of 'the fiction
factory' he worked with a dictaphone and a secretary and
before his death in 1932 he had produced around 200
money-spinning novels and stage plays. Profligate to the
last, he died in Hollywood while working on the script of
the film *King Kong*, and left debts of £150,000 which his
royalties paid off within two years.

Wallace never claimed that his success as a novelist owed
anything to his experiences in South Africa. Indeed, some

of his earliest biographical notes implied that he had served in South Africa as a soldier and that his young manhood had been spent exploring the remoter parts of the Empire. Nevertheless, he was proud of his years as a newspaperman; to the end of his life he always described himself as a reporter and never disclaimed his early years in Fleet Street.* Nor had he need to. Journalism, especially his years as a war correspondent, provided him with a useful literary apprenticeship by placing him in a position of authority which demanded a regular supply of newsworthy, pithy and colourful copy. He learned, too, the value of seeking out stories which people wanted to read and then telling them in an entertaining yet economical way. By the same token, the speed at which he wrote introduced a crisp superficiality which he carried over into his thrillers. When taxed on his vast output by his friend Willie Blackwood, editor of Harmsworth's magazine *Answers*, Wallace replied, 'I'm not writing for posterity. I'm writing for tomorrow's newspaper.' His very energy encouraged greater effort, for no sooner was he earning huge sums of money from his worldwide sales than the profits disappeared in a round of European holidays and expensive bets at Britain's race-courses. In the sense that his extravagances were fed by his creativity, journalism had proved to him that he could make a living from his pen.

An echo of the debt which Wallace felt he owed to Fleet Street can be heard in a letter he wrote to his old *Daily Mail* boss in May 1922.

I don't know whether you realize that when you gave me my chance I was semi-literate – a man entirely without education or

---

* The plaque put up to his memory at Ludgate Circus, where he sold newspapers as a boy, describes him as Edgar Wallace, Reporter.

any of the advantages which men had, even if they had only
graduated in Fleet Street.[3]

By then Harmsworth had been raised to the peerage as
Lord Northcliffe, and Wallace was nearing the height of his
fame, a wealthy and successful novelist whose only require-
ments for happiness were money, a string of winning
racehorses, a regular supply of exotic cigarettes and innu-
merable cups of weak sweet tea. It was all a far cry from
the poverty he had known as a child in the east end of
London.

4

Charles à Court Repington and the First World War

The turning point in the press's freedom to report wars as it saw fit came with the Russo-Japanese war of 1904–1905. On the face of it, here was a conflict which seemed to hold little interest for the Western powers: the battles were fought in the distant vastness of Manchuria and the reasons for the war were rooted in both countries' strategic ambitions in south-east Asia, at that time of little interest to Britain as a sphere of influence. But there was a novelty value to the war. Japan was in the process of self-modernization, having ended her centuries-long isolation from the West, and in 1902 she had signed a treaty of détente with Britain. On the other side, Russia was regarded in Britain as a backward-looking, yet still formidable giant, who had long been a threat to imperial interests in India. In London the newspapers' instincts led them to support Britain's gallant little ally: the David of Japan against the Goliath of Russia. (The mood was confirmed in October 1904 when the Imperial Russian Fleet, *en route* from the Baltic to the Pacific, opened fire on British fishing trawlers on the Dogger Bank in the mistaken belief that they were Japanese gunboats. From that ludicrous error war with Russia suddenly became a possibility: the Royal Navy's Home Fleet was mobilized and the popular press clamoured for revenge. Russia eventually paid suitable compensation.)

At the outbreak of hostilities well over a hundred press correspondents, mainly British and American, arrived in

Tokyo where they hoped to gain accreditation to the Japanese army in Manchuria. Amongst their number were the veterans Burleigh and Prior but, experienced or not, they all soon found that their presence in Japan was extremely unwelcome. Japan lacked a free press and the tenor of the country's autocratic rule discouraged the publication of much official information. Another reason for Japanese hesitation was that she had begun the war with a pre-emptive strike against the Russian naval base at Port Arthur and she was anxious to remain quiet about this piece of duplicity.

To cope with the sudden influx of foreign war correspondents the Japanese decided to stall by shifting the initial responsibility for accreditation on to the diplomatic corps. All the journalists had to be vetted by their country's ambassador who then had to make application for visas on their behalf. The necessary papers were then 'lost' in the machinery of Japan's bureaucracy, a delay which the Japanese hoped would force the journalists to give up and go home. Those who stayed the course and who were permitted eventually to visit Manchuria had to be accompanied by military attachés and were given little leeway in reporting the resultant battles. Ironically, those few correspondents who chose to cover the war from the Russian side discovered that they were permitted to come and go as they pleased. Autocratic in its dealings with its own press Russia might have been, but in Manchuria at least the Russians were prepared to give the foreign correspondents an open hand.

In May 1905 the Russian Baltic Fleet, after its voyage round the world, was annihilated in the Straits of Tsushima, one of the most decisive naval battles of modern times. It virtually ended the war and peace was signed in September 1905 at Portsmouth, New Hampshire: by its terms

Russia gave up claims to Manchuria, Japan took control of Korea and gained important fishing rights along Russia's Pacific coast. More importantly perhaps, Japan had informed the world that an emergent Asiatic country could take on one of the great powers and win. Japan's success in that respect owed much to her command of the sea and to the fact that Russia's lines of communication had been severely overextended, but what won the day in the land battles in Manchuria was the effective use of her modern army. Not only did the Japanese generals introduce modern technology to the battlefield, but they also evolved the right kind of tactics: for example, modern trench systems were used in the front lines to counteract the effects of heavy explosive shells and high-velocity small-arms fire.

The innovations and the scale of the war effectively defeated those war correspondents who did manage to get near the front. The size of the battlefields – the great conflict at Mukden was fought along a 90-mile-long front – made it impossible for them to get any overall view and the complexity of the Japanese tactics was difficult to grasp. Correspondents like Burleigh who had spent a lifetime reporting Britain's imperial wars were thoroughly perplexed by the war in Manchuria. For the first time in his career this experienced war correspondent found himself almost lost for words.

Secrecy in all things is an ineradicable Japanese trait. As a rule they made no display and tolerated no fuss when dispatching material or sending their troops to war. Nearly all the work was done silently, between the hours of midnight and four in the morning, so that only those who were awake and upon the watch saw battalions, batteries and regiments hurrying to railway stations to entrain. And the custom was to dispatch the men from wayside stations, never marching them through streets in the glare of day. Surely the Japanese have that Oriental fondness for doing things covertly, reminding one of the habit of the wily gardener who, if he wanted a cabbage, would try to steal upon it from behind, to cut its head off.[1]

Clearly, just as the face of war was changing, so too must the response of the war correspondent. One man who understood this change of direction better than most was Charles à Court Repington who wrote for *The Times*.

I had seen from the outset, that more useful work could be done by a man who remained at the London nerve centre than by war correspondents of the old type who sought to repeat the feats of Russell, Archibald Forbes and Steevens at the seat of war. I knew that they would be shepherded, almost imprisoned, and prevented from telling the truth owing to the regulations which had been established in all Armies to muzzle the press, whereas in London I had no censorship to control me and could speak my mind.[2]

The military correspondent – as Repington described himself – was an entirely different kind of journalist from the war correspondent, but he was no less professional in his approach. He was chair-borne, doing much of his work from the editorial office of a newspaper and only occasionally visiting the front line; for the most part his role was not news-gathering but the digestion of the information given to him by others. Whereas Burleigh and Prior rode around the Manchurian battlefields to little avail, Repington made an international name for himself through his shrewd comments on the Russo-Japanese war and through his brilliant interpretations of the main battles and the tactics employed by both sides. He did so by analysing and commenting upon what news was given to him and by utilizing his 'contacts' in the military and diplomatic communities who were often able to give him useful 'off the record' and confidential information.

The extent of Repington's contacts and his ability to use

them in place of direct experience can be gauged from his four volumes of autobiography – *Vestigia*, *The First World War* (vols I and II) and *After the War* – which divulged a mass of private conversations, indiscreet correspondence and dinner-table scandals. The books were hugely successful, but as the *Dictionary of National Biography* reminds us, they also lost Repington 'his social position'. Repington was a new kind of military commentator, a journalist who relied on contacts and his professional instincts instead of strength and stamina to take him round the battlefields. (When he visited the Western Front during the First World War Repington invariably stayed with Sir John French in the comfort of GHQ.)

He was born Charles à Court at Heytesbury, Wiltshire, on 29 January 1858 and was educated at Eton and Sandhurst. His family had a long tradition of service to the armed forces and after joining the Rifle Brigade in 1878, the young à Court moved easily up the Army's ladder. He saw service in Afghanistan and Burma, attended the Staff College at Camberley, and then moved into Military Intelligence, still then in its infancy; in that capacity he served with Wingate in the Sudan campaign and caught the eye of Kitchener. After a spell as a military attaché in Brussels and at The Hague, he joined Buller's staff in South Africa but in 1902 his military career halted abruptly. His affair with the wife of a British official in Cairo had caused an open scandal and he was asked to bring it to an end, on pain of leaving the Army. This he refused to do and when the aggrieved husband started divorce proceedings, à Court was forced to resign his commission: his own wife, the sister of an eminent cavalry officer, General Scobell, refused to divorce him and the whole affair caused a great deal of offence in military circles.

The following year, 1903, he assumed the name

Repington on succeeding to the family's estates – this
custom had been established by a great-uncle – and turned
his hand to military journalism. He wrote first for the
Westminster Gazette and the *Morning Post*, and after helping
L. S. Amery with *The Times History of the War in South Africa*
he was offered employment by the editor of *The Times*. Later
he was to say that it was one of the best things that ever
happened to him.

Mr G. E. Buckle, at that date editor of *The Times*, gave me an
extremely free hand, and permitted me to deal not only with the
purely military side of war but with its naval and political aspects
as well; and it is to this wise liberty which was accorded me that
I attribute mainly the success of my comments.

His astuteness as a military correspondent partially rehabilitated Repington's name in army circles – many senior
officers admired his professional approach to the problems
of modern warfare – and there were behind-the-scenes
moves to reinstate his commission. However, these came to
nothing when Repington divulged some private correspondence between Lord Tweedmouth, the First Lord of the
Admiralty, and the German Kaiser Wilhelm II. Far from
dismaying him, the forfeiture of that second chance merely
confirmed in Repington the belief that as a military correspondent he could have more influence on public opinion
than he ever could as a soldier.

It was a lesson worth the learning for in the immediate
aftermath of the Russo-Japanese war the subject of the
censorship of the press in time of war had taken on a new
importance. Britain had sent a number of military observers to Manchuria and they returned impressed not just by
Japan's military superiority but also by their no-nonsense
handling of the accompanying press corps. They sympathized with the Japanese approach and forward-looking

journals like the *United Services Magazine* began a campaign for the introduction of definite rules for press censorship in time of war. On the one hand they argued that modern war had become too complicated for the civilian journalist to understand and that it was not enough for him to trot around the battlefield making his own arrangements and generally getting in the way. On the other, they claimed that because news could travel so swiftly, some means had to be introduced of slowing it down or suppressing it altogether.

As early as December 1904, while the Russo-Japanese war was still in progress, the Committee for Imperial Defence (CID) had recommended that a bill should be drawn up which would place restrictions on the press in its reporting of military matters: only in time of war or national emergency would it be implemented by Parliament. To the military mind this would ensure the freedom of the press in peacetime but should war break out then censorship would become the law of the land. Initially, the newspaper proprietors were in favour of the CID's proposals but the exact terms of the legislation were difficult to work out. By 1908 the influential Newspaper Proprietors Association came down against the proposals, largely because under the terms of the bill the proprietors themselves would be made solely responsible for what appeared in their newspapers. As *The Times* pointed out, had such a bill been in existence in the 1850s Russell's exposures from the Crimea would never have been made public.

The debate rumbled on until the outbreak of the First World War when a War Press Bureau, under the direction of F. E. Smith (later Lord Birkenhead), was established to control the reporting of the war in France. In an attempt to bring some sense to the situation a policy of 'voluntary censorship' had been introduced in 1912 whereby the War

Office asked the press not to comment on the experiments
for embarking and disembarking the British Expeditionary
Force, but this papering over the cracks fooled no one.
Ideally, the Committee for Imperial Defence wanted a law
which would curtail the press in wartime only; this was
opposed by newspaper owners like Northcliffe who remembered that the *Daily Mail* had been threatened with the
removal of its access to official communiqués during the
Boer War. The stalemate was to prove doubly injurious to
the press because when war did break out in 1914 the
proprietors discovered that, had they accepted the CID's
proposals in 1908, they might well have been spared the
heavy-handed restrictions imposed upon them by a nervous
government.

A cable censorship and a postal censorship were established within Whitehall under the control of the Chief
Censor at the War Office; with the help of the Post Office
they were responsible for vetting all telegrams and letters
of a private, commercial or press nature. In the case of
press reports from the front, these would be censored locally
by an army officer and passed back to the Press Bureau in
London which had been formed on 7 August 1914. Situated
in the offices of the Royal United Services Institute opposite
the Admiralty, its main functions were to censor telegraphic
press reports from the front, to withhold news thought not
to be in the public interest, to distribute censored news and
to act as an advisory board for Britain's newspaper editors.
Originally it had been intended that the Bureau would
organize journalists' visits to the front under the aegis of a
Press Conducting Officer who would arrange censorship in
the field; but this well-intentioned scheme was dealt a blow
when Kitchener was appointed Secretary of State for War
on 5 August 1914.

A stranger to the workings of Parliament – he was the

first serving soldier to sit in the Cabinet since General Monck in 1660 – Kitchener was naturally secretive and dictatorial in his management of men and ideas. Unlike some of his colleagues, he also believed in acting in concord with his French allies (he was the only Cabinet member to speak fluent French) and when Marshal Foch decided to ban all French war correspondents from the front, Kitchener followed suit: one of his first decisions was to order the withdrawal of every British war correspondent from the Western Front. Some reporters did manage to stay on in France but such was the difficulty of gathering news and then sending it back to Britain, that they soon lapsed into silence. The first few weeks of the war went by largely unreported, prompting Repington to tell Lord Roberts that 'censorship is being used as a cloak to cover all political, naval and military mistakes'.

When Kitchener's appointment was announced most patriotic folk considered it a master-stroke. Even Repington thought so and he caught the mood of the country in a confident leader published in *The Times* the following day.

We need hardly say with what profound satisfaction and relief we hear of Lord Kitchener's appointment as Secretary of State for War. Since the suggestion has been put forward by *The Times* during the past two days there has been abundant testimony to the confidence which his name inspires in the public at this tremendous crisis. It was unthinkable, indeed, that so great a military asset should be wasted at such a time, and we heartily congratulate the Government on the promptitude with which they have confirmed the popular choice. In the huge task of equipping and dispatching our land forces, as well as perfecting the measures for protecting these shores, Lord Kitchener's services will be invaluable. Let us repeat that the appointment will be equally welcome to our friends on the Continent.

To the man in the street, all was well now that Britain had secured the services of her greatest soldier, and much of the anxiety which had gripped the country a few days earlier evaporated when the headlines proclaimed the new War Lord. Within a few weeks, though, Repington and his fellow journalists were to regret their heady words of welcome.

The public ignorance about the British war aims in France came dramatically into focus on 30 August 1914 in a special Sunday issue of *The Times* which published a story under the sensational headline: BROKEN BRITISH REGIMENTS BATTLING AGAINST THE ODDS. Written by a special correspondent called Arthur Moore who was in France while *en route* to Serbia, it told a dire story of the losses sustained by the BEF II Corps during the retreat from Mons; it was a report which was completely at odds with the bland assurances put out by the Press Bureau. Kitchener immediately issued a strongly worded rebuttal through the Press Bureau but the damage had been done. Other newspapers questioned the propriety of *The Times* to publish alarmist stories written by unqualified correspondents. Questions were also asked in Parliament about the right of the press to publish its own version of what was happening in France and for a time the freedom of the press hung in the balance.

Ironically, one of the factors which shielded *The Times* from further censure was that the publication of the despatch actually encouraged recruiting. F. E. Smith even admitted that he had added a sentence or two of his own invention pointing up the need for more volunteers. 'I have been asked by Lord Kitchener as far as possible to assist his object which was, of course, to obtain recruits,' said Smith by way of explanation during the debate in the House of Commons. The upshot of this undignified squabble was that Asquith promised to put the reporting of the war on a more professional footing.

The Government feel, after the experience of the last two weeks, that the public is entitled to prompt and authentic information (cheers) of what has happened at the front, and they are making arrangements which they hope will be more adequate.

The result was the appointment of an officer of the Royal Engineers, Colonel Ernest Swinton, to provide 'Eye-Witness' accounts from France for use by the press in Britain.

The Amiens Despatch – as Moore's report came to be known – had one other little-reported consequence. Because Repington enjoyed a longstanding friendship with Kitchener from their service together in the Sudan, he regarded the new War Secretary as his most important contact. Shortly after his appointment Kitchener had honoured that relationship with a series of interviews during which he outlined his hopes and fears for the long-term management of the war. These were published in *The Times* during August and their clear-headed tone excited a good deal of public interest, so much so that other newspapers began to complain about the unfair competition represented by Repington's 'special relationship'. In the aftermath of the Amiens Despatch, Kitchener had to inform Repington that in future he would have to deal with members of his staff instead of talking directly to him.

But it was not the same thing, and though I occasionally called to see FitzGerald [Kitchener's military secretary], most capable and loyal of Kitchener's men, great questions arose on which I could usefully speak to my old chief alone, and in the natural course of things, when I could not get things done which I knew ought to be done, I drifted away from him.[3]

Coming on top of the introduction of the 'Eye-Witness' accounts, themselves an unsubtle form of censorship, Kitchener's decision to cut Repington was to have a long-lasting effect on *The Times*'s military correspondent. From being a more-or-less faithful ally of the Secretary of State for War, Repington, abetted by Northcliffe, was to become one of his sternest critics.

Swinton's appointment was the kind of compromise the British always introduce when faced by conflicting claims. It neither provided a supply of news nor did it clear away the question of censorship. At the outset of the war Swinton held the post of Deputy Director, Railways, BEF, France, and it was from that workmanlike task that he was plucked by Kitchener on 7 September. He owed his preferment to two virtues: through his pre-war experience as Assistant Secretary to the CID he knew something about military administration and he was also the author of a cutting attack on British tactics during the Boer War which he had written under the pseudonym of 'Backsight-Forethought'.*

The manner of his appointment was typical of Kitchener's way of doing things: faced by any administrative problem, as Swinton noted later in his autobiography, he provided a military solution.

I had known Lord Kitchener in South Africa, and when I presented myself to him next day, as ordered, found him friendly, but quite brief. He kept to the immediate point, and did not enlighten me as to the general situation, of which I knew no more than was in the newspapers. His instructions to me were to go to GHQ – wherever it might be for it was moving forward – to report to the Commander-in-Chief for the duty of writing articles on the operations of the Army. These articles, after whatever censorship was deemed necessary in France, were to be sent direct to the Secretary of the War Office for Lord Kitchener's personal approval before publication.[4]

* *The Defence of Duffer's Drift.* He also used the pen-name 'Ole Luk-Oie' for his general military study, *The Green Curve.*

Armed with 'a packet of foolscap, some pencils and india rubber', Swinton left for France immediately and opened his office at Sir John French's GHQ at St Omer. Later he was joined by two assistants, Colonel J. E. Edmonds, later to be a Brigadier-General and responsible for *The Official History of the Military Operations in France and Flanders*, and Captain Lord Percy, later the Duke of Northumberland.

Between 11 November 1914 and 18 July 1915 Swinton and his small staff were to provide the Press Bureau with 103 articles describing the war in Flanders, but despite that conscientious output, Kitchener's experiment can hardly be counted a success. Swinton's arrival at GHQ was met with scant enthusiasm by Sir John French, the BEF's commander, who was suspicious of Kitchener and therefore regarded the 'Eye-Witness' as the War Office's watchdog.

Then there was the problem of censorship. As an experienced soldier Swinton knew what to report and what to omit, but he still had to show his despatches to the Director of Military Intelligence, Colonel Macdonagh. Once the articles had been vetted they were passed back to the War Office for examination by Kitchener and his departmental secretary, Herbert Creedy. Only then were they passed to the Press Bureau for final checking before release to the press. The resulting communiqués were a turgid catalogue of military terminology, devoid of place names or unit numbers which must have meant little to any but the purely military mind. Soon Swinton's civilian colleagues in the press corps were saying that 'Eye-Witness' wrote nothing but 'eye-wash'. The Newspaper Proprietors Association kept up pressure on the government to allow war correspondents to have access to the front and journalists like the outspoken Philip Gibbs of the *Daily Chronicle* denounced the loss of press freedom. In answer to the military leaders' bland assurance, 'Why don't you leave it all to us?' he had this to say:

We do trust you – with some misgivings, and we do leave it to you – though you seem to be making a mess of things – but we want to know what we have a right to know, and that is the life and progress of this war in which our men are engaged. We want to know more about their heroism, so that it shall be remembered by their people, and known by the world; about their agony, so that we may share it in our hearts; and about the way of their death, so that our grief may be softened by the thought of their courage. We will not stand for this anonymous war; and you are wasting time by keeping it secret, because the imagination of those who have not joined cannot be fired by lines which say, 'There is nothing to report on the Western Front.'[5]

In the absence of reliable information from the 'anonymous war' in France, Repington decided to cultivate his contacts in London. A tall, debonair man with a wide range of society, he was much in demand at dinner parties and *soirées* and it was at these agreeable social functions that Repington picked up some of his most useful information. During the early months of the war security was notoriously lax. Asquith used to tell his innermost secrets to his lover Venetia Stanley and on one occasion he distractedly threw a Cabinet paper out of the window of his car as it passed through Roehampton. Grey, the Foreign Secretary, had to remonstrate with Cabinet colleagues to keep secure their papers after sensitive files had been found by the police in St James's Park. The worst feature, though, of security in wartime London was society gossip.

Walter Page, the American ambassador, admitted that through his contacts in Mayfair and Belgravia he possessed the best intelligence-gathering unit of any of the neutral countries. Lloyd George, the Chancellor of the Exchequer, regularly shared the secrets of Cabinet meetings with

newspaper magnates like Northcliffe. Secret military movements were discussed openly at dinner parties so that senior
officers often found it easier to talk about their futures with
well-placed hostesses than to go to the relevant military
quarter. It was with good reason perhaps that Kitchener
joked that he would be more open in his dealings if only his
immediate staff would divorce their wives.

In such a friendly *milieu* Repington worked assiduously
and to good effect, hostesses, politicians and soldiers alike
succumbing to his easy charm. During the first week of the
war he was able to publish in *The Times* a passable map of
the German advance which outlined the encircling intentions of the Schlieffen Plan; from his contacts in the War
Office he was able to predict the British movements at the
Battle of the Marne. Fought on 3 September, it effectively
ended the German advance and introduced the stalemate
of the Western Front. More importantly, he had the ear of
Macdonagh and from him he was supplied with valuable
pieces of classified information about the state of the war in
France and the deployment of the BEF. Macdonagh also
allowed Repington to make his first unauthorized visit to
French's GHQ on 23 November 1914. 'It was the first of
many visits which I paid to the Army in France,' he
remembered, 'thanks to the friendship and hospitality of
the Field Marshal.'

Deprived of his personal access to Kitchener, Repington
turned to 'the little Field Marshal', Sir John French. It was
to be a momentous change of loyalties, for from the outset
of the war the relationship between Kitchener and French
had been awash with turbulent emotions. During the South
African war, when French had commanded the cavalry, the
two men had worked in harmony and they had remained
on reasonably friendly terms thereafter; but the war in 1914
had soured that friendship. French was the military

commander on the spot, Kitchener the civilian warlord in London; both should have worked on equal but different terms, but both were soldiers and very much aware of their ranks.

When French temporarily lost his nerve during the BEF's retreat from Mons, Kitchener rapped his knuckles and crossed over to GHQ to give advice to his commander in the field. To add insult to injury he wore not civilian dress but his Field Marshal's uniform. It was a move calculated to display his superior military authority, and one which had a terrifying effect on the increasingly insecure commander. French began to worry. He worried about Kitchener's motives in retaining two much-needed divisions at home in Britain for home defence. He worried about Kitchener's appointment of Sir Horace Smith-Dorrien to command II Corps in place of his nominee Sir Hubert Plumer. He worried about the possibility of being replaced. Above all, he worried that the BEF was being kept short of heavy artillery, high-explosive shells and machine-guns. Those shortages he attributed to Kitchener and in Repington he found a ready listener.

I had been able, during my frequent visits to France, to ascertain how lamentably short we were of high-explosive shells for our field artillery in particular . . . we were also short of heavy guns of all calibres, in which the enemy enormously outnumbered us, and of shells for those which we possessed, we were short of trench mortars, of Maxims, of almost all the necessary instruments and materials for trench warfare; and the trouble was that Lord Kitchener did not comprehend the importance of artillery in war, took no effective measure to increase our supplies of it, and concealed the truth of the situation from his colleagues in the Cabinet.

In his memoirs dealing with the First World War Repington not only laid the blame at Kitchener's feet, he also added that the situation had been exacerbated by the secrecy and censorship which surrounded the Government's dealings with the press.

Three times I endeavoured to see Lord Kitchener on this subject, and three times I failed. It was useless to see anyone else, and I found that my allusions to the subject in *The Times*, censored as everything inconvenient to the Government was censored during the war, were not enough to rouse the country to the facts. The Army in France knew the situation. Lord Kitchener and the MGO's branch [Master-General of Ordnance] knew it. The public knew nothing, and it was not certain that the Cabinet knew any more.

Repington's allegations, which appeared in *The Times* as vague allusions, were not without foundation. Kitchener was fully aware of the shortage of munitions and equipment needed for conducting a lengthy war, but the munitions industry at his disposal was out of date and byzantine in its operation. Perhaps the scale of the problem faced by him is best illustrated by the supply figures of weapons to the Army between 1902 and August 1914. During that period only 657 18-pounder guns, the Army's staple artillery weapon, had been manufactured and the total number of field guns and howitzers ordered and supplied amounted to 957, or an average of 80 per year. Quite simply, the War Office had been planning to fight a limited campaign as the Boer War and all previous colonial wars had been.

To counter those problems and to fill the gaps caused by the shortages Kitchener put in hand several far-reaching reforms: he reorganized the state munitions industry, he warned the private sector to think of supplying armaments and munitions in terms of years not months, he secured the support of the labour force but, typically, he maintained a cloak of secrecy around his moves. These improvements took time to implement and were constantly held up by bureaucratic interference with the end result that the supply of high-explosive shells did not reach full production until 1916. By the end of the first quarter of 1915 Kitchener estimated that 481,000 high-explosive shells should have been produced: due to the difficulties he inherited the actual figure was only 52,000. The knowledge that the goods had not been delivered only served to heighten the conflict between Kitchener and French. Had the latter known a little more about the Secretary of State for War's efforts all might have been well, but Kitchener could see no reason to bring French into his confidence.

As Repington had predicted, the problems caused by the shortage of shells came home to roost when the British began their spring offensive in 1915. On 9 May the French Army attacked along a four-mile sector of the front between Arras and Lens. Simultaneously, Sir John French's British forces launched an attack on the German positions at Aubers Ridge which was preceded by an artillery barrage of such intensity that it seemed to all who witnessed it to herald the complete destruction of the enemy's lines. Unfortunately for 11,500 British casualties that day, the heavily guarded German trenches and machine-gun emplacements had scarcely been harmed by the bombardment. When the main attack went in, line upon line of British infantrymen fell before the concentrated enemy fire, for the artillery had not only failed in their task, they had also given ample notice of the British attack. A week later, the battle was continued in the Festubert sector and the fighting lingered on until June, by which time the British had lost over 100,000 men.

For French, the battles at Aubers Ridge, Neuve Chapelle and Festubert were disasters which undermined his authority as commander of the British forces in France. He would

not have been human had he not tried to exonerate his
leadership or to find a convenient scapegoat. On 12 May,
three days after the first attack, French's military secretary,
Brinsley FitzGerald and his ADC, Captain Frederick
Guest, were back in London with a memorandum which
showed the number of shells requested against those
actually supplied. The implication was obvious: French
had failed not because his tactics had let him down but
because Kitchener had not provided him with enough high-
explosive shells. The document found its way into the
Conservative opposition camp and, as French intended,
into the hands of two of Kitchener's fiercest critics, Lloyd
George and Lord Northcliffe.

None of the three harboured any love for Kitchener at
that time. Northcliffe had become increasingly angered by
his refusal to allow war correspondents to visit the front
and on a personal level he blamed him, somewhat unfairly,
for the recent death in action of a favourite nephew. Lloyd
George, despite a surface cordiality to his Cabinet colleague, intrigued on a grand scale to undermine Kitchener's
authority and was particularly scathing about his handling
of the munitions industry. For his part, French had developed a paranoid hatred of his former friend. 'I devoutly
wish we could get rid of Kitchener at the War Office,' he
told his mistress, Winifred Bennett. 'I'm sure nothing will
go right whilst he is there. It is so hard to have enemies *in
front* and *behind*.' The passing of the sensitive document to
Kitchener's political enemies only provided them with
useful ammunition; it was not enough in itself to cause a
public outcry. To achieve that, French had to involve the
press and that is where his friendship with Repington came
in handy. Earlier, on 1 May, Northcliffe had already
written to him, advising him how to make best use of the
presence of his correspondent at the front.

A short and very vigorous statement from you to a private correspondent (the usual way of making things public in England) would, I believe, render the Government's position impossible, and enable you to secure the publication of that which would tell the people here the truth and thus bring public pressure upon the Government to stop men and munitions pouring away to the Dardanelles as they are at present.*

During the course of the Battle of Aubers Ridge, Repington, French's guest at GHQ, had been greatly upset by the casualties sustained by his old regiment The Rifle Brigade which had gone into action with twenty-nine officers and 1,090 other ranks. After the battle only one officer and 245 other ranks remained unwounded. Already hostile to Kitchener, he eagerly grasped French's offer to show him the confidential memorandum which showed the number of shells used in the battle.

Five days later, on 14 May, under headlines which screamed NEED FOR SHELLS/BRITISH ATTACKS CHECKED/LIMITED SUPPLY THE CASE/A LESSON FROM FRANCE, Repington laid the blame for the British losses on the lack of shells.

The attacks were well planned and valiantly conducted. The infantry did splendidly, but the conditions were too hard. The want of an unlimited supply of high explosive was a fatal bar to our success.

In an editorial published that same day Northcliffe, who had brushed aside his editor Geoffrey Dawson, was more forthright in his commentary on Repington's news. He hinted that the blame should be laid fairly and squarely on

* One of the problems facing Kitchener was that he had to supply men and munitions for the Western Front and for the newly-opened campaign against the Turks in the Dardanelles.

William Howard Russell of *The Times* in the Crimea.
Photograph by Roger Fenton

LEFT: George Warrington Steevens. From the portrait by the Hon. John Collier

BELOW: Modder River: the war correspondents with the press censor. Edgar Wallace second left, front row

OPPOSITE: Edgar Wallace in his first frock-coat before leaving for the Boer War

OPPOSITE: Charles à Court Repington arrives in New York

ABOVE: The tragedy of Neuve Chapelle: the front line trenches of the 2nd Scottish Rifles photographed by Captain R. C. Money, Adjutant of the Battalion

RIGHT: Claud Cockburn, photographed in 1973

ABOVE: Republican fighters under the leadership of General Varela getting ready for the assault on Madrid, 1936

LEFT: Chester Wilmot preparing for D-Day, May 1944

ABOVE: Two North Korean soldiers surrender to men of the Glosters. Ahead lies an uncertain fate

RIGHT: The classic image of the modern war correspondent: James Cameron writes a report from Korea, 1950

ABOVE: Lieutenant Macaulay Lamurde awaits his fate. 'What a great story he was going to make for them! A Page One Man'

LEFT: War reporting, Falklands' style: Max Hastings in action

the Government's shoulders. If the French Army was so well equipped, he asked, why was not the BEF?

This is a war of artillery, and more and more it is coming to depend upon the supplies of ammunition. From every source we are told that the new German infantry formations are in many cases inferior to our own, but that their artillery is good and lavishly supplied. If we equal the enemy in this respect our cause is won. British soldiers died in vain on Aubers Ridge on Sunday because more shells were needed. The Government, who have so seriously failed to organize adequately our national resouces, must bear their share of the grave responsibility.

Two days later, Repington was back in London and if we are to believe his memoirs, he was armed with 'enough high explosive to blow the strongest Government of modern times into the air'. His first port of call was Lloyd George's office; from there he visited the Conservative leaders, Bonar Law, Carson and Smith. Each received his eye-witness account of the shells shortage at Aubers Ridge, a report which backed up everything French had claimed in his leaked memorandum. The Opposition's next step was to request a debate on the shells crisis in the House of Commons.

The subsequent attack on the Government and the disclosures made by French and Repington were still not enough, though, to bring it down. All might have been well had not Admiral Fisher, the First Sea Lord, decided to resign over a disagreement with Churchill on the level of support needed for the Gallipoli campaign. This afforded the Conservatives the opportunity to end their wartime truce with the Liberals and to demand the formation of a coalition government. On 17 May, the day on which parliamentary questions were asked about Repington's disclosures, Asquith asked for his Cabinet's resignation and a separate battle began for the appointment of a Coalition

Cabinet. Other factors had also contributed to Asquith's decision: the recent sinking by a German U-boat of the passenger liner the *Lusitania*, the Zeppelin raids on London, the failure of the Gallipoli campaign and the high casualty lists from France.

Aware that Asquith was in the process of forming a new Cabinet and that the reshuffle offered an opportunity to get rid of Kitchener, Northcliffe stepped up his criticism of the munitions supply to the army in France. In a hotly worded editorial in *The Times* of 19 May he laid the entire blame for this mismanagement at Kitchener's feet.

Men died in heaps upon the Aubers Ridge ten days ago because the field guns were short, and gravely short, of high-explosive shells. Our sole purpose is to ensure that such a lamentable defect shall be made good as soon as possible. Lord Kitchener must bear his share of the responsibility, because against much wise advice he insisted upon keeping in his own hands the control of questions with which the War Office was far too preoccupied to deal. He could not raise new Armies, and direct industrial organization as well; yet that is what he tried to do, and the result was confusion.

Elsewhere in the newspaper the French and German supply systems were extravagantly praised, the inference being that Britain's was distinctly second-rate. In private, Northcliffe vowed to his friends that he would go on attacking Kitchener until he was finally driven from office; in public he used his newspapers to make the main assault. A few days later, the novelist John Buchan, who had just returned from France, added his voice to the controversy with a further report on the Battle of Aubers Ridge which ended with an oblique attack on Kitchener's administration of the war.

All the strategy and tactics of the war depend today upon one burning fact. The enemy has got an amazingly powerful machine and unless we can provide ourselves with a machine of equal vigour he will nullify the superior fighting quality of our men. That machine consists in a great number of heavy guns and machine-guns, and an apparently unlimited supply of high explosives.

Elsewhere, Northcliffe's other newspaper, the *Daily Mail*, povided sensationalism in place of good journalism to make its own comment on Repington's allegations. On 21 May its headlines announced, THE SHELLS SCANDAL/ LORD KITCHENER'S TRAGIC BLUNDER, and the ensuing articles demanded Kitchener's resignation. Its hysterical tone turned the tide. Shocked by the uproar in the press, the British public gave their support to Kitchener. Copies of both newspapers were burned by members of the Stock Exchange who also placed a placard outside the *Daily Mail*'s offices with the legend, 'The Allies of the Hun'.

The public display of affection and loyalty was not the only support which Kitchener received throughout the crisis. His friends rallied to his side and letters condemning French's behaviour flocked into the War Office. The Duke of Connaught expressed his 'disgust at the disgraceful campaign', and from France, the normally reticent Douglas Haig forthrightly laid the blame for the whole affair on the presence of British press correspondents at the Western Front.

I feel I must send you a line to tell you how thoroughly disgusted we all are here at the attacks which the Harmsworth reptile press have made on Lord K. [He wrote to FitzGerald, Kitchener's military secretary on 24 May.] It is most unfair and most unpatriotic at the present time. That 'Times' has published several articles for which the editor would have been shot in any other country but England. We in the First Army have a grudge against Repington who in an article on the 18th inst. gave away the position of our heavy batteries at Le Cateau with the result

that they were suddenly shelled and many casualties caused. I
think it was quite wrong to allow such a deceitful fellow to come
to the front at all.[7]

Throughout the crisis Kitchener behaved with dignity and
self-restraint even though he had been sorely provoked. His
only comment on the matter was to ask French why he had
allowed Repington access to GHQ. 'Unless war correspondents are allowed by the Cabinet,' he warned, 'I do not
think it is right for you to allow Repington to be out with
the army.' This rap over the knuckles met with a testy
reply. 'Repington is an old friend of mine,' replied French,
'and has constantly stayed with me for the last ten or
twelve years. He was here for a day or two in an entirely
personal capacity. I really have no time to attend to such
matters.'

And so ended the struggle that came to be known as
'The Battle of the Shells', a crisis that had been brought
about by political intrigue and by disclosures in the press.
In the ensuing Cabinet reshuffle Kitchener was confirmed
as Secretary of State for War but lost control of munitions
to Lloyd George who created a separate Ministry of Munitions. French stayed on as commander of the BEF although
he was never again to enjoy the same level of trust in
political circles: before the year was out he had been
replaced by Haig. Northcliffe turned his attention to other
things and Repington ensured that everyone would recognize the importance of his role in the affair.

Every endeavour was made to show that I had been engaged in
an intrigue against the Government, or was acting under the
orders of Northcliffe, and various reptiles bit one whenever they
could. It is not an intrigue to endeavour to save an Army from
defeat by a necessary public exposure when all official representations have hopelessly failed.

Repington was not being altogether honest. The disclosure of his story in *The Times* was certainly not enough to bring down Asquith's administration but it did bring into focus the problems caused by the shells shortage. This in turn led to the creation of a Ministry of Munitions and to an improvement in the supply of ammunition, improvements which had already been put in hand by Kitchener himself. That this was brought about by intrigue – in which Repington was involved – and by the use of underhand methods says more about British political life in 1915 than it does about the role of the press. Repington was a party to deceit, in spite of his later denials. He supplied the Opposition with sensitive information and acted in a manner that is not expected of the impartial journalist.

What can be said for Repington is that he had his reasons. His presence at GHQ was due to Haig's banning him from the First Army headquarters, he had been denied access to Kitchener, and he was a soldier by training. Although the lack of success at Aubers Ridge and Festubert was due mainly to faulty British tactics and to an inability to understand trench warfare, the shortage of shells did cause an unacceptable level of casualties. Repington understood that latter problem and was determined to expose the shortcoming. With press censorship so strict, he had to use *The Times* as best he could in public and then to take the battle into the underground of political intrigue. The very absence of press freedom, in fact, created the situation which the Government had been so anxious to avoid – the presence of journalists like Repington going to the front in 'an entirely private capacity'. As far as the press was concerned, the best outcome of the Repington affair was that the Government at last acted upon the newspaper industry's demands for more information about the progress of the war.

Typical of their complaints was this comment from Philip
Gibbs:

Even the enormous, impregnable stupidity of our High Command
in all matters of psychology was penetrated by a vague notion
that a few 'writing fellows' might be sent out with permission to
follow the armies in the field, under the strictest censorship, in
order to silence the clamour for more news.

From May 1915 onwards, journalists would no longer have
to enjoy a friendship with Sir John French in order to visit
the front line. War correspondents were placed on attachment to the British armies in France and Gallipoli; they
were given uniforms and the temporary rank of captain.
Green armbands distinguished their profession and in
France they were messed at GHQ. At the end of each
working day – which usually comprised a visit to the front
or a briefing by senior officers – they wrote their despatches
which were censored at GHQ before being sent to London
by King's Messenger. With their arrival Swinton's work as
'Eye-Witness' had come to an end, but as he was the first
to admit in his memoirs, the system he operated had paid
scant attention to the needs of modern warfare.

In regard to the recording of news for the public in a future war
arrangements should be made similar to those in existence before
August 1914, to include photography, films, sound films, and in fact
all known methods. This would ensure a close, sympathetic and
understanding co-operation of all concerned, such as would enable
the nation to be told as much of the situation and of the progress of
events as it might be possible to reveal. To this it has a right.

Throughout his stint as 'Eye-Witness', Swinton had been
scrupulously fair. Although he often resented the butcher-
ing of his despatches by the military censor, he was also
aware of the delicacy of his position. 'The principle which

guided me in my work was above all to avoid helping the enemy,' he later admitted. 'This appeared to me even more important than the purveyance of news to our own people.' Given that self-censorship, the necessary outcome of his own military training, it is hardly surprising that Swinton's reports lacked the urgency and drama required by the newspapers. It was, therefore, with high hopes that the first officially accredited war correspondents crossed over to France: amongst their number were such fine journalists as Gibbs, Basil Clarke of Amalgamated Press, Perry Robinson of *The Times*, Percival Phillips of the *Daily Express* and Beach Thomas of the *Daily Mail*. As in previous colonial wars literary men also served their country as war reporters, John Masefield in Gallipoli, Rudyard Kipling in France and Arnold Bennett in the Ministry of Information. A further innovation was the commissioning of artists to delineate the war in paintings: they were known as official war artists and amongst their number were men of the calibre of Sir D. Y. Cameron ('The Battlefield of Ypres'), Paul Nash ('The Menin Road'), J. D. Ferguson ('A Damaged Destroyer'), C. R. Nevinson ('Harvest of Battle'), Eric Kennington ('The Kensingtons at Levantie') and Sir William Orpern ('Changing Billets: Picardy').

The government also began to value the propaganda aspects of press reporting. John Buchan was attached to Haig's staff in France in 1916 to provide short written reports of the fighting for consumption by the British and foreign press. The following year saw him appointed Director of Information, responsible to the new Prime Minister, Lloyd George, for providing all aspects of press propaganda through official communiqués, pamphlets, books and photographs; he also commissioned the war artists and introduced film-makers to the Western Front. In 1918 his department became a separate ministry under the leadership

of Lord Beaverbrook and Buchan went on to complete
Nelson's History of the War, which was published throughout
the war in fortnightly instalments.

Although the reporting of the war had been put on a
professional footing in May 1915, the press and the various
propaganda agencies still faced well-nigh insurmountable
problems in capturing all its aspects. Quite simply, the
First World War was fought on a scale and with numbers
of men never before experienced in the world's history: the
public could not make sense of all its ramifications and
despite their efforts neither could the war correspondents.
The battlefields were large and confusing places which
frequently denied observers an overall view; campaigns
were fought in Gallipoli, Palestine, Salonika and Mesopo-
tamia as well as in France; there was a long-lasting war at
sea. And then there were the technical innovations. Air-
ships and aeroplanes introduced war in the air, submarines
and wireless telegraphy changed the face of war at sea,
tanks and heavy artillery the war on land. It was also a
difficult war to report unemotionally. The fighting on the
Western Front was a barbarous affair, men died horrible
deaths after artillery bombardments or in frontal attacks
against heavily defended machine-gun emplacements; in
Gallipoli, disease and idiotic tactics caused thousands of
unnecessary deaths. The actuality of war could not always
be reported with any decency and censors struck out
truthful, yet over-realistic, descriptions of the horrors of
trench warfare: had the war correspondents been permitted
to tell their readers the truth about battles like the Somme
or Passchendaele, there is no telling what effect the public
revulsion might have had on the direction of the war.

All too often, the war correspondents took the side of the
armies in the field and this tendency had a detrimental
effect on their reports. For instance, neither the British nor

the French public were ever given the real casualty figures and reports tended to speak of heroism and glory in place of the killing which was actually happening; even in Germany the numbers were fudged to such an extent that the exact casualty figure is not known to this day. One of the problems was that the war correspondents relied over-much on GHQ for their supply of news: inevitably friend-ships would be made and then journalists would baulk at exposing harsh realities which, had they been published, would damage the Army's prestige. Sometimes it seemed to the fighting men, who read the newspapers and could see the distortions, that the censorship system had been introduced not to prevent information reaching the enemy but to withhold the truth from the British public. After the war, journalists like Philip Gibbs tried to square the matter with their own consciences by putting the dilemma in a human context.

There is not one word, I vow, of conscious falsehood in them [his despatches]. But they do not tell the truth. I have had to spare the feelings of men and women who have sons and husbands still fighting in France. I have not told all there is to tell about the agonies of this war, nor given in full realism the horrors that are inevitable in such fighting. It is perhaps better not to do so, here and now, although it is a moral cowardice which makes many people shut their eyes to the shambles, comforting their souls with fine phrases about the beauty of sacrifice.

If the First World War was a war in which the journalists, like the armies, had to learn as they went along, it was also a time when they had to come to terms with death on a previously unheard-of scale. And no one, not even the public, was ready for that.

At home in London – he was banned from France and was not to visit the front until March 1916 – Repington was left to add to his comments on the war from his wide range of social contacts. His regular column, 'The Military Situation', was a mine of sound sense and demonstrated his firm grasp of the strategic situation, but to his disgust the censor still removed information considered to be too sensitive. To Repington those cuts were both a slur on his professional competence and a means of keeping the truth from the public. 'The ignorance of the people concerning the war, owing to the censorship,' he wrote in his diary early in 1916, 'is unbelievable.' He also considered the politicians to be equally ignorant or naïve and in his attempts to promote his own beliefs, he became increasingly indiscreet.

Learning of the huge losses suffered at the Battle of the Somme, while at Haig's headquarters, he confirmed them in London from friends at the War Office, but his attempts to print the story came to nothing. In turn he became a committed supporter of universal conscription and throughout 1916 and 1917 he urged that the army should be properly supplied with men and reserves, an idea which was becoming increasingly unpopular as the war progressed. His diary for that period reveals the extent of his interests: he urged the importance of the Eastern Front and Russia's part in the war, he supported the convoy system to reduce heavy shipping losses and he took an active interest in the campaigns in Palestine and the Near East. Manpower, though, remained his central concern and it was his support for increased levels for the army in France that led him to break with *The Times*.

Alone amongst the British press corps Repington had understood the extent of the losses suffered by France and the heavy price paid by her armies. For every British soldier in the colours there were two French and their casualties were correspondingly higher: the French were not joking when they claimed that the British would fight to the last drop of French blood. By the end of 1917, though, the British public was becoming chary of the war of attrition waged by their military leaders. The heavy losses sustained at Cambrai and Passchendaele had convinced Lloyd George that the generals were too profligate of British lives and the Prime Minister responded to the sense of disillusionment by cautiously promoting moves which would husband British manpower. A Cabinet Committee on Manpower was established in December 1917 and it recommended not only a reduction in the men allotted to the Army but also a reorganization of the BEF. Although opposed by the Army Council, Lloyd George's Cabinet pushed through both proposals with the result that the BEF, instead of being reinforced, had to reorganize itself from within by reducing the size of its division and brigade structure. 'This was too much for me,' wrote Repington in his diary. 'I should deserve to be hanged as a Boche agent if I remained with these imbeciles any longer.' Angered by the Government's actions and further enraged by the failure of *The Times* to support him, Repington tendered his resignation to Geoffrey Dawson, telling him that his constant deletion of paragraphs was 'dishonest to the public, since it prevented the country from knowing the truth'.

Repington resigned on 18 January 1918; within two days he had joined the staff of the *Morning Post*, then edited by H. A. Gwynne. There he continued his fight against the Government and narrowly missed prosecution when an article on military manpower was published on 24 January without being sent to the censor for prior approval. Within a fortnight, though, he was in trouble again when he leaked the decision of the Supreme War Council to form a joint Anglo-French reserve, which would be under the control of an Executive Committee chaired by Foch. Haig and Pétain were less than satisfied with the outcome and both generals refused to risk the safety of their armies by parting with their reserves. On 6 February Repington dined with Pétain and from him learned that if the strategic reserve were created 'he would not remain in command' because he believed (wrongly) that the entire strength of any future German assault would be directed against his lines. The commanders' pessimistic warnings were echoed in London by Sir William Robertson, Chief of the Imperial General Staff, who told Repington, off the record, that in the opinion of the Army Council the creation of a joint reserve would be unconstitutional.

Repington's revelations of the allied discussions and of the subsequent disagreements sparked off a controversy which had all the makings of another shells crisis. In the uproar which followed, Lloyd George threatened to resign, Robertson was removed from the War Office to command the home defence forces, Pétain backed down and the question of joint reserves was allowed to drop. This time, though, the law took its course and under the terms of the Defence of the Realm Act Repington and Gwynne were prosecuted by the Crown. Both men were fined £100 each. The relatively mild sentence was undoubtedly influenced by the defence put forward by their counsel, Tindal Atkinson KC, who argued that neither man had erred as the findings of the Supreme War Council had already been reported in the French and German press.

Within a month, Repington's warnings about a lack of adequate manpower in France became a reality when three German armies opened a spring offensive on the British lines between Arras and St Quentin. Following a fierce artillery barrage on 21 March 1918 the Germans broke the British line and swept forty miles into territory previously held by the allies, taking prisoners and capturing guns. The fighting continued into the following month but by then the Germans had over-reached themselves in some of the fiercest fighting of the whole war. Although they had made substantial advances into enemy territory and at one stage had threatened to break through to the Channel, it had been achieved at a cost: their casualties numbered 348,300.

For the British, who had borne most of the fighting, it had been a near-run thing. The manpower shortage, the lack of suitable reserves and the absence of a unified command had placed a tremendous strain on the soldiers in the field. Lloyd George might have criticized Haig and his generals for wasting lives in the autumn battles of 1917 but the casualty list in April/May was equally appalling: 351,793. As Repington had said all along, sooner or later the Germans would take advantage of the weakened state of the British forces on the Western Front. On hearing of Repington's sentence, General F. M. Maurice, the official historian of the Boer War, wrote to him expressing the army's thanks for his efforts: 'I have the greatest admiration for your courage and determination, and am quite clear that you have been the victim of political persecution such as I did not think was possible in England.'

When the war came to an end in November 1918 Repington was an enthusiastic supporter of the idea that the natural frontier between France and Germany should be the Rhine and he promoted the creation of an independent Rhineland state. He also lent his weight to the demands for a League of Nations and was in favour of disarmament, provided that it could be properly controlled. But even Repington, a reasonably tolerant and mild-mannered man, did not escape the tendency to 'hate the Hun', a demand for 'implacable hatred'* against the

* The phrase is Arthur Conan Doyle's in a letter to *The Times* published in December 1917.

enemy which swept through the country during the summer of 1918.

We have most of us lost by custom the capacity for surprise, joy or sorrow. A dead, numb, implacable feeling of seeing the thing through fills all minds. There has not been a flag raised, nor a bell rung, for all the victories of these past four months, unequalled though they be. The feeling is so strong that most people have shut it up in their own hearts and give little open expression to it. The thousands of casualties which fill the papers daily shut out all pity for the vile enemy. The murders, lootings, crimes of every sort, the memory of the *Lusitania*, of Nurse Cavell and Captain Fryatt, of the poison gas and the ill treatment of our prisoners, are never out of our minds, and terrible retribution is in store for Germany. The cold and terrible implacability of the English is the deadliest hate of all. This is the frame of mind in which we approach the end of this bloody, prolonged and horrible war. *Vae victis!*

Repington was not alone in expressing such angry sentiments – most newspapers rang to demands for executions, reparations and imprisonment – but it is sad to see his hitherto dignified voice being added to the chorus. To many men at the front where the victory was still being won in the autumn of 1918 it seemed that the fire-eaters who had sent them off to war had now resurfaced to replace the miseries of war with the miseries of peace. Certainly there is little evidence to suggest that the men who did the fighting shared the attitudes of the commentators at home. Instead, their response was one of muted joy and relief that the whole dreadful business had finally come to an end. As an American correspondent, George Sandes, reported, men were finally able to stand up in their trenches without being shot at; the British troops shouted out that they had come through and the French responded that they were all still alive. Only the civilians and the politicians at home, Sandes remarked, shouted Victory.

From our line I saw helmeted heads of German soldiers appearing over the parapets. The Germans came into No Man's Land shyly, awkwardly, still frightened, but the Americans, followed by the French, rushed into the field and extended their hands in welcome. The Americans gave away food and cigarettes.

This was all a far cry from the implacable hatred preached by Repington and others at the war's end.

As it was, Repington did not live long enough to see the lasting futility of the peace-making. His finances being in a parlous state, he set about writing the record of his life, his books delighting an audience avid for the crumbs of gossip he dropped from a lifetime's eating at the nation's high tables. He died of apoplexy on 25 May 1925 at Hove in Sussex, having been previously reconciled to his wife. The last years of his writing career were spent with the *Daily Telegraph*, but it was left to his original employer, *The Times*, to put his life and work into perspective:

Certain aspects of temperament and judgement detracted from his very real talent, and led to some later development in his career [his books] which his friends could only regret. But at his best he was a brilliant writer on his special subject, and deserves to be remembered for the ability with which he illustrated and enforced its lessons to a public which, at any rate before the war, was much in need of such stimulation.

A professional soldier, Repington brought a trained mind to his interpretation of war. He showed that the military correspondent in his editorial office could present a different, though no less realistic, perspective and he proved his worth by twice drawing attention to the head-in-the-sand attitude taken by the government at two crucial junctures: the shortage of shells in 1915 and the withholding of men in 1918. In both cases he had to side-step the censorship and face the consequences. The strength of his reputation and his impeccable connections with 'the best people' (as he called them) might have provided a safety net but he deserves to be remembered as one of the few journalists to have raised his voice against some of the greater futilities of this most futile of wars.

5

Claud Cockburn and the Spanish Civil War

Although Britain played an important role at the peace
settlements which concluded the First World War she was
not otherwise engaged in the problems of post-war Europe;
one of the most far-reaching policies of Lloyd George's
government was to withdraw from any further military
commitment to the European mainland. Conscription,
which had been introduced in 1916, was brought to an end
and the mass armies were disbanded. The British Army
became once more a small professional concern, a society
apart; its officers and men went back to regimental duties
in hot out-of-the-way places, resuming their former role as
members of a worldwide imperial police force. A strong
tide of pacifism and disillusion with war quickened the
process and stagnation quickly set in. Many of the tactical
lessons learned so painfully in the mud of Flanders or in
the heat and dust of Gallipoli and the Middle East were
laid aside; even such vital innovations as the tank were
allowed to remain undeveloped for many years. One of the
few journalists to question this policy of *laissez-faire* was
Basil Liddell Hart, the military correspondent of the *Daily
Telegraph* who advocated the modernization of the British
Army as a fully mechanized force capable of fighting a war
of movement, but his was a lone voice. (Within the army a
similar doctrine was preached by General J. F. C. Fuller.)

Victory also led to a complacency amongst the country's
leaders that Britain's withdrawal from European affairs
would enable her to concentrate on her world position and
to consolidate her imperial responsibilities. With Germany

and France weakened and Russia isolated by the Soviet
revolution, another war in Europe seemed to be little more
than a distant and far-fetched possibility; few people realized, though, that far from being totally defeated, Germany
retained military ambitions which would surface again
within twenty years to threaten that illusory stability.
Britain's insularity was, therefore, bought at a price. It
contributed to a vacuum in European politics which fascism
was allowed to fill and the emergence of fascist dictatorships
in Germany and Italy was to weaken European stability
and threaten another global conflict.

For many people – especially for politicians, intellectuals,
trade unionists, writers and journalists – the major factor
which helped to delineate the European situation in the
1930s was the Spanish Civil War which broke out in 1936
and lasted until 1939. Although the major British political
parties all supported non-intervention at first, left-wing
sentiment in favour of the Republican cause did not take
long to gain strength. The Communist Party of Great
Britain recruited a British battalion for the International
Brigades – the 1st Battalion of the 15th Brigade – and in all
there were around 2,000 British volunteers, of whom some
500 were killed and 1,200 wounded. The British labour
movement as a whole responded warmly to Republican
appeals for funds to purchase guns and ammunition, medical supplies and food. More importantly, perhaps, the
conflict in Spain convinced many young people that this
was a 'just war', that the forces of international Communism could be harnessed to fight against the fascist powers
of darkness. They called for a Popular Front uniting
France, Russia and Britain against Hitler's Germany and
Mussolini's Italy: their hopes found one expression in the
young men who fought in the International Brigades,

another in the intellectual response of the writers who supported the Republican, or Loyalist, cause.

There are many reasons why the writers of Britain, France and America responded to the war in Spain. To begin with, it was a civil war free of national or patriotic constraints; it was also easy to visualize, the war being confined to one country, and just as the battle areas were easy to comprehend, so too did it seem that the ideological battle lines were equally clearly drawn. On the one side were the Nationalists, abetted by Germany and Italy, the apogee of fascist intolerance; on the other were the Loyalists, bolstered by the Soviet Union, who seemed to represent the socialist future. Thus the clash between the two sides crystallized the rival ideologies of the 1930s and signalled a terrible warning for the future should fascism be allowed to triumph. Above all, the war in Spain provided the writers with evidence, albeit tenuous, that they could make a worthwhile contribution to the struggle through their work. However naïve those aspirations might have been – the stark simplicity of their ideals led quickly to disenchantment in the wake of the Nationalist victory – many writers in 1936 felt as John Cornford did when he wrote *Full Moon at Tierz: Before the Storming of Huesca*.

> Freedom is an easily spoken word
> But facts are stubborn things. Here, too, in Spain
> Our fight's not won till the workers of all the world
> Stand by our guard on Huesca's plain,
> Swear that our dead fought not in vain,
> Raise the red flag triumphantly
> For Communism and for liberty.

Cornford, a young Communist who was one of the first writers from Britain to throw in his lot with the forces fighting the Nationalists, was killed in action shortly after the war began and was quickly regarded as a martyr to the cause. Other courageous young writers met similar fates, amongst them Christopher Caudwell, the literary critic whose *Illusion and Reality* (1937) attempted a Marxist theory of art, and the young poets Julian Bell, Charles Donnelly and Ralph Fox. Many of the writers were either members of the Communist Party or at least looked upon themselves as a left-wing *avant-garde*, and in the early stages they regarded the war as the first violent test of the usefulness of Marxist dialectics as a means of ordering experience. For them, Marxism provided a radical solution to the problems of the world, whereby they would be permitted to participate in events which would allow the down-trodden to claim their heritage. ('Raise the red flag triumphantly . . .') If it was impossible to serve in Spain on the Loyalist side, then at least it became *de rigueur* to visit the country or to organize petitions and rallies. The American novelist Theodore Dreiser spoke for many when he said: 'to remain a pacifist while a democratic government was under attack by the combined forces of fascist dictators was tantamount to being pro-fascist'. Given such simplistic, yet heady, ideals it was hardly surprising perhaps that, when the disillusion did set in, it set in very rapidly and conclusively. Many of the young left-wing writers who either served in Spain or sympathized with the Republican cause later renounced their association with the Communist Party or distanced themselves from any political extreme.

This is not the place to chronicle the impact of the Spanish Civil War on the legions of British, European and American writers who involved themselves in the struggle or allowed themselves to be affected by the aims of its main protagonists: suffice it to say that very few writers of the 1930s were not affected in some small way. What is certain is that the writers who went to Spain, either as war correspondents or to seek out realistic material for their novels and poems, found it difficult to remain impartial. As a result much that was written about the war was highly coloured, much of it was fiercely partisan and, as we shall see, a good portion of it was pure fabrication.

The war itself had its immediate origins in the intervention of a group of right-wing generals in Spain's affairs during the summer of 1936. Ostensibly they made their move to prevent the country sliding into anarchy and this was sold to the rest of the world as an attempt to restore order and to save Spain from a Republican government dominated by Communists. As seen by Claud Cockburn, the editor of the radical journal *The Week* and a staff journalist on the *Daily Worker*, the war in Spain fitted the pattern of 'right-wing violent intervention in the supposedly normal course of democratic development, and also the classic formula for justifying this violent intervention to the public opinion of the older-established Western democracies'.

In February 1936 Spain had gone to the polls and brought to power the Popular Front, an alliance of Republicans, Socialists and Communists. They had collected 263 seats. Opposing them had been the National Front, the focus for right-wing groups and composed of monarchists, landowners and Conservatives who had won 133 seats. By July rebellion was in the air as the different factions within the two main parties jockeyed for power in the *Cortes*, the country's parliament. At the same time General Francisco Franco, living in semi-banishment in the Canary Islands, led a military coup with the backing of the Spanish Army in Morocco and by late summer the battle lines between the Nationalists and the Loyalists had been firmly drawn. Spain, the one major European power to have escaped involvement in the First World War, had fallen into a state of bloody civil war. There were, of course, other historic causes for the outbreak of fighting – the monarchy, the church, the growing falangist movement, the aspirations of the Catalans and the burgeoning strength of the trade union movement – but to the world outside the war in Spain represented the brutal crushing of democracy by the military machine. In other words, Spain had become a cause, a last chance to maintain a Republican government and a pluralistic society in a Europe which was in danger of turning towards fascism.

From the very outset of the war few British politicians were prepared to argue for intervention on one side or the other, although the Labour leader Clement Attlee spoke sympathetically in favour of the Republicans and later visited the British battalion of the 15th International Brigade. Outside political and intellectual circles public opinion was fairly evenly divided; the left-wing *avant-garde* might have greeted the war as a second French Revolution or as a repeat of the year of 1848 but for the most part the British middle and upper classes viewed the struggle as an unwelcome interruption and something to be avoided. Many supported the Nationalists. The division of opinion was reflected in the attitudes of the press. The *News Chronicle*, *Daily Mirror*, *Manchester Guardian* and *Daily Express* generally supported the Republican cause, while the *Morning Post*, *Daily Mail*, *Daily Sketch* and *Observer* were pro-Nationalist. *The Times* and the *Daily Telegraph* attempted to keep a middle path and to offer a disinterested view of the war. However, as many correspondents found when they got to Spain, preserving a state of impartiality for either side was one of the first problems they had to confront. Some correspondents actually joined the Republican forces and served in a military capacity while continuing to file despatches, others wrote articles in support of one side or the other, a few passed on information which could be strategically important. Looking back at the war from the vantage point of 1943 George Orwell put the problem into perspective when he claimed that 'history stopped in 1936'. In other words he believed that in Spain history was recorded not in terms of what happened but of what ought to have happened.

Early in life I have noticed that no event is ever correctly reported in a newspaper, but in Spain, for the first time, I saw newspaper reports which did not bear any relation to the facts, not even the relationship which is implied in an ordinary lie. I saw great battles reported where there had been no fighting, and complete silence where hundreds of men had been killed. I saw troops who had fought bravely denounced as cowards and traitors, and others who had never seen a shot fired hailed as the heroes of imaginary victories; I saw newspapers in London retailing these lies and eager intellectuals building emotional superstructures over events that had never happened.[1]

Although Orwell does not mention the specific instance he had in mind when he claimed that battles had been reported 'where there had been no fighting' it is probable that he was thinking of Claud Cockburn's imaginary report of non-existent fighting in the Moroccan town of Tetuan in March 1938.

Cockburn had been in Spain from the very beginning of the war, having gone there on holiday in July 1936, 'unaware', as he said later, 'that this was going to be far from a holiday'. Good journalist that he was, one of his first acts was to seek out an interview with the somewhat unlikely figure of General Julio Mangada, one of the few senior army officers who supported the Republicans. A poet who believed in the benefits of nudism and vegetarianism, Mangada had earlier served a prison sentence for shouting out '*Viva la República!*' at a mess dinner and he cut a somewhat inglorious, though undoubtedly eccentric, figure. Cockburn thought that he looked like 'some sort of cross between Gandhi and Gandhi's goat' and although the interview revealed little – Mangada being too fond of confusing fantasy with reality – it did help to show him that the war in Spain was to be as much about emotions as it was about the intellect. That early persuasion was to have a considerable bearing on Cockburn's attitudes to reporting the war in Spain.

Of all the war correspondents who covered the Spanish Civil War, Cockburn was perhaps the most quirky and provocative. Born on 12 April 1904 in Peking, he was the great-grandson of Lord Cockburn, the eminent Scottish advocate and judge who was one of the decorations of the period of intellectual growth known as the Scottish Enlightenment. His father served in the Eastern Consular Service working as British Agent in various cities in China and Korea and from him Cockburn appears to have picked up several traits which served him well in later life – such as a delight in the precise meaning of words and a distaste for superficial interpretations of ideas and events. He was educated at Berkhamsted School and at Keble College, Oxford, a fellow undergraduate and contemporary at Hertford College being his relative Evelyn Waugh who referred to Cockburn as 'my communist cousin'. After graduating he was a Travelling Fellow of Queen's College and spent a year in Berlin where he made his first steps as a professional journalist, eventually being employed as an assistant foreign correspondent of *The Times*. In 1929 he joined the paper as a full-time journalist and worked as a foreign correspondent in New York and Washington, but by 1933 he had swung to the left and his political disenchantment persuaded him to resign and to return to London.

There he established *The Week*, a crudely printed stencilled news-sheet which published the kind of story other newspapers would not touch. What it lacked in typographical style, though, it made up for with an adventurous editorial policy, printing confidential information and challenging fixed opinion in a style that was more akin to the *samizdat* than to any other kind of publication. It was never prosecuted under the terms of the Criminal Libel law or the Official Secrets Act but, as Cockburn frequently admitted, his policies sailed close to the wind on more than one occasion; soon it became *de rigueur* for politicians, diplomats, industrialists and intellectuals to subscribe to *The Week* and many brought with them new sources of information.

When it was seen what kind of stories *The Week* uniquely would handle, all sorts of people – for motives sometimes noble and quite often vile – would approach *The Week* to draw its attention to the most extraordinary pieces of more or less confidential information. Sometimes it came from frustrated newspapermen who could not get what they considered vital news into their own papers. More often such confidences were the outcome of obscure financial or diplomatic duels. They would come, for instance, from the Councillor of an Embassy who was convinced of the wrong-headed policy of the Foreign Office and the Ambassador, and wished, without exposing himself, to put a spoke in their wheel.

The savage tensions of the 1930s naturally produced a situation favourable to this type of development.[2]

One of the 'savage tensions' which *The Week* reported ahead of the rest of the British press was the growing unrest in the Spanish Army during the early summer of 1936. From Spanish friends Cockburn heard at first hand reports of the slide towards anarchy and the firmly held belief that, sooner or later, the army would intervene. This was confirmed by the Spanish Foreign Minister, Alvarez del Vayo, and Cockburn printed the information in *The Week* of 4 June 1936.

Intensive underground activity suggests that the long delayed attempt at a fascist putsch by the higher ranks of the army officers is not likely to be delayed much longer. The re-organization of the army, which will in fact amount to a certain democratization of the army, is due this month. The disorderly elements of the right are believed determined to try to get in their blow before the re-organization can be carried out.

Cockburn did not follow up the story but six weeks later he was in Spain. Ostensibly he had decided to take a holiday in Villefranche in the south of France but had fetched up instead at Tarragona on the Costa Brava, having taken the wrong train in Paris. Years later he would tell disbelieving friends that it was a genuine mistake, that his real destination had been the south of France, but given Cockburn's sense of mischief one could never be sure.

Following his interview with General Mangada Cockburn hurried to Madrid where the Republican press corps had taken up residence at the city's Hotel Florida; at one point or another throughout the war it was to be occupied by writers like Ernest Hemingway representing the North American Newspaper Alliance, Sefton Delmer of the *Daily Express*, Herbert Matthews of the *New York Times* and Jim Lardner (son of Ring Lardner) of the *New York Herald*. The Spanish capital was to remain the focus of Republican sympathies throughout the conflict but it was typical of Cockburn that no sooner had he reached Madrid than he joined up as a soldier in the Fifth Regiment, one of the best organized of the Communist militia groups, then under the political guidance of an Italian Communist, Vittorio Vidali, also known as 'Carlos Contreras'. (The Fifth Regiment had adopted the Red Army's system of political commissars whose purpose it was to reinforce Republican political ideals. Cockburn regarded Carlos as 'an almost super-human power with an unbreakable gaiety'.)

Cockburn was not alone amongst the journalists who took up arms. Orwell went to Spain as a reporter but joined the fighting in Barcelona, Hemingway gave lessons – largely unsuccessful, it must be said – in arms drill and Jim Lardner was killed fighting in an International Brigade at the Battle of the Ebro in September 1938: to men like them service was a simple extension of their ideological convictions. Later in life Patricia Cockburn put her husband's actions into a more human context.

He was tired, he said, of sitting there in Madrid exhorting other people to fight like tigers and if necessary to lay down their lives for the Cause. He was sick of writing stories praising other people's sacrifices.[3]

With the Fifth Regiment Cockburn served for some weeks on the Sierra front before being persuaded that he could best help the Republicans by employing his journalistic talents in the propaganda war. He returned to London to address the Labour Party and the Trades Union Congress on the necessity to speak out against the policy of non-intervention and turned his pen to that cause. For the Communist Party of Great Britain he wrote an emotive account of the war in Spain under the pseudonym of Frank Pitcairn: called *Reporter in Spain*, it was written quickly and betrays the speed of its creation. In his autobiography Cockburn claimed that he had been locked up in a nursing home and ordered not to come out of his room until it was finished: 'A nurse was in attendance to give me shots in the arm in case I fell asleep or dropped dead from exhaustion.'

The publication of *Reporter in Spain* and the revelation of Cockburn's obvious pro-Communist sympathies did not endear him to the British government. When he applied for a visa to return to Spain he was refused permission on the grounds that he had breached Britain's non-interventionist policy by serving as a soldier in the Republican militia. The matter was taken up on his behalf in the House of Commons, but to no avail. Typically, Cockburn was sitting in the Strangers' Gallery during question time and after listening to the outcome he simply took a bus to Victoria Station and caught a boat-train to France. The border with Spain might have been closed to all travellers without visas but there were secret routes if one had the right contacts and by the time the British press was reporting the Government's decision Cockburn was sending *The Week* his first despatches from Spain.

For all that Cockburn sent back regular reports to *The Week* and to the *Daily Worker* – he had become their diplomatic and foreign correspondent in 1935 – it is as a propagandist rather than as a war correspondent that he is best remembered. Some of his work was done for the western section of the Comintern which was run by the brilliant German propagandist Willi Muenzenberg. His assistant and bodyguard was a Czech Communist called Otto Katz who operated under the name of André Simone. From Paris Katz conducted a worldwide, anti-fascist, pro-Popular Front press and propaganda campaign which frequently fell foul of accepted journalistic practices. 'In journalism,' he was fond of saying, 'one should always try for clarity of impact': to achieve that aim he placed stories in unlikely places, subverted journalists and politicians and was prepared to use lies and rumours in his stories when hard facts were either unavailable or not to his taste. Cockburn fell in with many of Katz's notions, especially with his idea that journalism was simply a means to an end.

In this I found him sympathetic. Long before, in New York and Washington, I had come to the conclusion that the real humbug of the press begins only when newspapers pretend to be neutral, impartial fact-purveyors, 'servants', so help me, 'of the public'.

Early on in his editorship of *The Week* Cockburn had decided that rumours were just as vital as facts in piecing together a newspaper story. After all, he reasoned, a good journalist started off with a point of view and then organized the available facts to fit that perspective. He did not just pick up all the facts and then present them without comment: he organized them according to his taste and then presented them in a palatable way. From a coterie of British, American and European journalists who provided snippets of information from conversations and other unattributed sources, Cockburn was able to publish stories which were part supposition, part fact. His methods 'shocked people horribly' but as Cockburn always argued, if *The Week* were only to print confirmed facts it would print little that was of interest to its readership. Added to his anti-fascist editorial policies and to his belief that newspapers remained impartial at their peril, it goes some way to explaining why so much of his writing on the Spanish Civil War has come to be regarded as simple propaganda.

One incident above all others has encouraged the judgement that Cockburn broke journalistic conventions by turning war reporting into a propaganda exercise: it happened at a crucial stage of the war and it involved the use of the press to subvert the normal course of events. From August 1936 the Franco-Spanish Pyrenean border had been officially closed to the traffic of arms, although Léon Blum, the French socialist Prime Minister, later admitted that the French 'voluntarily and systematically shut [our] eyes to any smuggling and even organized it'. The inability to channel Russian and French arms supplies into Spain in any quantity, though, was a considerable drawback to the

Republicans, especially as the Nationalists had easy access
to modern German and Italian military hardware. By early
1938 the Republican armies were falling back in Aragon
and the absence of *matériel* was becoming crucial. Only an
immediate delivery of arms – in this case Russian field guns
waiting on the French side of the border – could stave off
defeat; to avoid that eventuality the Republican leadership
lobbied Blum to open the border. It was an apposite
moment for in the wake of Hitler's annexation of Austria
Blum was considering the possibility of French intervention
on the Spanish Republican side. Although he was talked
out of the idea by his military leaders he was prepared to
listen to the Republicans' argument and the border was
reopened on 17 March 1938.

According to Cockburn, Blum's decision also owed a
great deal to a story which was then breaking in the French
press revealing a major Nationalist setback in Morocco.
Any hint of Franco facing fresh difficulties would be enough
to persuade Blum to meet the Republican demands and to
allow the field guns to cross the border. The problem was
that the story, originated by Cockburn and Katz, was a
complete fabrication.

The ploy took shape in the second week of March when
Cockburn passed through Paris on his way back from
Spain. Calling at Katz's office he was told that the Comintern agency wanted him to provide 'a tip-top, smashing,
eye-witness account of the great anti-fascist revolt which
occurred yesterday at Tetuan, the news of it having been
hitherto suppressed by censorship'. When Cockburn
demurred and said that he knew of no such battle, Katz
replied gleefully that that was not the point: the important
thing was to persuade the French government that Franco
had suffered a major defeat. Such a story would surely
persuade them to smile kindly on the requests made by the

visiting Republican delegation. What better, continued Katz, than to concoct a story 'of a sudden revolt against Franco at the very origin and source of his first onslaught, Spanish Morocco'? The obvious place for such a battle would be Tetuan, the scene of Franco's arrival from the Canaries in July 1936.

Initially Cockburn expressed doubt that they could put together a believable story. He had never visited Tetuan and knew nothing of the layout of the town; neither did he know anything about the disposition of the Nationalist garrison nor of any Republican opposition. Tetuan was in any case firmly pro-Nationalist and the Caliph Mulay Hassan had provided Moroccan troops for Franco's armies in Spain. Katz, though, was not to be dissuaded by such sensible logistical considerations. By using a guide-book the fighting could be confined to short streets and open squares so that no eagle-eyed night editor with a knowledge of Tetuan would become suspicious of any topographical inconsistencies. Encouraged by Katz's enthusiasm the two men worked through the night to produce a workmanlike and credible story.

As we saw it, the important feature of the affair was that sections of the Moorish soldiery, sickened by losses in Spain, had joined with civilian victims of colonial oppression and Spanish anti-fascists in united, if desperate, action. It meant that the same thing might happen in Spain itself. Katz was insistent we use a lot of names, of both heroes and villains, but express uncertainty over some of them – thus in the confusion of the struggle outside the barracks it had been impossible to ascertain whether the Captain Murillo who died so gallantly was the same Captain Murillo who, months ago in Madrid . . .

In the end it emerged as one of the most factual, inspiring and yet sober pieces of war reporting I ever saw, and the night editors loved it.

Not just that, but it had the desired effect. The story was
released to the French press and published on the day that
Blum met the Republican delegation.

When the deputation saw Blum in the morning he had been
reading it in newspaper after newspaper and appreciating its
significance. He was receptive to the deputation's suggestions.
The guns got through all right, and the Republicans won that
battle.

And so the fraud seemed to have worked. Encouraged by
the possibility that the tide might be turning against
Franco, Blum opened the border and allowed the guns to
go through. Cockburn was proud of the part he had played
in the concoction of the story and firmly believed that its
publication played a major part in framing French policy
at that crucial juncture. He repeated it in his autobiography, *Crossing the Line*, and remained unrepentant when
friends and colleagues accused him of producing lies and
distortions and of using the press to achieve a political goal.
To him it was enough that his story appeared to have been
instrumental in persuading Blum to alter his policy and
that the guns had been allowed to pass over the border.
When Blum's supporters claimed later that the French
Prime Minister would not have been swayed in that way
Cockburn was prepared to listen to their argument
although he continued to believe that such a supposition
was 'quite mistaken'.

What then did happen? Katz and Cockburn did write a
story about an uprising in Tetuan which they knew to be
untrue and this was released to the French press and
published. How greatly it influenced French policy, though,
is open to doubt. A week before meeting the Republican
delegation Blum had been returned to office for a second
term of government and amongst his first considerations

was the future level of French support for the Republicans in
Spain. Although he had subscribed to the Non-Intervention
Agreement of August 1936, by which the major powers had
agreed to keep out of the war, he had continued to
sympathize with the Republican cause. As a radical himself
who headed a Popular Front alliance in France he was in
favour of the Spanish government and from a strategic
point of view he was concerned that a Nationalist victory
would endanger France by sandwiching it between two
fascist powers. Hitler's invasion of Austria on 12 March
had also alarmed him, convincing him further of the need
to prevent a Nationalist victory and of countering German
and Italian intervention in Spain. Military support was
discussed but discarded on the grounds that Germany
would treat any French mobilization as a threat to her own
security; besides, Blum was far from sure that Britain or
Russia would support France in any ensuing conflict.

With France unable to offer active military support to
the Republicans, the reopening of the border to supply
arms was as good a means as any of aiding them without
rocking the boat. Thus the strictures of *realpolitik* played as
great a part as any other factor in helping Blum and his
colleagues to reach their decision. Naturally, Blum would
have read in the newspapers the story of the supposed
setback to Franco in Morocco and that may have stiffened
his resolve but the point is that he was going to help the
deputation anyway: the appearance of Cockburn's story
confirmed that he was doing the right thing.

Years later, Cockburn's revelations and the obvious
pleasure he took in his part in the affair were the cause of a
good deal of affront amongst his fellow journalists. To them
the substitution of propaganda for a hard news story was a
heinous crime and one of which a responsible writer like
Cockburn should have been thoroughly ashamed. Richard

Crossman attacked him in the *News Chronicle* and a more recent critic has been Phillip Knightley in his study, *The First Casualty:*

There can be no validity in Cockburn's attitude. If readers are to have no right to facts, but only to what a war correspondent feels it is in his side's best interests to reveal, then there is no use for war correspondents at all . . . In the event, the outcome of the war revealed the basic flaw in Cockburn's approach to war reporting. If a correspondent writes not what is true, but what he wishes was true, he has a fifty-per-cent chance that the tide of war will change and he will be proved right. But, equally, it may not change, and he will be seen to have got the whole thing wrong. That is what happened to Cockburn. Examined today, *The Week*'s reports about Spain appear accurate in detail, but grossly wrong in terms of the overall situation, misleading in their optimism and in their confidence of an eventual Republican victory.[4]

Knightley was writing in the context of the war correspondents' historical relationship to the wars they covered and to the problems they had to face in their work – press censorship, government propaganda and so on. In those circumstances his strictures are valid enough. If it is the duty of a war correspondent to follow the guidelines first laid down by Russell – 'All that a newspaper correspondent wants is to see what is done and to describe it to the best of his ability' – then in the Tetuan incident Cockburn certainly broke many rules. He was not being objective; he used the press to achieve a political aim and he told lies to do so. If he wanted to take sides, Knightley seems to be saying, then he should have given up journalism and joined the army of his choice.

In a sense, of course, that was precisely what Cockburn had done. While at Oxford he had been attracted to Communism and had joined the Communist Party during the early 1930s, feeling that it offered the only means of resolving the political and economic difficulties of the day. In Spain the Republican cause had become his army and it had many powerful allies. From the outset of the fighting the Soviet Union had supported the Republicans: although they had been signatories to the Non-Intervention Agreement they maintained a formidable presence in Spain. As well as a diplomatic corps containing several military advisers, there were two war correspondents – Ilya Ehrenburg of *Izvestia* and Mikhail Koltsov of *Pravda* – who undertook a variety of espionage, para-military and propaganda duties in addition to their journalism. Both were influential party members – Koltsov was thought to be Stalin's personal adviser on Spain – and both were committed to the Stalinist view that only the creation of a Popular Front involving Britain, France and Russia could prevent further fascist expansion in Europe. For that reason Stalin wanted the war in Spain to continue in order to tie down Germany and Italy.

Koltsov's ideology is well summed up in a story told by Cockburn himself. During the siege of the Alcázar in Toledo in the early months of the war, Koltsov reprimanded the American journalist Louis Fischer for writing about the low state of morale amongst the besieging Republican forces. Such disclosures, he said, damaged the Republican cause in the eyes of the world; far better to distort the truth for the sake of preserving unity and maintaining discipline. Cockburn went along with Koltsov's argument, believing that liberal susceptibilities had to be put to one side in a war whose outcome would decide the future course of European politics. If Britain and her allies had used propaganda in the First World War then there was no reason why similar techniques should not be employed in the Spanish Civil War and therein lay the nub of the matter; Cockburn not only considered himself to be a

journalist but a journalist working as a propagandist in the
Communist cause. Or as he himself expressed his position:

To me, at least, there seems something risible in the spectacle of
a man firing off his propaganda-lies as, one presumes, effectively
as he knows how, but keeping his conscience clear by 'detesting'
his own activities. After all, if he does not think the cause for
which he is fighting is worth lying for, he does not have to lie at
all, any more than the man who sincerely feels that killing is
murder is forced to shoot at those enemy soldiers. He can become
a conscientious objector or run away.

To Cockburn the war in Spain represented one of the
great divides in European politics. He believed that were
Franco to defeat the democratically elected Republican
government his victory would expedite Hitler's ambitions
to dominate Europe. France would be threatened by her
immediate neighbours – fascist Spain and Nazi Germany –
thus allowing Hitler to attack the Soviet Union with
impunity. Fascism's threat to democracy was one of the
causes which had prompted the brief though passionate
flirtation between the writers of the 1930s and the Soviet
Union, but with Cockburn this belief was more broadly
based.

From his days in Berlin and from his journalistic contacts
in Paris and elsewhere, Cockburn had come to understand
the threat posed by Hitler to the future stability of Europe
and all his instincts told him that the creation of a Popular
Front was the only course for Britain to adopt. He could
also see through the sham of non-intervention and he
believed that British and French neutrality should be
brought to an end for the sake of preserving the Republican
government in Spain. If that was a cause 'worth lying for',
then so be it: the Tetuan story loses its identity as a straight
war report and becomes instead a ploy in the propaganda

war which was being fought with equal intensity by both sides. On that historical canvas the invention of the uprising at Tetuan was but a detail, contributing to the picture as a whole, but was little in itself.

Cockburn was neither the first nor the last journalist to see his work as a war correspondent in terms of propaganda for the side he supported. During the Boer War there had been jingoists aplenty amongst the British press corps in South Africa and during the First World War the British press had at one time or another produced stories about the Germans boiling down human corpses for glue, about nuns being used in place of bell clappers and about Belgian children being casually bayoneted to death. None were true: all were believed.

Similar types of stories originating from official sources also found their way into the reporting of the Second World War. The extent of the allied losses in France in 1940 was never revealed for fear of damaging British morale; by the same token, the Air Ministry exaggerated the number of enemy planes shot down during the Battle of Britain and during the great Crusader tank battles in North Africa Britain claimed to have destroyed more tanks than Rommel possessed. All three stories were used by the government to lend support to the allied war effort, whereas German counter-claims could be dismissed as enemy propaganda. The technique, therefore, had a military justification which was recognized by the allied leaders. 'In wartime,' Churchill told Stalin, 'truth is so precious that she should always be attended by a bodyguard of lies.' Sometimes, though, it was the bodyguard which had the final say.

Even Richard Crossman, who attacked Cockburn for his part in the Tetuan story, had himself played a role in the war of deception, lies and disinformation which the British waged against the Germans during the Second World War.

The planning of official deceptions was put on a regular footing by the British government and was managed by the London Controlling Section, a highly secret department of the War Cabinet. Amongst its greatest coups was the case of 'The Man Who Never Was', which involved the body of a dead British naval officer carrying false information about the allied landings in Sicily. This was floated ashore on the Spanish coast and, as expected, the papers found their way into German hands. Another ruse was 'Monty's Double', which involved the employment of an actor to 'understudy' General Montgomery in a successful attempt to deceive the enemy about British intentions in the prelude to D-Day. Because it was considered a patriotic duty such deceptions were morally acceptable: where Cockburn went wrong in the eyes of his critics was to apply those rules to a war in which war correspondents were supposed to be objective. That was missing the point. Cockburn believed that the Spanish Civil War was a war for civilization against Nazism and that it had to be won – using whatever measures he considered to be necessary. In that respect he was assuming a role which many other war correspondents have adopted down the years: playing the propagandist for the ideals of the side he supported.

Later, the extent of the propaganda war in Spain was exposed by writers like George Orwell who noted that the press propaganda issued by both sides was frequently too fallacious to be taken seriously.

One of the dreariest effects of this war has been to teach me that the Left-wing press is every bit as spurious and dishonest as that of the Right. I do earnestly feel that on our side – the Government side – this war was different from ordinary imperialistic wars; but from the nature of the war propaganda you would never have guessed it. The fighting had barely started when the newspapers of the Right and Left dived simultaneously into the same cesspool of abuse.

The Republicans went to considerable lengths to treat war correspondents well by providing decent accommodation and excellent communications facilities. They were greatly helped by having control of the principal international telephone and cable lines which ensured that 'Republican' news always reached the outside world before 'Nationalist' news. In contrast, the correspondents attached to Franco's forces worked under conditions which would have been familiar to the British journalists of the First World War. Press censorship was controlled by the despotic Louis Bolin and journalists were only allowed to visit the line in the company of a conducting officer. The Republican side was less formal in its approach although they took good care to sanitize visits to the front or to take journalists to quiet areas or places where victory had already been assured.

Both sides made considerable use of atrocity stories, providing 'evidence' of massacres, rape and pillage, some of which were true, many more fabricated to further the aims of whichever side presented them. Many journalists accepted the evidence without question and some, especially those with Republican sympathies, believed that to tell the truth about what was happening in Spain would prejudice the world in favour of Franco and thereby aid the fascist cause. Objective reporting reached a nadir in Spain, mainly because war correspondents allowed themselves to become mouthpieces of the side to which they were attached. As a rule, only right-wing correspondents were allowed into Franco's camp and liberal and left-wing reporters covered the war from the Republican point of view: neither made much effort to remain unbiased.

Against that background, and taking into account his
political ideology at that time, Cockburn's part in the
Tetuan invention assumes less significance, perhaps, than
his critics have accorded it. It should also be seen in the
wider context of his work in Spain for the *Daily Worker*.
According to Patricia Cockburn, while Cockburn was in
Spain much of the writing for *The Week* was done by other
hands. This may account for the over-confidence in a
Republican victory noted by Phillip Knightley, a good
example being this remark in *The Week* which followed a
report of the arrival of modern military equipment for the
Nationalist army in September 1936:

> Competent observers both friendly and unfriendly to the Govern-
> ment's cause are agreed that the rebels would have no chance of
> effectively ruling the country if they were to secure a military
> victory.

This was wishful thinking, albeit expressed early in the
war, and seen from the perspective of today and our
knowledge of Franco's victory, *The Week*'s attitudes are
naïve and almost pathetically over-optimistic. More
enlightening and more indicative of Cockburn's writing
from Spain are the reports he filed for the *Daily Worker*.

As the mouthpiece of the Communist Party of Great
Britain the *Daily Worker* took a fiercely pro-Republican line,
supported the trade union and Communist elements in
Spain and promoted the concept of the Popular Front.
Throughout the war in Spain it helped to organize support
for the International Brigades and encouraged British
workers to raise funds and provide comforts for the Republican cause as a whole. It never enjoyed a large readership
– Cockburn described the conditions there as a 'raw
financial blizzard which blew continuously through the
offices for months on end' – but it was required reading for

those on the left who preferred the Communist approach to that offered by Attlee's Labour Party.

Cockburn had been recruited into the *Daily Worker* by Harry Pollitt, the Secretary of the Communist Party of Great Britain, and had made a good fist of his commitment, using many of the journalistic techniques which served him so well on *The Week*. The move meant that he had to forgo other lucrative contracts – he continued to edit *The Week* – but there was the compensation of working for his chosen party which, although 'small, poor and adventurous', was in his opinion the most creative force in British politics. Partly, then, it was a sense of idealism which prompted his decision; partly, too, there was an aura of drama attached to the move, but the mainspring was Cockburn's committed opposition to fascism. At a time when Britain and France were standing by and timidly preaching appeasement while Hitler raped Europe, only the left appeared to be lifting its voice in protest. Throughout the 1930s, too, the Comintern represented the issue as a struggle between democracy and the dictators and although we now know the extent of the subversion and the propaganda practised by Stalin's agents in the West, at the time it was a difficult call to resist. Later, Cockburn was to admit that his membership of the Communist Party was as much due to his opposition to fascism as it was to any prevailing political ideology. He left the party shortly after the end of the Second World War.

Cockburn was not the only *Daily Worker* reporter in Spain – at various times the war was covered by William Rust, Tom Wintringham and Elizabeth Wilkinson, as well as by notables on the left who went to Spain to see for themselves – but writing under the name of Frank Pitcairn he was the most consistent of the team.

Very little of his work was actual reporting of the fighting; this was carried out mainly by William Rust who later wrote *Britons in Spain* (1939), an uncritical account of the part played by British volunteers. Cockburn spent much of his time in Madrid where he met, amongst others, Ernest Hemingway and observed shrewdly that the great man's presence there helped to foster the illusion that if a famous American author could take the Republican side then the rest of the world would surely follow. Of all the writers in Spain Hemingway was perhaps the most apolitical; nevertheless, Cockburn could not fail to underestimate the presence of such a larger-than-life character at the heart of the fighting.

At breakfast one day in his room at the Florida Hotel, which more or less overlooked the nearest part of the front, Mr Ernest Hemingway was very comfortable about the shelling. He had a big map laid out on the table, and he explained to an audience of generals, politicians and correspondents that, for some ballistic reason, the shells could not hit the Florida. He could talk in a very military way and make it sound all very convincing. Everyone present was convinced and happy. Then a shell whooshed through the room above Mr Hemingway's head – the first actually to hit the Florida – and the ceiling fell down on the breakfast table. To any lesser man than Mr Hemingway the occurrence would have been humiliating. While we were getting the plaster out of our hair, Mr Hemingway looked slowly round at us, one after the other. 'How do you like it now, gentlemen?' he said, and by some astonishing trick of manner conveyed the impression that this episode had actually, in an obscure way, confirmed instead of upset his theory – that his theory had been right when he expounded it and this only demonstrated that the time had come to have a new one.

Cockburn's reports from Spain were discursive and informative and there was little of the sense of over-optimism which found its way into *The Week*. In favour of the creation of a Popular Front and consequently wrong in many of his judgements he might have been, but he never lost sight of

his political objectives and opinions. In common with the
rest of the British press the *Daily Worker* did not publish his
story about the uprising in Tetuan; instead it carried 'Frank
Pitcairn's' thoughtful analysis of the possible course of
events should the fighting in Aragon in March 1938 bring
to an end Republican resistance in Spain. It appeared
under the headlines: FASCIST PLAN TO END SPAIN,
ATTACK FRANCE:

The events of the last few days in Austria and Spain and the ever-
increasing German pressure on Czechoslovakia have made perfectly clear, competent observers are agreed, the strategic line now
being pursued by the Fascist Powers. It is an attempt to paralyse
the Western democracies by the enormous joint intervention and
offensive against the Spanish Republic, while, at the same time,
building as fast as possible a Fascist war bloc in Central Europe.
This new long-scale intervention and offensive in Spain has,
however, a long-term, as well as an immediate significance for the
Fascist Powers:

The destruction of the Spanish Republic and the consequent
consolidation of Germany and Italy in Spain and the Mediterranean would not only render France vulnerable to the enemy on
yet another front and unable to assist Czechoslovakia, it would
completely isolate both Britain and France from their sources of
manpower in their most important colonies when the Fascist
attack on them directly is launched.

This was Blum's fear too: encirclement by the fascist
powers, thus rendering France powerless in the face of
further German aggression. As Cockburn saw it, a Nationalist victory in Spain would prevent France and Britain
from acting in concert with Russia to save Czechoslovakia,
then already under threat at the time of the Tetuan story.
It was of paramount importance, therefore, for France to
allow the guns to cross the border, even if they did not turn
the tide of war as Cockburn hoped they would. This was
the overriding policy in all of Cockburn's journalism from

Spain: the necessity to shake Britain and France out of their policies of non-intervention and appeasement and to encourage them to oppose the fascist dictators. It was for that purpose that he adopted such a partisan approach, for in the early part of the war at least few people in Britain were prepared to believe the extent of the German and Italian involvement in the struggle.

As it was, the main thrust of Cockburn's political arguments was seen to be off-course by the end of the Spanish Civil War. Czechoslovakia did fall but the much feared encirclement of France never took place as Franco refused to throw in his lot with Hitler during the Second World War. By that time Cockburn was disillusioned, as much by the Nationalist victory as by the cynical in-fighting amongst the Spanish left. The creation of the Russo-German pact was also a bitter blow. By that time, too, Katz and Koltsov were both dead, executed in 1941 on Stalin's orders during the notorious purges of the 'volunteers of liberty'.

In 1940 the *Daily Worker* and *The Week* were suppressed, the latter never to return, as the Communist Party was becoming increasingly nervous about Cockburn's dual responsibilities. When the *Daily Worker* was rehabilitated in 1943 Cockburn decided to close down *The Week*, feeling that it had no role to play in a world at war. After the war Cockburn was to live in Ireland and to become a regular contributor to *Punch*, the *New Statesman*, *Private Eye* and the *Irish Times*, confirming his reputation as a lively and occasionally acerbic columnist, a rapper of knuckles and a believer in the basic decency of common humanity. He died on 15 December 1981.

Fifty years after it first began, the Spanish Civil War still remains a subject of intense interest both within and without the country. In particular, speculation continues to surround the intellectual response to the war, especially the part played by the left-wing sympathizers of the Republican cause who saw the struggle as the final confrontation between democracy and intolerance. In that respect the war was as much an international conflict involving different ideologies as it was a civil war between rival political factions.

Partly, the reason for this response lies in the nature of the war itself: by 1939 and Franco's eventual victory the surface simplicity of the original motives had become blurred and confused. It was no longer a matter of need to protect a democratically elected government against the threat of authoritarianism. Three years of war had seen squabbling break out amongst the supporters of the Republican movement, the fighting between the Communists and the anarchist factions being particularly long-lasting and bloody. It had also become clear by then that the war in Spain had been affected by the concerns of international diplomacy whose needs were dominated by the prevailing power structure of Europe. In that sense Spain had become a testing ground for the larger international conflict which would break out within months of Franco's victory.

Partly, too, the abiding interest in Spain stems from the myths which have grown up around the civil war. Many of these have their origins in propaganda stories concerning atrocities which may or may not have taken place. Of course, thousands of people were executed by rival political groups and horrible events did take place but so powerfully ingrained in the popular imagination are many of the stories that even today it is difficult to separate fiction from fact. Arthur Koestler reported the war for the *News Chronicle*; like Cockburn he was recruited by Katz into the Comintern's Western European propaganda agency and like Cockburn he wrote a book about the war in Spain. Called *Spanish Testament* (1937) it was later found to be

largely a work of invention; many of the atrocities ascribed
to the Nationalists never took place and in his later study,
Invisible Writing (1954), Koestler admitted that Katz had
persuaded him to introduce the distortions. He was not
alone in being duped: many journalists on both sides
accepted stories as facts and deliberately presented them in
a sensational manner to assist the side they supported.
After the bombing of Guernica in April 1937, for example,
Louis Bolin, the Nationalist censor, was still able to present
the story to the world as a non-event and to claim that the
damage had been caused by Basque incendiarists. He was
even able to cast doubt on the evidence of George Lowther
Steer who wrote a first-hand account of the raid for *The
Times*; and it was not until 1970 that official credence was
given by the Spanish authorities to the blazing truth that
Guernica was bombed from the air.

Elsewhere countless lies were told about the murder of
priests or the slaughter of trade unionists, the victims
varying according to the political persuasion of the reporter:
in some cases such reports were further disfigured by a
pornography of violence. Thus stories appeared in which
barricades were constructed from human corpses, naked
nuns were raped by Moorish soldiers and children were
torn limb from limb. George Orwell called this kind of war
reporting 'a substitute for fighting' but many journalists
found that the public had an insatiable appetite for stories
tinged with sadism. At one stage in the war the *Daily Mail*
carried a headline which read REDS CRUCIFY NUNS,
while the *Daily Worker* claimed that Franco's Foreign
Legion was composed of 'murderers, white-slavers, dope-
fiends and the offal of every European country'. The
excesses were probably no worse than those committed in
previous wars but in Spain they only added to the many
myths surrounding the war.

Finally, the war retained its fascination from the sense of disillusionment which permeated most of the sympathizers to the Republican cause. They had entered the struggle in 1936 with high hopes, yet by the war's end none of their ideological goals had been achieved. The defeat of the Spanish Republic and the subsequent signing of the Russo-German pact signalled for many the end of their flirtation with Marxism and the beginning of a new cynicism in which politics were seen to be either unworkable or incomprehensible. For them it had become evident, too, that even had the Spanish Republic beaten off Franco's rebels, Soviet interference would have made Spain little more than a puppet of Moscow. Furthermore, those who had taken part in the fighting had seen at first hand the horrors of modern warfare and had been sickened by the gulf between the ideals of a heroic struggle and the reality of facing machine-gun fire on the ground and bombs from the air. While serving with the Spanish militia, Cockburn was fascinated by the way in which the men had charged enemy positions holding their rifles high above their heads with one hand and giving the clenched fist salute with the other: 'It emerged that they had taken the highly stylized and symbolic posters designed by the Madrid intellectuals, showing a Soldier of the Republic in this posture, as illustrations of correct military practice.'

For many writers like Cockburn the outbreak of the Second World War helped to put the Spanish War into perspective. Throughout the 1930s Cockburn had warned that sooner or later Hitler would attempt to dominate Europe; his fight against fascism, therefore, was a personal crusade and Spain one of the many battles which had to be fought. By the time he had gone to Spain as a correspondent he had come to the conclusion, too, that it was impossible for the press to remain neutral or impartial. In that light it was a weapon to be used in the Republican cause and the Tetuan invention a notable, though dubious, victory. Perhaps the strength of the pro-Republican passions can be best summed up by the American war correspondent Herbert Matthews: 'Those of us who championed the cause of the Republican government against the Franco Nationalists were right. It was, on balance, the cause of justice, legality, morality, decency.'

Cockburn applied for credentials as a war correspondent during the Second World War but was turned down by the Ministry of Information on the grounds that he was a Communist and, therefore, likely to whip up agitation amongst the British servicemen.

Although, politically, I naturally welcomed the turn of events and the end of the nerve-racking period between the signature of the Nazi-Soviet Pact and the outbreak of the Nazi-Soviet war, from a strictly personal viewpoint the new situation, as it developed during the following couple of years, left me feeling increasingly at a loose end. Things were suddenly so cosy that one had the sensation that nothing one might write was really necessary – everyone was rushing in the right direction anyway.

It was naturally irksome to keep writing so much, so encouragingly, about the war effort without oneself getting into battle.

He also believed that Labour leaders opposed his application because they feared that he would use the opportunity to promote the *Daily Worker* and, as Cockburn admitted, 'anything was better than that'. In despair he made a direct approach to Brendan Bracken, the Minister of Information, and mischievously suggested that a solution to the problem might be found in sending him to an RAF bomber squadron. As he would have little contact with the crews during raids over Germany he would be in no position to 'subvert' them, and in between raids he could be kept in solitary confinement in another part of the base. Bracken was much amused by the proposal and although he promised to pursue Cockburn's request, it fell on stony ground. It was not until April 1945 that Cockburn was given official accreditation when he covered the first meeting of the United Nations in San Francisco.

In retrospect, the decision not to give Cockburn employment as a war correspondent was probably a mistake, for given his committed stand against fascism and his quicksilver mind he would no doubt have made a useful contribution, either as a reporter or a propagandist. It is tantalizing to think what he might have made of officially approved deceptions like 'The Man Who Never Was' or 'Monty's Double' which were dreamt up to sow the seeds of doubt and confusion in the minds of Britain's enemies.

Chester Wilmot and the Second World War

When Britain declared war against Germany in support of Poland on 3 September 1939 she was unprepared to offer any ready military assistance to the country she was supposed to be helping. The British Army could only put together four divisions as an expeditionary force for Europe, six infantry and one armoured division in the Middle East, a field division and a brigade in India, two brigades in Malaya and a modest scattering of imperial garrisons elsewhere. Years of neglect and tolerance of old-fashioned equipment meant that the army in particular was ill-prepared to meet the modern German forces in battle, and British industry was not geared to make good those deficiencies. The Royal Navy had started rebuilding in 1936 and entered the war with a numerical superiority over the Germans, but it was still woefully short of escorts for convoy duty. Only the RAF had prospered with the intro-duction of radar and the huge fighter-building programme which had resulted in adequate supplies of Spitfire and Hurricane aircraft for home defence. Once again in the nation's history it seemed that Britain was going to war with the equipment and the mentality of previous conflicts.

A ruthless opponent was ranged against Britain and her French ally. Germany had crushed Poland within 18 days of Britain's declaration of war, allowing Hitler to turn his leisurely attention to the invasion of France. The German leader had based his strategy on appeasing the Soviet Union through the Russo-German pact which had been signed on 25 August 1939: this allowed Germany to invade

France in the spring of 1940 without incurring the danger of a second front in the east. France had duly fallen by 21 June, and had paved the way for Hitler to implement the second phase of his plan – an attack against the 'menace of the Soviet Union'. 'My pact was meant only to stall for time,' he told his senior advisers at a conference at Bad Reichenhall on 29 July, 'and, gentlemen, to Russia will happen just what I have practised with Poland – we will crush the Soviet Union.'

A year later, on 22 June 1941, the German Army attacked across the Soviet border from the Baltic to the Black Sea, in so doing creating an eastern front which for three years was to be the major battleground of the Second World War. The collapse of France had left Britain isolated in the west, able only to take the war to Germany through bombing raids and isolated attacks on fortress Europe. By winning the Battle of Britain in the air, the danger of immediate invasion had been staved off but the country was desperately short of raw materials, equipment and food with which to continue the struggle. Roosevelt's promises of assistance through the Lend-Lease agreements of March 1941 heralded the day when America would herself enter the war – Japan's attack on the Pacific fleet at Pearl Harbor helped to settle the issue – but the creation of the British Isles as a 'floating aircraft carrier' to arm and supply the projected invasion of Europe meant that British forces would play a subsidiary role in the war. As described by military historian Correlli Barnett, Britain's part in the Second World War was to help the Russians and the Americans to beat Germany, and the Americans to defeat Japan. Against that strategic background the major theatre of Britain's war against Germany was to be the campaign in North Africa which lasted from December 1940 to May 1943.

Although Hitler never attached much importance to
North Africa, being preoccupied with Russia, it was central
to British thinking. Partly, the theatre of war in North
Africa was determined by Britain's need to safeguard the
Suez Canal, the imperial jugular to the Far East. Partly,
too, it was regarded as the one area in which the enemy
could be engaged and victories won; but the overriding
principle was Churchill's belief that victory there would
open up the Mediterranean, thereby permitting an allied
attack on Italy, the axis powers' exposed southern flank.
To Churchill, the campaign would also restore to Britain
strategic freedom of action, the historic principle which
allowed the Royal Navy to command the seas while her
armies attacked the enemy in vulnerable positions. In *The
Struggle for Europe*, his highly regarded study of the Second
World War, Chester Wilmot believed that the North African campaign freed British strategic thinking from the
shackles of being forced to wage a war in continental
Europe.

The influence of Britain in war has always been most effective
when exerted, not in an effort to match the mass armies of the
more populous European powers in continental warfare, but in
the precise application through command of the sea of small yet
highly trained forces at vital or exposed points in the enemy's
flank or rear. Used in close conjunction with the Royal Navy,
British armies throughout modern times have been able to
produce a strategic effect out of all proportion to their size.

The Middle East was promoted in the order of British
strategic priorities and towards the end of 1940 prep-
arations were made to sweep the Italians out of Libya
which had been their colony since 1912. Victory there
would preserve the Mediterranean as a British sphere of
influence, protect the Suez Canal and in the longer term

stop any enemy pincer attack on the Persian Gulf, Britain's principal source of non-dollar oil. When it went in on 9 December 1940, the British attack was a resounding success. General Sir Richard O'Connor's army, which included the 4th Indian Division, the 6th Australian Division and the 7th Armoured Division, crushed the Italians at Sidi Barani and drove through Cyrenaica to take Bardia and Tobruk. At the same time Italian forces were ejected from Abyssinia, thus bringing to an end Mussolini's influence in East Africa.

Both victories did much to restore British morale, so badly dented after the fall of France; had they been capitalized upon, North Africa could have fallen at a stroke, but two new ingredients were then added to the war. Firstly, in pursuit of creating a front in the Balkans the British offensive in Libya was halted and units of Wavell's victorious army were despatched to Greece where they were badly mauled by the invading German forces. Secondly, Hitler decided to lend assistance to Italy by despatching to North Africa two armoured divisions under the command of the experienced Lt-Gen. Erwin Rommel. British gains quickly turned into losses as the Germans and Italians counter-attacked in April 1941 to threaten Britain's hold on Egypt; from that point onwards, British interest in the Desert War – as the campaign in North Africa was also known – became an obsession.

One ingredient of the British infatuation with this theatre of war was the persona of Rommel who was grudgingly admired both for his dashing style of leadership and for the sense of gentlemanly purpose he seemed to bring to the war. Nicknamed 'The Desert Fox' by the British press, he was a spectacularly successful battlefield general, a modern Hannibal, who inspired affection amongst his own men and respect from his enemies. It was due to his presence in

North Africa that the Germans were able to tie down the weight of the British Empire with only two panzer divisions and a motley collection of Italian troops. Secondly, the Desert War was sold to the British public as 'a gentleman's war', a glamorous confrontation between the armoured might of two great nations, fought against the backdrop of the neutral desert. To Alan Moorehead, a war correspondent with the *Daily Express*, the first year of the Desert War was . . .

. . . an *annus mirabilis*. Like a backward sapling that is transplanted into a rich soil I began to sprout with new growth, and I was probably happier than I had ever been before. At a moment when most people's lives were being frustrated and ruined by war everything conspired to give me confidence . . . even the very wartime air of the desert itself and the sense of freedom it conveyed – the feeling of being able to travel out into the distance far beyond the range of money, of bosses and jobs, and of responsibilities.[1]

Moorehead had been born in Melbourne in 1910 and after leaving university had worked for the *Melbourne Herald*. At the age of 26 he had come to London and had been employed as a European correspondent for the *Daily Express*, occasionally visiting Spain to cover the civil war; with him in North Africa was his friend and rival, Alexander Clifford, whom he had met in 1938. At the outbreak of war, Clifford, formerly Reuters' chief correspondent in Germany, had been appointed 'Eye-Witness' by the Ministry of Information and his duties were similar to those exercised by Swinton during the early days of the First World War. It was not a happy experience. Recoiling from the confused motives by which the British government had attempted to manage the dissemination of news during the fall of France and the retreat from Dunkirk, Clifford had resigned his post and had joined the army of first-class journalists who had arrived in North Africa to record – and, in many instances, to glorify – the fighting. Amongst their number was Chester Wilmot, like Moorehead an Australian, who was covering the war for the Australian Broadcasting Commission (ABC).

Born on 21 June 1911 in Melbourne, the son of a newspaperman, Reginald William Winchester Wilmot had been educated at Melbourne Grammar School and the University of Melbourne, graduating with an arts degree in 1935, followed by a law degree in 1936. The year after leaving university he had been part of a two-man Australian student debating team on a round-the-world tour, an experience which had taken him to the Far East, the USA, Britain and Europe and which had given him his first steady work as a broadcaster; amongst his freelance assignments for the ABC he covered the 1938 Australian cricket team's tour of England. Early in 1939 he was back in Australia working as an articled clerk; he joined up shortly after the outbreak of the Second World War but his military career was cut short in August 1940 when the ABC recruited him as a war correspondent to cover the part played by the Australian forces in the Middle East and Greece. Initially, he worked as number two to Lawrence H. Cecil, an experienced Australian radio producer who had served in the British Army during the First World War, and who had won a Military Cross on the Western Front.

To this task Wilmot brought a good conceit of his own abilities. At university he had proved to be a forceful debater and his history professor, Sir Ernest Scott, had instilled in him the virtues of tracking information back to primary sources, essential qualities for any good radio journalist. As a fledgling broadcaster he had given early

evidence of his ability to channel basic facts into the
confines of a radio talk without ever losing the listeners'
interest in his main points – before commentating on the
Australian cricket tour of England he had been obliged to
dig deeply into the arcane lore and the background statistics which he knew to be the life and breath of all committed
supporters. All those abilities, his capacity for absorbing
detail, his preference for hard facts in place of hearsay and
his good broadcasting voice, gave him a head start as a
radio war correspondent and quickly brought him to the
attention of the BBC in London which monitored all the
reports from North Africa. Donald Boyd, the Home News
Talks Editor, said after the war that 'the qualities which
distinguished him [Wilmot] were utmost observation and
fidelity to detail, a far-reaching perspective view and an
ability to relate the two'. He was not alone in holding that
judgement.

Other characteristics also distinguished Wilmot. According to those who knew him well, he could be overbearing
and self-opinionated, others thought him bumptious or
nakedly ambitious; yet he seems also to have been possessed
of the easy charm that often goes with people who assert
themselves in public life. In short, he had the ideal temperament for the modern broadcaster.

The North African campaign to which he and the other
British and Commonwealth war correspondents had been
assigned had few comparisons with the other theatres of
the Second World War. To begin with, the terrain was
harsh, barren, inhospitable, yet strangely compelling, a
landscape which imprinted itself on the minds of the men
who fought there. Soldier poets like Hamish Henderson
described it in *End of a Campaign* as the 'brutish desert . . .
this landscape for half-wit stunted ill-will', and Jocelyn
Brooke in *Landscape near Tobruk* declared that 'this land was

made for war'. In fact, few of the men who served there, writers or not, failed to be affected by the sheer size of the desert arena over which the two opposing armies fought, its absence of definition and the seemingly limitless horizons with no roads or tracks to break up the bare expanse of sand and scrub. Responding to its similarities with a classical sporting arena, the war correspondents tended to report the conflict in an imagery which spoke of a courtly tournament involving valiant rivals. Even the military operations carried codenames smacking of gallantry and derring-do – 'Battleaxe', 'Crusader', 'Torch'.

The war correspondents covering the campaign in North Africa were allowed a freedom of movement which would have astonished their Great War predecessors on the Western Front. Because the vast tracts of desert encouraged a war of movement correspondents teamed up with individual units and developed, not unnaturally, a feeling of sympathy and *esprit de corps* with their compatriots. By that time of the war all correspondents were on attachment from the Ministry of Information and were suitably kitted out; they wore officers' uniforms with green epaulettes and their cap badge was a gold-lettered 'C'. (The War Office had originally proposed 'WC'.) In North Africa they adopted the easy and unofficial uniform of pullover, corduroy trousers and desert boots worn by most British and Commonwealth units and later made something of a fashion by General Montgomery. By then, too, the authorities regarded the war correspondents as vital cogs in the allied war effort and went to great lengths to provide them with up-to-the-minute information, on the understanding that this would be transformed into favourable copy. Shortly before the 'Torch' landings in Tunisia in November 1942 General Eisenhower, in his first address to the press, went

so far as to tell them that he regarded them as military
personnel and would treat them as such.

I regard war correspondents as quasi staff officers, and I want to
emphasize that, in my opinion, each newsman has a greater
responsibility than that of a competitive newsman. I am not
prepared to treat you as if you were my enemies or a bunch of
commercial gentlemen. If I thought you were, I tell you here and
now I would do nothing for you. It is for that reason I do not
worry if I see you in the corridors of my headquarters, or passing
my window or anywhere else. I trust you. As staff officers your
first duty is a military duty, and the one fact which you must
always bear in mind is to disclose nothing which would help the
enemy. He is always looking for every bit of information to help
him make his calculations, and many things appearing inconse-
quential to you may help him. It would be a distinct disservice to
let such things get out, particularly when the enemy gets them
with such little effort.*[2]

Eisenhower clinched the issue by adding that he regarded
a mass of copy covered with blue pencil marks as failure.
Stay on our side, tell our story, he seemed to be saying, and
we'll treat you well. Give your own version, and you're out
on your own. Most of the 92 allied journalists in North
Africa favoured the former approach, and those who
attempted to file 'bad news' stories – defeats or setbacks,
criticism of commanders, descriptions of agonizing deaths,
for example – soon discovered a formidable array of military and civilian censors to cut their material.

Another reason why most journalists maintained their
partnership with the military was that the war was exceptionally difficult to follow. Operations were carried out over
a long front and flying sand and dust obscured both the
view and intelligence. One way to keep in touch was to
rush from one headquarters to another to interview com-

* Compare this with General Alexander's words in Chapter One.

manders in forward positions and to create a general
picture from the information received. Another was to talk
to senior commanders before the battle, to come to a basic
understanding of their tactics and of the expected gains and
losses, to keep close to the front-line units during the battle,
to have a clear channel of communication to the senior
commander and to accept nothing that could not be
reconciled with the facts. This was the method adopted by
Chester Wilmot and, according to Donald Boyd, it helped
to make him the outstanding war correspondent of the
Second World War.

His reasoning was his brilliance. Few men observed with such
accuracy and retentiveness and at the same time could maintain
the long perspective view. His writing was vigorous and clear but
only concerned with his observations and conclusions. It was not
in any way meretricious – it was not designed to attract; it was
used only to report and explain. His artistic inclinations, so far as
he had any, were used to construct an exposition. He was not,
therefore, so sympathetic a speaker as some others. But that didn't
matter. He knew what was going on, and why, and where it was
going to; and this knowledge could almost be felt in the decisive
drive and tone of his voice. Even the slight hesitation – it could
not be called a stammer – was a sign of the pressure behind, never
of doubt.[3]

Unlike many of the other war correspondents in North
Africa, Wilmot was not particularly concerned with filing
'colour' pieces. Cavalry metaphors rarely invaded his copy;
instead he concentrated on analysis and interpretation,
preferring broad political and military issues to the heroic
minutiae of the soldier's life in the desert. His experiences
in North Africa also helped him to evolve two basic rules:
go on your own and always establish – and then maintain
– contact with the senior commander. Not that his serious-
ness of purpose or his concern with the wider issues of the

battle kept him out of the front line. While in the company
of Randolph Churchill in a forward position he came under
British artillery fire and was wounded in the leg; during the
siege of Tobruk he dragged out into the open a Type C disc
recording machine (weighing 500 lb) so that he could
record authentic battle sounds; and while with the
Australian forces in Palestine he caused something of a stir
by living in a one-man press camp near the front and
scorning the luxury of a hotel in Haifa or Jerusalem. There
was nothing vainglorious in these gestures, neither was he
demonstrating any personal fearlessness – on the contrary,
he frequently admitted to being 'bloody scared' – but he
did feel that it was essential to be near the front to
appreciate any military situation, whatever the circumstances. (He was not alone in showing personal, even eccentric,
courage in pursuit of his newsgathering. While accompanying an RAF sortie over Sicily, Alexander Clifford had
taken the place of a wounded air-gunner and had shot
down an enemy fighter. Ronald Monson of the *Daily
Telegraph* had rescued a badly wounded private under
enemy fire, a feat that would have brought him a medal
had he been wearing a soldier's uniform. North Africa was
that kind of war.)

Wilmot's early days with the Australian forces were
spent in Libya and he covered the first campaign there
from Bardia to Beda Fromm, the great tank battle which
broke the back of the Italian armour. Although he was the
only correspondent to be present at the battle it was typical
of the man that he should have shared his 'scoop' with the
other war correspondents. He also commented on the
operations in Greece and had critical words to say about
the lack of air cover and about the decision to send the
better part of O'Connor's army to the area in pursuit of
Churchill's Balkan ambitions. This judgement, which was

shared by many, was borne out by subsequent events. After the war German Supreme Command papers expressed surprise that 'the British did not exploit the difficulties of the Italians in Cyrenaica by pushing on to Tripoli. There was nothing to check them.'

At the end of March 1941, taking advantage of the allies' weaknesses, especially in armour, the Germans and the Italians under Rommel advanced into Cyrenaica. Within a fortnight the British and Commonwealth forces had surrendered most of their gains of the previous months and the smell of defeat was in the air. The depleted British armour – provided by the inexperienced 2nd Armoured Division – collapsed in the face of Rommel's onslaught and by 8 April its resistance had come to an end. After that, only the Australians remained to hold the enemy at Tobruk where the main part of the garrison consisted of the 9th Australian Division, the 18th Australian Infantry Brigade and detachments of the British 1st and 7th Royal Tank Regiments. All in all, there were about 36,000 men within the Tobruk perimeter.

Fortunately for that garrison, the town's strongpoints had been left intact and were largely proof against the German artillery. More significantly, perhaps, the garrison's Australian commander, General Leslie Morshead, was a man of iron. 'There'll be no Dunkirk here,' he told his men. 'If we should have to get out, we shall have to fight our way out. No surrender and no retreat.' Throughout the summer the Tobruk garrison lived up to that order and withstood all of Rommel's and the Luftwaffe's attacks on the port – which held the key to any German advance on Egypt – but at great cost to men and equipment.

The men of the Tobruk garrison had always regarded their predicament as being the period required to drive off the investing German forces, but by July General Sir

Thomas Blamey, Commander-in-Chief of the Australian forces, was voicing disquiet about the physical decline amongst the Australian troops. He also believed that the Australian Corps should fight as a single force and that the 9th Division should therefore be allowed to regroup in Palestine with the 6th Division (Greece, Libya and Crete) and the 7th Division (Syria). On this second point he had the support of the Prime Minister Robert Menzies who protested to Churchill that such a move would 'give immense satisfaction to Australian people for whom there is great national value and significance in knowing that all Australian soldiers in any zone form one Australian unit'. After a fair display of prevarication by Churchill and his military leaders, the 18th Australian Infantry Brigade was relieved in August, followed by the 9th Division in October;* by then Menzies' Liberals had been ousted by John Curtin's Labour Party. After a period in reserve in Syria the 9th saw further action in North Africa during Montgomery's successful 1942 campaign, while the rump of the Australian forces returned home to defend their country against the threat of Japanese invasion from New Guinea.

With them went Chester Wilmot who was recalled to Australia by the ABC after the fall of Pearl Harbor. During the siege of Tobruk and the related British operations in the Western Desert, his radio broadcasts had been well received in Australia. More to the point for his future career, perhaps, they had also been monitored by the BBC in London, re-recorded, transcribed and circulated by them to any department which might find them useful. In that way, Wilmot had begun to acquire a reputation within the BBC for the accuracy and soundness of his reports. Within

---

* Only the 2/13th Battalion remained to take part in the subsequent Crusader operation. It left Tobruk on 16th December 1941.

the space of a four-minute package he was able to capture the reasons for a battle and which direction it seemed to be taking. News sub-editors were quick to latch on to the fact that this unseen Australian could make sense of items which otherwise seemed to be obscure or over-burdened with technical information. Wilmot's obvious ability as a war reporter made them look out for his despatches – and make use of them. Soon his reports were being heard all over the world for, as Desmond Hawkins explained in *War Report*, his compilation of wartime broadcasting, the BBC had become an international organization.

For in addition to the multitude of transmissions from London in English, beamed to the Empire, to British forces in the many theatres of war, and to English-speaking people in occupied and neutral countries, there was the vast range of foreign language broadcasts – ranging from French and German to three separate dialects of Chinese. For millions of people London was the voice of freedom – and very often the only voice.

By May 1941 messages and cables were reaching Wilmot recording the BBC's appreciation of his work and it is a measure of the regard in which he was held that Donald Boyd noticed his absence and regretted it. 'Then he disappeared. No more messages from that Australian chap.'

He had ample reason to miss Wilmot's regular despatches. During the siege of Tobruk his reports from inside the perimeter had provided the world with a vivid picture of the trials faced by the garrison and of the position's strategic importance to the allied effort in North Africa. With his radio mechanic, Bill MacFarlane, he had covered a good deal of ground to understand the complexities of Morshead's defensive strategy; above all, he had spent time and trouble interviewing the men themselves so that his listeners could be provided with first-hand accounts of the fighting. This was not a question of providing a blood-and-guts story. As Wilmot had discovered, the quickest way to lose a soldier's confidence was to misrepresent him or to 'shoot a line'; rather it was a question of making a thorough check on the action and then allowing the soldier to pick up the story. In most cases, as in this extract from an account of an Australian attack on a German patrol led by Lieutenant F. A. Mackell, the results could be singularly impressive.

They [the Germans] left their guns and scattered. In their panic some actually ran slap into the barbed wire behind them and another party that was coming through the gap turned and fled. We went for them with the bayonet. In spite of his wounds Edmondson [Corporal J. H. Edmondson, VC] was magnificent. As the Germans scattered, he chased them and killed at least two. By this time I was in difficulties wrestling with one German on the ground while another was coming straight for me with a pistol. I called out – 'Jack' – and from about fifteen yards away Edmondson ran to help me and bayoneted both Germans. He then went on and bayoneted at least one more.[4]

The Australian patrol accounted for at least twelve Germans and took one prisoner before the rest fled, leaving behind all their weapons. Edmondson was wounded in the stomach by a burst of German machine-gun fire and died the next day; for his action he was awarded the Victoria Cross, the first to be awarded to an Australian during the Second World War. In itself the skirmish was a minor enough operation but the Australians' resolute action had helped to disrupt a major German assault on the Tobruk perimeter at the El Adem Road.

That was the key to Wilmot's success as a war correspondent: he could read a battle, understand the tactics and was then prepared to stay with the front-line troops, in the case of Lieutenant Mackell winning a reluctant interview from the participants. At its simplest, Wilmot took the microphone to the battle for Tobruk when things were happening and let it listen to the sounds of war and to the reactions of the men who were doing the fighting. Above all, his style of war reporting was not an official statement; it was the voice of the observer and the interpreter who had been to the action and could then report what he had seen.

Within four months of entering the war in 1941 Japan had achieved most of her offensive aims. Malaya, Hong Kong and the Dutch East Indies had fallen into Japanese hands; the Americans had been driven out of the Philippines, the British out of Burma, and China had been isolated from her allies. Anxious to secure supremacy in the South-West Pacific and to prevent an allied counter-attack, the Japanese Navy proposed the elimination of Australia and Hawaii: to do that, New Guinea and Papua would have to be taken as well as the Pacific island chain which ranged from the Solomon Islands to Samoa. There is little doubt that Australia stood in danger of an assault by Japanese forces: were New Guinea and Papua to fall, northern Australia and Queensland would then be under threat of Japanese air and sea attack. Pitted against them was an Australian garrison of brigade strength in Port Moresby, the capital of Papua and the springboard for any Japanese invasion plans, as well as small garrisons on the north coast and surrounding islands in the Bismarck Sea. In March 1942 these isolated units had to be withdrawn when Japanese forces successfully stormed Rabaul in New Britain and from there leap-frogged into New Guinea at Lae and Salamaua.

The Japanese Navy, flushed by its easy successes, wanted to proceed with an invasion of Australia; they had already bombed the north-western coast without meeting any opposition and believed, correctly, that the defending forces were thin on the ground. Only eleven divisions were available for the defence of the homeland and of these only two were combat-ready: the remaining nine were composed mainly of militia men, Australia possessing no great tradition of a standing professional army. Reinforcements were on the horizon in the shape of the Australian forces returning from their service in the Middle East, but, realistically, Australian defences were in dire straits. The RAAF had no fighter support until May 1942 when the Boomerang fighter was evolved hurriedly from the outdated Wirraway trainer, and the Royal Australian Navy possessed no aircraft carriers. In short, the Australians had little capacity either to defend themselves or to carry the attack to the Japanese. Had it not been for the successful repulse of the Japanese forces by the US Navy at the Battles of Midway and the Coral Sea early in May 1942, Papua and New Guinea could have succumbed to a seaborne attack. As it was, the two defeats led Japan to abandon its plans for a naval attack on Port Moresby and to concentrate instead on a land assault over the high peaks of the Owen Stanley Range in the eastern tip of Papua.

What the allies lacked in fire-power in Australia they compensated for with a well-oiled propaganda machine. General Douglas MacArthur, fresh from his defeats in the Philippines, had been appointed allied Commander-in-Chief of the South-West Pacific area and to his task he brought a good deal of Hollywood-style bravura. Soon the press was being told that a mighty army was being assembled to drive the Japs out of their island fortresses; everything was done to promote MacArthur's image and his historic utterance, 'I shall return',* was dragged out on

* His actual words on arriving in Melbourne were: 'I have come through and I will return.'

every conceivable occasion to demonstrate his iron resolve and determination to win. Moreover, MacArthur possessed a slick press department and operated a military censorship which, according to the journalists accredited to his headquarters, was the strictest operated by any commander of the Second World War. Even in the New Guinea front line, which attracted the majority of the Australian press corps, the censorship rules stood in the way of reporting the reality of the fighting in any great detail.

Censorship in the Western Desert had been noticeable largely by its absence, the commanders preferring the reporters to operate their own self-censorship; in New Guinea it was a fact of life as impenetrable and inhospitable as the mountainous jungle terrain over which the fighting took place. Most of the journalists were critical of the lack of preparation for the defence of Port Moresby but they were permitted to say little. To them it was clear that official stories which spoke of the build-up of great allied armies were little more than a public relations bluff. The reality, they knew, was rather different. In his book *Green Armour*, written after the war, journalist Osmar White revealed that the concentration of Australian strength in the Middle East had left the armed forces ill-equipped to deal with the Japanese threat in Papua and New Guinea.

It has been publicly admitted by Australian politicians that at this time there were not enough rifles to arm the forces drafted for home defence, not enough bullets to fill their ammunition pouches and only enough shells to keep all field artillery in action for 36 hours. It is difficult to imagine a nation more completely open to even the most hastily prepared invasion than Australia was in the first three months of 1942.

Until the reinforcements of experienced soldiers from the Middle East arrived to bolster the New Guinea force

the Australian garrison in Port Moresby was in a parlous
state. The men were badly equipped and trained and could
not match the Japanese man for man in jungle warfare;
they also lacked air power, the one sure means of stemming
the Japanese advance and of taking the war to the enemy
in the difficult jungle conditions. White, who accompanied
Wilmot into the forward fighting areas, was critical of the
conditions endured by the Australian forces but censorship
prevented him from giving the public a realistic picture. As
White realized, it would have been impossible – and
perhaps inadvisable for morale – to have described the Port
Moresby garrison in words like these, which he wrote but
never filed:

The strength, equipment, training and leadership of the New
Guinea force is inadequate for the task it has been briefed to do.
It is enervated by tropical diseases and it is badly fed, overworked,
discouraged and very nearly hopeless. It is without reserves or air
support. If the Japanese come, organized defence will not last
more than forty-eight hours.

In fact it was a close escape. Helped by reinforcements
and increased American air support, the Australians not
only defended Port Moresby and Milne Bay but broke up
the Japanese attack over the Owen Stanley Range. By the
end of August the enemy had been halted thirty miles short
of its objective, superior Allied air power having played
havoc with the Japanese lines of supply and communication. By then, too, plans had been made for General Sir
Thomas Blamey, the Australian commander of the Allied
land forces, to take over personal direction of the fighting
from Port Moresby. Wilmot had already crossed swords
with him in the Middle East; in New Guinea the confrontation was almost to bring to an end his career as a war
correspondent.

Blamey was a man who inspired widely different emotions in those who knew him. Born in 1884, he had served as a staff officer in the 1st Australian Division during the First World War and had worked his way up the command structure to lead the Australian forces in the Middle East in 1939. Although his career had been interrupted between 1925 and 1936 when he was Commissioner of the Victoria Police Force, he was still considered to be the country's foremost military strategist and administrator, fully justifying his appointment as MacArthur's deputy. As a human being, though, he was something of a conundrum. Vain, ambitious, and overbearing, he courted publicity, yet frequently fell foul of the press on account of his odd behaviour. It was said of him, with no little truth, that his greatest handicap was not his private life but the fact that it fell so short of being private. As John Hetherington, his biographer, admitted: 'It was inevitable that a man of his full-blooded and personally indiscreet character should give his enemies plenty of ammunition.'

One of those 'enemies' was Chester Wilmot, who made little secret of the low regard in which he held the Australian commander. During the Middle East campaign he had clashed with Blamey over the right of correspondents to make informed criticism of the direction of the war: on one occasion Wilmot's comments on the poor standard of reinforcements arriving from Australia was censored by Blamey because he felt that the report reflected badly on himself; on another, Blamey attempted to kill a report which criticized some aspects of the fighting in Crete. On each occasion Blamey reminded Wilmot that it was not part of the war correspondent's job to be critical of the Australian high command as this promoted the wrong image of the Australian war effort.

A further point of conflict was Wilmot's suspicion that

Blamey might have made money out of a motion picture contract and that he had covered up cases of graft involving military contracts. Blamey always denied the allegations but Wilmot refused to let the matter drop and on his return to Melbourne from the Middle East, made further enquiries. At one point a mutual friend, a lawyer called Krcrouse, intervened on Blamey's behalf and there the matter might have ended had not both men found themselves together in New Guinea.

At the end of September Blamey arrived in Port Moresby to assume personal command of the Australian forces. Almost immediately the tension between the two men was heightened when Blamey sacked Lt-Gen. Sydney Rowell, the commander of the New Guinea force and a man whom Wilmot liked and admired. Believing that he was the only person who could present an objective account of the problem, Wilmot left for Canberra to lay the facts before the Prime Minister. Although he was given a fair hearing, Blamey's position was unassailable and when he got back to New Guinea Wilmot found that his own working conditions had deteriorated: Blamey had denied him access to his headquarters and had ordered his staff to snub him. A week after Wilmot's return, following the successful Kokoda operations which finally broke the Japanese offensive, Blamey called Wilmot into his headquarters, removed his accreditation and ordered him back to Australia forthwith. Although Wilmot had denied making mischievous statements about the general, Blamey was an implacable enemy. 'We should give thousands of pounds to have someone in your position in Japan trying to undermine the C-in-C there,' Blamey told Wilmot. 'Your accreditation to Allied Land Forces is forthwith cancelled. You will return to Australia at once.'

It was of little balm to Wilmot's injured pride that the

real reasons for Blamey's actions should have been quite different. In a long memorandum to the managers of ABC Wilmot explained that his accreditation had been removed because he chose to make criticisms of the way in which the war was being run in New Guinea: 'the real reason was my insistence on the right of a correspondent to criticize and to enquire freely and the fact that I had been critical of the military conduct of the war in New Guinea and when I could not get my criticism published I went to the Government.' Furthermore: 'this is not just an individual case affecting me alone. The basic freedom of correspondents in General Blamey's command is at stake. If this is unchallenged he has succeeded in placing himself above criticism.'

This was the nub of the war correspondent's problem. Working in close liaison with the very armed forces which provided him with material and information – and in most cases with cover and protection, too – he was supposed to act on their behalf, to be one of the team. If he told the truth, then he was out in the cold, accused of damaging morale at home or of helping the enemy in the field.

Such was the length of Blamey's arm that he could, and did, prevent Wilmot from serving as a war correspondent for Australia's national broadcasting system. On his return to Australia Wilmot continued to work for the ABC as a news commentator in Sydney but it irked him that he was forbidden to earn his keep at the front. Almost by way of compensation he turned to authorship and in his spare time wrote *Tobruk*, an authoritative account of the siege, based largely on his own experiences and on the interviews he had conducted with the serving men and their commanders. He also wrote the commentary for a documentary film, *Sons of the Anzacs*, but it was the book which signalled the major change of direction: this was no 'instant' account of the siege written from a journalist's point of view for rapid consumption, but a rounded and accurate history which revealed Wilmot as a first-rate military historian. The publication of *Tobruk* was generally well received by reviewers and by military men alike, and convinced Wilmot that he could write a different kind of historical record, based on hard facts and analysis but transformed by his first-hand experience.

Throughout the period of his 'exile' Wilmot tried, unsuccessfully, to have his accreditation restored but Blamey was deaf to all requests, official or off the record. When help did come, it arrived in the shape of the BBC in 1944 when plans were being finalized to cover the forthcoming invasions of Europe. A separate War Report unit, transcending departmental boundaries, had been established and it needed experienced reporters. Wilmot's name was remembered and, according to Donald Boyd, steps were taken to find him.

When we in Home News Talks heard that Chester was going round reinforcement camps in Australia and would not be tolerated as a war correspondent by General Blamey we were at first dismayed, and then saw it as a golden opportunity. We suggested (as quietly as possible) that the BBC should beg ABC to second him to us for the duration. We felt a good deal of warmth over this prospect and were overjoyed when it was accepted.

Behind the scenes, it had been a close-run thing. On hearing that Wilmot was to be seconded Blamey had sent a signal to the War Office warning them not to give him accreditation. The message, though, fell into the hands of General Rowell who gladly gave the background to the BBC and the War Office. No action was taken and on 12 April 1944 Wilmot was on his way to London.

The War Report unit which Wilmot joined had been set up solely to cover the D-Day invasion and the expected

fighting in north-west Europe; and it was a unique amalgamation of talents from news and current affairs, depart-
ments normally antagonistic to each other's work. Its aims
were summed up by Desmond Hawkins who wrote after
the war that it 'was the task of this unit to select and deploy
the correspondents and equipment necessary to supply
dispatches, recordings and material suitable for documentary treatment, to all the programmes engaged in presenting war news'. The first War Report was broadcast on 6
June 1944 immediately after the 9 P.M. news and it continued until 5 May 1945 with one gap between 4 February
and the Rhine crossings of 23 and 24 March.

War Report had the enthusiastic backing of the senior
British and allied military commanders; indeed, General
Montgomery, who commanded the 21st Army Group,
made considerable use of the BBC's facilities. His orders of
the day were frequently broadcast to the nation and in
interviews and talks he was able to inform both the public
at home and his army in the field about the allies' progress
after D-Day. So close was the co-operation between Montgomery and the BBC's reporters that, like Eisenhower, he
came to regard them as military men, and in return seems
to have won their total loyalty and commitment. Wilmot
came to enjoy a reasonably good relationship with Montgomery: he also had a fruitful friendship with Lt-Gen.
Brian Horrocks, the commanding officer of XXX Corps.
(After the invasion Horrocks provided Wilmot with an
Auster observation aircraft for his own use.)

Altogether the BBC employed forty-eight correspondents
in its War Report team for D-Day. They were given special
training by the army, wore uniform and were assigned to a
particular unit; they were also given additional practice in
broadcasting techniques and sound engineering so that
they could service their own equipment, should anything

happen to their engineers. In place of the old and unwieldy
recording equipment which had seen service in North
Africa, the BBC had evolved lightweight portable recording
machines which weighed 40 lb and which provided the
reporter with one hour's recording on twelve double-sided
discs. It was to change the face of combat reporting,
enabling a war correspondent to get into front-line positions
by himself, without the attendant paraphernalia of a radio
truck.

Receiving and transmitting posts were also established
along the south coast of England and plans were laid to
take additional recordings across the channel by speed-boat
or aircraft. Later, once a foothold had been made, high-
power transmitters were set up on the European mainland,
thus enabling reporters to broadcast live to the BBC.

Wilmot was assigned to the 6th Airborne Division whose
task was to hold the left flank of the allied bridgehead along
the River Orne which would face the brunt of the expected
German counter-attack. Made up of two paratroop brigades and an airborne glider force the division had been
detailed to hold the Orne bridges and to destroy a
menacing-looking battery at Merville. It was considered to
be a hazardous operation: quite apart from the scale of the
German opposition, airborne operations were still in their
infancy and the limitations of dropping lightly armed
formations straight into the heat of battle were well enough
known. During the Sicily landings of the previous year
paratroopers had suffered high casualties, not only in battle
but also because their pilots had dropped them over the sea
or on to windswept mountains far from the dropping zones.

Nevertheless, for all those dangers, Wilmot came to terms
with his assignment, telling himself and other doubters like
David Woodward of the *Manchester Guardian* who was also
attached to the airborne forces that it would get them closer

to the action and the stories. This was not simple bravado: Wilmot had accustomed himself to glider flying and had come to admire, if not love, the large wooden Horsa gliders which would take them to France. Especially intriguing to him was the technique by which the pilot landed the machine – diving to earth at a steep angle before pulling out into a perfectly controlled short landing.

At D-Day itself Wilmot accompanied 29 men in a Horsa glider which was pulled over to the dropping zones by an RAF Albemarle: it was part of the 24,000-strong British and American airborne forces which would be first into France as the vanguard of the later seaborne landings. So that he could record in flight, Wilmot took up his position behind the two pilots and with an army public relations man holding his torch he made his first recordings for War Report. Even across the passage of the years and through the crackle and hiss of the original recordings it is still possible to experience Wilmot's sense of awe as the glider plunged into the darkness of the waiting French countryside.

With grinding brakes and creaking timbers we jolted, lurched and crashed our way to a landing in northern France early this morning. The glider in which I travelled came off better than most. The bottom of the nose was battered in, the wings and tail assembly were slashed here and there, but she came to rest on her three wheels, even though she had mown down five stout posts that came in her path, and although we virtually crash-landed in a ploughed field. As the tug left us we dropped speed and went into a slow gliding descent. Five hundred feet up it was just clear enough for the pilot to distinguish the white roads bounding the field where we were to land. For an instant we caught a glimpse of the guiding lights at one end of the rough runway. We put the nose down and we stiffened ourselves for the jolt of the touchdown and lifted our feet clear of the floor in case something might rip through the belly. The touchdown itself was perfect but as the

wheels bounced and lurched over the furrows and ditches we
heard the harsh straining of the wooden fuselage, the crash of
posts hitting the nose wheels and undercarriage. No one was even
scratched.[5]

Just as he had come to the end of his first disc the glider
received a direct hit by flak, but, fortunately, little damage
was done and the glider was able to put down in a ploughed
field littered with obstacles. It was one of the lucky ones.
That night, 71 out of the 196 glider pilots became
casualties.

Although the airborne operations at D-Day were criticized later for the high losses – caused mainly by inexperienced aircrews – they did play a vital role by sowing
confusion amongst the defending German forces in Normandy. The gallantry displayed by the airborne troops –
British and American – was also outstanding, the 6th
Airborne Division achieving all its objectives on the River
Orne. 'This victory accounted for the broad smiles on the
faces of the men who were manning the forward positions
yesterday,' Wilmot reported on 12 June. 'They're in splendid heart, even though they've been through the great
strain of the initial landing and attack, and the further
strain of six days' fighting in nerve-racking country. And it
is nerve-racking country.'

Shortly after D-Day Wilmot teamed up with the 9th Bn.
Parachute Regiment who were fighting a fierce action at
Château St Come east of the River Orne. The Germans,
realizing that the airborne bridgehead had to be broken,
fought with great ferocity and in several recorded incidents
resorted to subterfuge. Using the uniforms of dead paratroopers, they infiltrated British positions, causing chaos
and making the exhausted defenders trigger-happy. At one
point, Wilmot and his team found themselves in front of

the fighting and only the speedy action of Lt-Col. Terence Otway prevented a tragedy. It was not the only dangerous incident in which Wilmot was to be involved during the D-Day operations. On the day after the landings he ignored a German attack on the British divisional headquarters at Château de l'Heaume in order to record the arrival of the allied glider reinforcements. Some weeks later, in mid-July, south of Caen, he dug a slit-trench to record the leading tanks of the 11th British Armoured Division as they punched their way into the Goodwood offensive. As the tanks rattled by, an officer shouted out to him: 'What the hell do you think you're doing?' When Wilmot gave his reasons the tank commander replied politely, 'Would you mind getting out of the way, Mr Wilmot, as we're about to open fire.'

Not unnaturally, perhaps, the story improved with the telling and soon gained a common currency amongst the invading British forces. Incidents of that kind also added to Wilmot's name and, to his mild astonishment, he discovered that he had become something of a celebrity. Just as had happened in the desert, his reputation was linked to iron nerves and total fearlessness, attributes which he insisted he did not possess. He once told David Woodward that he followed General Horrocks into a forward area and only stayed with him out of a sense of duty. 'There was Horrocks without his brass hat,' he admitted, 'so what could I do?' On another occasion he told his recording engineer, Harvey Sarney, that he agreed with Field Marshal Viscount Gort's remark that being a soldier involved long periods of extreme boredom and short periods of intense fear. Characteristically, Wilmot added, 'Only a fool is not frightened.' (Although anxious to avoid tags, Wilmot was intensely proud of the red beret which had been

awarded to him by the airborne forces shortly after the
initial landing in Normandy.)

At home in London the BBC was quick to spot the
potential of Wilmot's style of reporting and after his first
leave he returned to the front as a 'special events' correspondent to cover the allied push into Germany. Instead of
asking Wilmot to continue reporting the day-to-day events,
Boyd decided to use him as an analyst and interpreter, who
would provide up to three minutes of comment after the
main news item of War Report. He was also working for
the ABC and in odd moments it amused him to think that
his old adversary, General Blamey, would be hard pressed
to avoid hearing him on the airwaves. For by the end of
1944 Wilmot had established himself as one of the best
known 'voices' of the BBC. Listening to the recordings of
those leading broadcasters some forty years after the event
there is little to choose between their despatches from the
front. Richard Dimbleby and Guy Byam both risked their
lives providing thrilling commentary from RAF raids over
enemy territory (Byam was killed while flying with the 8th
United States Air Force in February 1945) and reporters
like Howard Marshall and Frank Gillard supplied authentic first-hand accounts of the fighting in France, but it was
Wilmot's ability to absorb detail and then to reveal it that
made his contribution different. During the Ardennes offensive at the tail-end of 1944, for example, he was quick to
praise the contribution made by British air command to
stemming the German breakthrough into the American
lines.

We can see now the effect of these air attacks in what has
happened and is happening beyond Rochefort. The reinforcements haven't arrived, and those reconnaissance tendrils which
were pushed out [by the Germans] towards the Meuse have
withered for lack of nourishment and are now being lopped off

and destroyed. Here, our people are on the offensive and the enemy is being driven back from the Meuse towards Rochefort. And so we now have this position along the front. At the western end of the salient the Germans are being forced back. On the southern flank we have a solid wedge driven in as far as Bastogne, so that at its waist their salient is now only eighteen miles wide.

On 20 December Montgomery had been ordered by Eisenhower to take charge of the American front in the Ardennes, a position which also gave him command of allied tactical air support. There is little doubt that those air attacks – provided mainly by rocket-firing Typhoons of the RAF – were instrumental in stopping the German offensive and bringing about an eventual withdrawal. Over the Christmas period American and British air forces flew 15,000 sorties, according to Wilmot in *The Struggle for Europe*, 'striking not only at traffic in the Ardennes, but also at roads, railways and airfields throughout the Rhineland. The German "railheads" in the Eifel were soon rendered useless and Model's [the German commander] forces became dependent on supplies brought up by road from distant depots.' Although Wilmot was also to admit in the same book that the reaction of the allies to the German counter-attack was one of 'disagreement and incredulity', his assessment of the value of allied air support did not differ radically from the broadcast he had made for War Report on 29 December 1944.

Gradually a trend began to develop in Wilmot's broadcasts from the allied advance into Germany. Less interested than the other reporters in human interest stories or in rumours which spoke of the war's end, he was gradually assembling material which could be used later for analysis and interpretation. At the beginning of 1945 Collins, the London publishers, had commissioned him to write the book which would be published under the title of *The Struggle for*

Europe. 'They want a full, thorough job – written after the war when the documents, or some of them, are available,' he told his sister. 'They don't want a correspondent's book, but to use their own words, "another *Tobruk*". That's very nice and I am looking forward to settling down in a cottage near London with Edith and Jane [his wife and first daughter] and taking six or eight months off as soon as the battle ends in the west.' Although the bulk of the research for *Struggle* was indeed carried out after the war – both Eisenhower and Montgomery allowed Wilmot to see confidential papers and to interview them at length – much of Wilmot's work as a correspondent in 1945 was carried out with the book in mind.

By the spring of 1945 Wilmot was in charge of the BBC's Brussels transmitter and had the task of organizing the broadcasting coverage in the 21st Army Group and 2nd Tactical Air Force. As he was then in charge of four other reporters and also responsible for the technical side, Wilmot had to deal with organizational problems in addition to his own broadcasting duties but, more importantly as far as he was concerned, the post made him senior man in Montgomery's sector with free access to the British high command. Not unnaturally, perhaps, Wilmot's sudden rise to prominence – he had been with the BBC less than a year – irked some of the other reporters, but none could deny his professionalism or the accuracy of his reports.

Wilmot admitted that he owed much to his close relationship with the senior British generals who trusted him with confidential information – but it was not a one-way affair. Horrocks frequently confided in Wilmot and in turn valued his opinion. If Wilmot made a comment on the troops' performance, for example, Horrocks would take it seriously. 'I think you should watch such and such a formation,' Wilmot once told him. 'They have been in the line rather a long time and their morale isn't as high as it should be.' Horrocks usually acted on the information and told friends later that, had Wilmot been a soldier, he would have made an admirable staff officer.

However time-consuming Wilmot's administrative duties might have been, they never prevented him from doing his fair share of war reporting. With his sound man, Harvey Sarney, he was never far away from the front line during the last months of the war, on one occasion even finding himself ahead of it. During the Reichswald battle in February 1945 he and Sarney contrived to get so far ahead of the 15th Scottish Division's advance that they almost blundered into the German lines. Stuck in a narrow lane with the Germans some 200 yards ahead of them, they were forced to reverse their Humber radio truck with Wilmot guiding it by hand-signals. It took them two hours to cover the mile-and-a-half stretch of roadway. On another occasion near Cleve they were accosted by enemy troops but made their escape by shouting out to their would-be captors in German. As Sarney recalled after the war, confusions of that kind often happened to the reporting teams travelling over unknown roads in the heat of battle. The only time he ever saw Wilmot lose control of himself was when there was an interruption in his transmissions to London. 'It's only five minutes, Chester,' he would say whenever enemy bombardment knocked them off the air. 'You'll be back again soon.' Wilmot, though, would be inconsolable, either swearing in anger or weeping tears of frustration.

Using the BBC's high-power transmitters Wilmot and his team were often able to break into War Report or other programmes with up-to-the-minute news of importance. From the MCN ('Mike Charlie Nan') transmitter he broadcast an account of the fighting for the bridge at Nijmegen; although it was officially 'off-air', Wilmot persisted with his broadcast on the medium wave and eventually alert listeners passed on this information to the BBC. Less dramatically, he broke into Radio News Reel with news of the Reichswald offensive just as it was about to begin transmitting to the USA and Canada. The end result was that North American listeners received the information before the following day's newspapers – a notable scoop for Wilmot.

The decision whether or not to take a report lay with the War Report editor who had to weigh the virtues of the material offered against the balance of the programme as originally planned. He also had to take into account the demands of the other war correspondents in the team. According to Donald Boyd, Wilmot was unusually persistent and as he was known to deliver the goods it was well-nigh impossible to gainsay him: 'Chester quite rightly believed that everything he was doing at the time was important,' he recalled. 'If it had not been important he would have done something else.' Now, while it is in the nature of every journalist to believe that his or her work is more vital, more interesting and more accurate than anyone else's, and to demand more space for it, Wilmot was prepared to fight to the bitter end for his beliefs. At the war's end, that persistence was to pay handsome dividends.

On 3 May, with Montgomery's forces firmly established in north Germany, Wilmot was able to tell War Report: 'The general surrender of the German forces opposing the Second British Army may now come at any hour.' As it happened, the first steps had been taken that very day. With Hitler dead, power had passed to Admiral Dönitz who ordered a four-man delegation to discuss surrender terms with Montgomery at his tactical headquarters on Lüneburg Heath. The British field marshal treated the plenipotentiaries with some disdain and made it clear that he was only interested in an unconditional surrender of the northern German forces; he gave them to the following day to discuss that demand with their superiors. By showing the Germans the tactical situation on his headquarters' maps and threatening the north German towns with further air bombardment, Montgomery was able to demonstrate to the delegation the hopelessness of their position. 'They had no idea of this situation and when they saw the map they at once gave in,' he told Sir Alan Brooke later that day.

Shortly before five o'clock in the afternoon on Friday 4 May the Germans returned to offer their surrender, just as Montgomery had predicted. Never averse to publicity, he had briefed the accompanying war correspondents and by giving the news in advance to Chester Wilmot he allowed him to prepare his recording equipment for the historic moment. Everything went according to plan. A conference tent had been set aside with six chairs and a table covered by an army blanket and each German officer from the five-man delegation (an intelligence officer had been added overnight) was invited to sign the instrument of surrender. Then Montgomery added his signature, a matter of some moment for him as a soldier, for the document made it clear that the Germans had surrendered to him personally. An excited Chester Wilmot recorded the whole scene and added his own comments. It was just before 6.30 P.M.

The triumph of the British armies in Europe is complete. Tomorrow morning at eight o'clock the war will be over for the British and Canadian troops, and for the airmen of Britain and the Commonwealth who came to liberate the occupied countries and to conquer Germany. Tomorrow morning their victory will be complete.

Having finished his recording Wilmot rushed to the MCN transmitter to get it back to London without thought

of editing any of the material. War Report was half-finished
by the time that he managed to get through with the news
that he had an important message and would require at
least ten minutes of air time. Boyd replied cautiously that
he would have to scrap the running order and that time
was running out, but when he heard Wilmot 'struggling
with his impatience at the other end of the beam', he gave
in, thus allowing the wonderful news to be broadcast.

Hallo BBC, hallo BBC, this is Chester Wilmot speaking from the
Second Army front in Germany. This is not so much a description
of what happened this afternoon, but the actual thing – recorded
at Field Marshal Montgomery's headquarters this afternoon – the
full ceremony which took place when the German plenipotentiaries came to sign the instrument of surrender. I've just got to the
transmitter and so I haven't had time to edit these recordings and
will play them to you as we recorded them on the hill of the
Lüneburg Heath this afternoon at Field Marshal Montgomery's
headquarters. There is an opening description of the arrival of the
plenipotentiaries, and then you hear Field Marshal Montgomery
himself reading the terms of surrender. These are the recordings
we made.

No sooner had the broadcast begun than a circuit broke
and MCN went off the air. In London a children's choir
singing hymns could be heard in place of Wilmot; Boyd
made a gesture of despair to his announcer who took it as a
signal for a closing comment and all at once it seemed that
Wilmot's momentous tidings were not to be heard. However, a minute or so later the circuit was re-established and
Wilmot's words were broadcast to the nation.

The following day, 5 May 1945, War Report was broadcast for the last time and the MCN transmitter was closed
down a fortnight later. Its last operational broadcast was
made by Wilmot and included the news that Himmler had
committed suicide. (Ever alert to the news value of a first-

hand account, Wilmot had interviewed the British sergeant-major on duty but he dried up and had to be 'encouraged' with alternating cups of coffee and brandy. Eventually Wilmot got the recording he wanted but the censors cut out the sergeant-major's last words: 'And I spat in his eye, the dirty bastard.')

Wilmot's reputation and his good working relationship with Montgomery allowed him to record the surrender ceremony in its entirety and thereby to gain a notable scoop. Montgomery knew the value of good publicity and there is little doubt that he made the most of the opportunity presented by the presence of the microphone. Shortly before the ceremony he had crowed to the war correspondents that the Germans would be surrendering 'a million chaps' to him personally, but when the time came to go on air his demeanour changed. According to Nigel Hamilton, his latest biographer, 'a quite different Monty was in evidence – the ruthless Army Group commander who brooked no disobedience or vagueness, whose life had been devoted to the study and practice of the art of war'. Montgomery had in fact played a part in ensuring the BBC's presence at Lüneburg. Early that morning he had instructed his Intelligence Officer, Colonel Joe Ewart, to telephone Wilmot, who had then woken Sarney with the words: 'Come on, this is it.' In that way Wilmot got a memorable broadcast and Montgomery received a sizeable slice of personal propaganda.

It has become fashionable in recent years to play down the performances of the war correspondents of the Second World War and to accuse them of being little more than cogs in the military machine, of being Montgomery's and Eisenhower's 'quasi staff officers'. To some extent that was the role extended to them by the allied armies as all 'news' and press briefings came from military sources. This tended

to make correspondents feel that they were essential ingredients of the allied front. For example, correspondents
living in close proximity to the armed forces, whether at
tactical headquarters or in the front line, naturally sided
with the 'home team'. Not only did they want to lend them
their support but they knew, too, that the fighting men with
whom they lived would resent misreporting or 'bad news'
stories. Then there was the enemy. Most war correspondents, like most of the protagonists in the struggle, regarded
the war as a righteous war and the Germans as an
unparalleled evil. In those circumstances it was often
difficult to present objective reports. Censorship, too,
played a heavy-handed role, with the result that disasters
like the Dieppe raid or the Arnhem landings were never
fully reported, because the military authorities did not want
to dent civilian morale.

To a great extent the failings of the war correspondents
of the Second World War can be excused because the
nation itself was at war, locked in a struggle with a vicious
and unbending enemy. That being so, most war correspondents believed that they had a loyalty to their country and
its armed forces which transcended their duties as objective
journalists. Some abused the system and wrote 'colour'
pieces from the safety of comfortable hotels while purport-
ing to be 'on the western front'; others did their best to get
to the heart of the fighting and to describe it as best they
could to the people at home. A handful – Alexander
Clifford, Christopher Buckley, Alan Moorehead and Chester Wilmot – found out for themselves, analysed the course
of the fighting and were more interested in the battle itself
than in the impression their reports were making. At the
war's end, Lt-Col. Graham Jackson, the press briefing
officer of the Second Army, regarded those four as the
'aristocrats of the correspondents', men who were accurate

and thorough and who took a keen interest in the wider questions of the conduct of the war.

Wilmot stayed on in Europe to cover the War Crimes trials at Nuremberg and continued to work for the BBC. By then, November 1945, he was working hard on *The Struggle for Europe*, acquiring his 'own collection of documents dealing with the strategic, diplomatic and economic aspects of the war'. He also had access to German military, naval and economic records, the latter having been made available to him by Eisenhower; and he was allowed to interview high-ranking German battlefield commanders. With justifiable pride he was able to tell his family on 11 November that he had the field to himself.

> I shall, I hope, be able to disclose for the first time what went on in the German High Command during the last critical years . . . So far as I know no one else is tackling the story from these sources, and no one else has access to them except the official historians and of course their work won't be finished for years.

At this period in his life Wilmot's prestige as a correspondent was second to none and a staff job with the BBC or any national newspaper would have been his for the asking. Instead, he decided that his first priority must be the book and that he would buy time by supplying freelance work for the BBC, broadcasts which in fact helped him to put his research into perspective. Laurence Gilliam, for whom Wilmot often worked at the BBC, described the process as: 'mutual self-interest. Chester wanted rent money to keep himself going while he worked on the book.' Gilliam, on the other hand, wanted what Wilmot had got: 'his intensive research and unique mastery of both the radio and historical techniques. Other historians were ignorant of radio, or afraid of it; and other correspondents lacked the qualities of the historian; only in Chester was this dual expertise

synthesized.' As it turned out the 'mutual self-interest' was
of immense help to the book: parts of *The Struggle for Europe*
possess a brevity and clarity which read like a radio script
and the book as a whole has a sense of unfolding story in
the best tradition of radio narration.

The Struggle for Europe was six years in the writing and
was not published by Collins until January 1952. It was
worth waiting for. The first edition sold 154,671 copies in
three printings and an additional 91,000 copies were sold
in a book club edition. It also sold well in North America
and was translated into several foreign languages, including
German. It was well received by the critics and a particular
interest was taken in Wilmot's argument that the allies'
pursuit of absolute victory and unconditional surrender led
only to confrontation in Europe with the Soviet Union.
This policy, and its results, Wilmot laid at the feet of the
Americans; his conclusion being that at the war's end, 'the
Americans had to find out for themselves that to strive for
victory alone is not enough and that the balance of power
must be the basis of peace.' Later, Wilmot was to modify
that view but he did not shift significantly from the main
critical thrust of his last chapter, that by mismanaging the
latter stages of the war the allies replaced Hitler with Stalin
as the principal threat to western European security. By
concentrating solely on victory, he claimed, and by taking
their time at the end of 1944, the allies gave the advantage
to the Soviet Union and put themselves in the invidious
position of making a bad peace.

In strategy, as in diplomacy, Stalin's policy was always in tune
with his post-war ambitions. Once military victory was assured,
Stalin was less interested in bringing about Hitler's early downfall
than he was in securing for the Soviet Union a commanding
position in the heart of Europe. Although the timing of his various
offensives in the last nine months of the war may have been

governed very largely by tactical and logistic considerations, it is surprising how clearly these offensives fitted into the strategic pattern most likely to secure his political objectives.

Expressed in blunter terms, this view was shared by Montgomery who described the arrival of the Red Army in Berlin as the 'onrush of the barbarians'. At the conclusion of his war diary he wrote: 'The point to understand is that if we had run the show properly the war could have been finished by Christmas 1944. The blame for this must rest with the Americans.' (Although he was quick to add the rider: 'To balance this it is merely necessary to say one thing, i.e. if the Americans had not come along and lent a hand we would not have won the war at all.')

The success of *The Struggle for Europe* and his own abilities as a correspondent brought Wilmot substantial reward. He continued to work for the BBC, broadcasting for radio and the fledgling television services, and in 1952 he became the military correspondent of the *Observer*. Television, though, seems to have been the most likely medium for his talents – in its early days the BBC relied heavily on its experienced radio presenters – and for BBC Television he was commissioned to write and present a series of films on the impact of Communism in Asia during the winter of 1953–54. It was to be his last assignment.

Returning to London from Rangoon on 9 January 1954 he joined a BOAC flight from Singapore to London, then operated by a Comet airliner, the world's first commercial jet transport. Shortly after leaving Rome at 9.31 A.M. on Sunday 10 January the Comet, G-AZYP, carrying twenty-nine passengers and six crew, exploded and plunged into the Mediterranean off Elba. By a sad coincidence, at Rome airport Wilmot met a party of fellow journalists who were travelling back to London in a slower piston-engined

airliner. He was almost persuaded to accompany them but
chose instead to get back to London as quickly as possible
as Edith and his daughters had arranged to meet him at
Heathrow. During the course of their flight home, his
colleagues heard the news that the Comet had crashed.

At the time of his death Wilmot was at the height of his
powers and a great career lay ahead in which he would
have undoubtedly combined his twin talents as a broadcaster and military historian. The *Observer*, for whom he
had recently written an incisive article on the use of ballistic
missiles in modern war, took the unprecedented step of
devoting a full page of obituary notices written by Wilmot's
fellow professionals. Amongst the tributes paid to him by
Basil Liddell Hart, Randolph Churchill and Michael
Davie, Sir Ian Jacob, Director-General of the BBC, got
near the heart of the matter when he said that Wilmot's
success rested 'upon his intense mental and physical
energy, upon his tenacity and thoroughness, and upon his
integrity'. It was left, though, to his fellow Australian, Alan
Moorehead, himself a distinguished war correspondent and
historian, to deliver the keenest assessment:

Always he had been where no one else had been, and always he
was eager to share his news with anyone else who would use it
well. And because he was so clear and incisive, and so utterly
professional he became in the end a correspondent's correspondent, and even more than that: a correspondent trusted by the
soldiers themselves.
   In other words, he concentrated upon the battle and not upon
the effort he was making with his broadcasts and writings. I
cannot remember a man who kept his mind in such steady focus
in what he considered to be the essential things and the truth.

Other tributes spoke of Wilmot's thoroughness, integrity,
steadiness, energy and his analytical mind; but more
importantly for his reputation as a war correspondent,

those were the virtues respected and trusted by the very men whose actions he had reported in the course of his short career. Three weeks after his death a memorial service for Wilmot was held in All Souls' Church, Langham Place, opposite the BBC: with good reason the order of service opened with John Bunyan's words, 'Mr Valiant-For-Truth passed over and all the trumpets sounded for him on the other side.'

James Cameron and the Korean War

The British servicemen who saw action in Korea between 1950 and 1953 had to fight their way over a barren, remote and barely known peninsula which was almost as far away across the globe as it was possible for them to travel. Much of the fighting was reminiscent of the trench warfare which their grandfathers had encountered on the Western Front; the weather was usually awful, freezing cold in winter yet hot and wet in summer and they faced an enemy who asked for, and offered, no quarter. The most common reaction of the men of the Commonwealth Division, which provided three British, Canadian and Australian infantry brigades to the United Nations forces, was bewilderment: bewilderment about the identity of their enemy and bewilderment that they should have been fighting the war in the first place.

Korea had been annexed by Japan in 1910 and had remained a Japanese colony until 1945 when the country had been split into two halves along the 38th parallel, the north becoming a Communist régime and the south a hastily organized democracy. Although the United Nations entertained hopes that the two Koreas might be united in the future, the opposed régimes were antagonistic to each other's existence and to the artificially created boundary which divided them. Any idea that they might find a means of living in harmony was shattered on 25 June 1950 when North Korea invaded its southern neighbour. Shocked by the abruptness and unexpected power of the attack, the United States of America successfully persuaded the United

Nations to oppose the invasion – their argument in favour of armed intervention was helped by the absence of the Soviet Union from the Security Council in protest at the UN's refusal to recognize Communist China. The United States acted quickly: General Douglas MacArthur, Commanding General of the US Army in the Far East, was despatched from Japan to appraise the situation and by the end of July the Americans had four divisions in South Korea. Although the US task force had command of the air and the sea, it was powerless to halt the North Korean advance and by August the UN forces were desperately defending the Pusan Perimeter, their last line of defence in the south-east of the country.

By then the first British contribution to the UN forces had also arrived in Pusan – the 1st Bn. Middlesex Regiment and the 1st Bn. Argyll and Sutherland Highlanders. According to Eric Linklater, author of the official government publication, *Our Men in Korea*, what the British units lacked in numbers they made up for in enthusiasm and experience.

Neither the Middlesex nor the Argylls could muster more than three rifle companies and there was no military principle to justify the despatch and committing to battle of two weak battalions that had neither their own necessary transport nor their proper supporting arms. It was the desperate plight of the Americans in the Pusan bridgehead that had compelled their sudden embarkation and as military principles were overridden by moral need so were the difficulties of their strange campaign to be overcome by recruitment, as it seemed, from the regimental spirit to which they were heirs. In the months to come both the Middlesex and the Argylls – though nearly half of them were youngsters doing their national training – were to enhance the pride and reputation, not only of the Diehards and the 91st, but of all the Army.

Both regiments were thrown quickly into battle as the confused UN forces attempted to stabilize the Pusan bridgehead. During the course of the fighting, a tragic accident occurred when an air strike by USAF Mustangs hit the wrong target, killing Scottish troops. Two companies of Argylls were holding a redoubt known as Point 282 and although their recognition panels were clearly displayed, the USAF fighter-bombers pressed home an attack, using napalm. In the subsequent confusion the North Koreans also attacked and the remaining Argylls were driven from the hill. They sustained eighty-six casualties, including the loss of the battalion's second-in-command, Major Kenneth Muir, who was awarded the Victoria Cross posthumously. The incident was a grim reminder of the problems of forming a unified UN command from scratch; it also helped to breed a suspicion that the Americans were liable to make basic battlefield mistakes when under pressure, or, more seriously, that they could not always be relied upon to hold their ground. Later in the campaign a similar mistake happened when USAF Shooting Stars strafed a Greek position, again causing unacceptable casualties. Like the Point 282 incident it was plastered over, with both sides issuing conciliatory statements in the interests of UN solidarity. No mention was made of any ill-feeling amongst the Allies, but after the war some British war correspondents admitted that they had come across senior officers in the United Nations forces who had a low opinion of their American colleagues.

In the early stages public opinion was largely in favour of the United Nations' stance; later it came to be felt that the war was being prolonged in the interests of American global strategy. More significantly, the reasons for the fighting had become confused and the reporting of the war in that distant corner of the world was sketchy and inaudible in comparison to the standards set during the Second World War. As Hal Boyle, an American war correspondent, was to remark, Korea was the worst reported war of modern times.

Some 20,000 British servicemen fought in Korea and although they were smaller in number than the American contribution, their role was not without importance. A number of RAF pilots flew on attachment with Commonwealth or American units, three squadrons of Sunderland flying-boats flew reconnaissance sorties from their bases in Japan, ships of the Royal Navy patrolled the Korean coastline to prevent infiltration and a carrier task force provided air cover for the battle ashore. The main contribution, though, was provided by the Army: in all, sixteen infantry battalions served in Korea, backed up by four armoured regiments and eight regiments of artillery with engineering, ordnance, transport and tactical support. By July 1951 the Commonwealth Division had been formed, providing three infantry brigades for the UN forces – 25th Canadian, 28th Commonwealth and 29th British. It was a hard, bruising war with high casualties: 71 officers and 616 other ranks were killed in action, 187 officers and 2,311 other ranks were wounded and 52 officers and 1,050 other ranks were listed as 'missing', of whom 40 officers and 996 other ranks were prisoners-of-war and eventually repatriated. By comparison, 33,000 US lives were lost and the total UN casualty list was 447,697 officers and men killed in action.

In the immediate aftermath of the North Korean invasion, most sections of the British press were prepared to support the United Nations' initiative. On 5 July 1950 Parliament, too, agreed to support the government's policy of taking action in concert with Britain's allies; on the following day, *The Times* leader spoke for those who feared that the North Korean attack heralded an escalation of global Communist aggression.

The resolve to resist aggression is necessary, so, too, is the ability
to resist successfully. The news from Korea is still not good. In
every country which has made the decision to stand against
attack, whether in Europe, across the Atlantic, or in the Pacific,
an alarm bell is sounding. Separately and together, the free
countries have to ask how far the defences which they have set
down on paper exist in fact. The aggression in Korea represents a
double challenge. The first is to the United States and her allies
in the United Nations to frustrate the Korean attack. The second
is to their readiness to meet attacks wherever they may come.

The threat of Communist expansion in the Far East and
South-East Asia was keenly felt in the Western world.
Britain had been fighting a counter-insurgency war against
Malayan-Chinese Communist terrorists since 1948; the
victory of the Communists in China in the civil war against
Chiang Kai-shek had transformed the political situation in
neighbouring countries; and there was evidence to suggest
that the war in Korea had been triggered by Soviet
intervention in North Korea and by the withdrawal of US
forces from the south during the summer of 1949. Quite
simply, many people in the West thought that UN intervention in Korea was justified because a Communist victory
there would start a chain reaction in the Far East. Those
fears were not lessened when China lent 'volunteer' military
support to North Korea towards the end of 1950, thereby
adding a formidable opposition to the overstretched UN
forces.

For many people in the USA, mesmerized by the
McCarthy régime, any defeat in Korea would herald the
beginning of worldwide Communist domination. That
mood was caught by MacArthur's conclusion that the war
in Korea had 'come at the right time', in that it would
allow the West to confront the Communist powers before
nuclear superiority was lost to the Soviet Union. He

advocated the extension of the war into China in the interests of securing a total victory in South-East Asia and was in favour of using atomic bombs to achieve those aims. Although he enjoyed some military support for his theories he was opposed by both President Harry Truman and Secretary of State Dean Acheson who advocated a limited war in Korea on the grounds that the Western powers could easily outpace the Communists in the area. In April 1951 MacArthur was dismissed from the post of UN Commander-in-Chief and was replaced by General Matthew Ridgway. The subsequent Congressional hearings came down on the side of the Truman administration and MacArthur's strategy was discredited.

Although the British press echoed much of the American disquiet about the possibility of a Communist victory in South-East Asia, the war in Korea never occupied the same space as it did in American newspapers. In the first months of the war the fighting was reported on a daily basis and considerable coverage was given to actions such as the defence of the Pusan Perimeter, MacArthur's successful landings at Inchon and the subsequent invasion of North Korea. As the war progressed, though, the reasons for the British involvement became blurred and the fighting itself turned into a stalemate of entrenched positions, artillery barrage and frontal attacks as the opposing armies slogged it out while the politicians argued. Thus the reporting of the war tended to centre on the details of individual incidents involving British troops, and became less concerned with the overall condition of the war. Wide coverage was given, for example, to the gallant stand of the Gloucestershire Regiment – the 'Glorious Glosters' – during the Battle of the Imjin River at the end of April 1951, an action which won the regiment two Victoria Crosses and, later, a US Presidential Citation. Other actions were given a good

deal of publicity such as the defence of the Maryangsan
Ridge by the King's Own Scottish Borderers and the Third
Battle of the Hook involving the Black Watch and the Duke
of Wellington's Regiment; but by the middle of 1951 the
war in Korea did not possess a high news rating and most
of the British journalists had come home.

Such was the interest in the war in its early stages,
though, that by the end of 1950 around 270 correspondents
from nineteen different countries had arrived in South
Korea to report the United Nations' initiative. Only two,
including Alan Winnington of the *Daily Worker*, covered the
war from the Communist point of view. Amongst the
sizeable British contingent were veterans of the Second
World War, such as the talented Christopher Buckley of
the *Daily Telegraph* and Ward Price of the *Daily Mail*. Rene
Cutforth covered the war for BBC radio, Jack Percival for
the *News Chronicle*, Michael Davidson for the *Observer* and
James Cameron for *Picture Post*.

Like most of the British press corps Cameron had been
sent to Korea at the outbreak of the war and had arrived in
time to report the breakout from Pusan and MacArthur's
subsequent seaborne attack which had broken up the North
Korean offensive. With him he had taken Bert Hardy, a
first-rate photographer who had served with the Army Film
Unit during the Second World War and who had been at
one time Mountbatten's personal photographer in the Far
East. Together, Cameron and Hardy made a formidable
team.

From the very outset they made it their business to paint
a realistic picture of war-torn Pusan and of the confusion
that reigned there as the UN forces began arriving in
Korea. Hardy's photographs showed the crowded Pusan
docklands and the arrival of the Argylls; they also revealed
the bewildered faces of the Koreans fleeing from the fighting

– all the stark reality of civilians caught up in the tragedy of war. Cameron's accompanying essay was a masterful piece of writing, a counterpoint to Hardy's photographs. In common with the other correspondents on Korea, the first thing that had struck them was the dreadful smell that pervaded Korea. Coupled to the desperation of the civilian population and the confusion, it was to leave a lasting impression: later, in his autobiography *Point of Departure* Cameron was to admit that he 'loathed Korea and to this day it lives perversely in [my] mind as though I loved it'. Quite apart from the dismay he felt at the squalor that was Korea, Cameron did not mince his words about the war which he believed to be futile, wrong and, but for its tragedy, ridiculous. He was also inclined to believe that the blame for the war lay with those 'wonderful, terrible people', the Americans.

It is fair to say that not many people are trying to feel ideological about it [the war]. I would not imagine that the GI in Korea is an excessively complex personality; nevertheless he is hard to judge. If his imposition of the jukebox civilization on Korea jars, at least it must be said that there was nothing much to impose on it anyway. It might be an impoliteness to say that the American is puzzling, with his generosity and hospitality and open friendship, his perversity and barren-mindedness, his conversational reliance on the old worn-out obscenity – apposite enough in Korea I must say – nourished in the body by lavish rations and in the mind by the practised back-slapping, catch-in-the-voice jargon of newspapers. Everything combines to form a standard Hollywood approach to war, a boy-scoutishness that finds expression in dangling .45s and daggers, and the routine phrases of toughness, but which is no armour against the dark dread that comes down from the hills in the night.[1]

Cameron was not the only British correspondent in Korea to be sceptical of America's war aims. Reginald Thompson of the *Daily Telegraph* was critical of Mac-

Arthur's leadership, reporting that 'his assumption of a kind of divinity' had alienated him from the majority of the press corps: to him, and to others like Ian Morrison of *The Times* and Rene Cutforth of the BBC, the war was a morass of confusion in the front lines and confused motives amongst the high command.

Other aspects of the war were also disquieting – racist attitudes to the Koreans, atrocities committed by both sides, a general anti-Communist hysteria in the American contingents and badly managed attempts to control the transmission of news. After December 1950 MacArthur's headquarters introduced a censorship, having relied previously on the voluntary principle, and throughout the war the correspondents were stymied by the system of passing all despatches through military channels of communication. On returning to Britain, Thompson admitted in his book *Cry Korea* that none of his colleagues had dared to write the truth as they saw it and instead had committed 'their thoughts and the true picture of events to their confidential airmail'. Because the Americans made up the bulk of the United Nations forces it was natural perhaps to find fault with their contribution, but as the war progressed it also came to be felt that the fighting in Korea was being continued less for the ideals of the UN Charter than to bolster US fears of a Communist take-over in the Far East.

Although James Cameron was only in Korea for the opening rounds and did not stay on to cover the long slogging match which followed China's entry, he made a signal contribution to reporting the war for British readers. He was an experienced foreign correspondent, having worked for the *Daily Express* until a disagreement with the proprietor had driven him out of the Beaverbrook stable into Edward Hulton's *Picture Post*.

Cameron had been born of Scots parentage in London in

1911 and his childhood had been spent in Brittany and England. In common with not a few British journalists he became a newspaperman by working for D. C. Thomson, the Dundee-based publishers whose list includes *Dandy*, *Wizard*, *Beano*, *Weekly News*, *Secrets*, *People's Friend* and the *Scots Magazine*. For Thomson he worked in Manchester and Dundee before being transferred to Glasgow as a reporter for the *Sunday Post*, writing 'articles of a character almost excruciatingly homely and domestic'. Passed unfit for call-up at the outbreak of war, he spent the next ten years with the *Daily Express*, becoming, in his own words, 'an itinerant bagman of what most of the time were dreary tidings'.

In that guise he helped to chart the making of the post-war world, covering events like the partition and independence of India and Pakistan and the American nuclear tests in the Pacific. The latter experience helped to reinforce a belief that the Americans were fully capable of alarming the world into all-out war; it made him a life-long opponent of nuclear weapons. He was also a committed pacifist, yet was uneasily aware that some wars, like the Second World War, might be justified if they put down greater evils like fascism. (The dilemma of putting his ideals to the test had been spared him when he was passed unfit for military service.) By his own admission, he was a subjective reporter who believed that any journalist worth his salt had to be fully engaged with his subject to do his job properly. This was not the writer as propagandist: rather, he felt that it was the writer's duty to present his argument and all counter-arguments as vigorously as possible, but then to make certain that his point of view was paramount.

There is a way of being scrupulous about this which every thinking journalist understands. He has at least the resources to present his liberal principles for consideration and debate, and to argue

the basic importance of moral independence – which includes, to
be sure, the need to question *him*. Surely the useful end is somehow
to encourage an attitude of mind that will challenge and criticize
automatically, thus to destroy or weaken the built-in advantages
of all propaganda and special pleading – even the journalist's
own. The energetic argument for liberal thought must by definition, I should imagine, embody the machinery for its own
conquest, since it presents itself as equally vulnerable.[2]

During the course of his time in Korea Cameron was to
discover just how exposed the position could be for the
journalist caught up in the cut and thrust of a vicious
modern war.

One of the first soldiers whom Cameron met in Korea
was General Walton H. Walker, the commander of the 8th
US Army. His headquarters were in Taegu, the temporary
administrative capital of South Korea following the loss of
Seoul, and the scene of some of the fiercest fighting in the
north-west corner of the Pusan Perimeter. Walker had
proved himself to be a first-class battlefield commander
during the fighting in north-west Europe in 1945 but there
he had been on the offensive; at Taegu he was defending a
bridgehead whose loss could have brought about the end of
the UN involvement in Korea. Aggressive by nature, he
was not popular with the US forces in his command,
mainly because he insisted on a highly personal style of
leadership – one of his favourite ploys was to hector and
bully junior commanders in front of their fellows. For all
those personal drawbacks, his tenacity and his ability to
move men and armour quickly from position to position, as
the situation demanded, undoubtedly saved the UN position in Pusan. When Cameron met him Walker was at his
most genial, proffering his arm and passing him on to a
brigade major who, he promised, would fix him up with
details of the defence of Taegu.

Walker's promise, no doubt well meant, turned out to be wishful thinking. As Cameron was to discover, the fighting in the area was confused and difficult to follow; even the 8th US Army headquarters could not be relied upon to provide useful information as attack followed counter-attack in routine succession. Victory for the North Koreans would mean that they controlled the strategically vital road and rail lines of communication to Pusan. To achieve that aim they had committed five divisions plus armoured support to take Taegu and to capture the Naktung river crossings which ran along the eastern boundary of the Pusan Perimeter. Their failure to break through the UN lines after a summer of easy victories came as something of a surprise, especially to the American correspondents who had witnessed the débâcle of earlier US setbacks. There was, in fact, no one easy explanation. Partly it was due to Walker's command and the new-found ability of the 8th US Army and its South Korean allies to hold their ground, thus preventing North Korean flanking attacks; partly it was the superior air power and the greater resources enjoyed by the UN forces. In contrast, the North Koreans had over-extended their lines of communication and could not make good their losses of men and material. It was almost as if the pace and depth of their earlier actions had burned them out: they had covered too much ground too quickly without the necessary logistical back-up.

The very speed of the fighting made this stage of the war very difficult to follow, even for the front-line journalists who generally resorted to first-hand accounts of the fighting as they saw it. Less interested in filing up-to-the-minute combat reports – which were, in any case, liable to be contradicted within hours of being filed – Cameron's concerns were with the overall effect of the war on Korea and its people. Taegu, he admitted, had no charm, a mean and

nondescript place hardly worth defending, but it was full of
refugees, a grimly stoical people caught up in the tide of
war. Their plight seemed to epitomize all the futility of the
war in Korea. Small things, unimportant in themselves,
took on a new significance when placed alongside events
which would linger longer in history's pages. An old man
caught up in a fire fight died naturally in front of Cameron
'without any confusion or excitement at all; it was the most
composed and deliberate action I had seen that day, and
certainly the most graceful'. Later amongst the devastation
of bombed Pohang he came across a school jotter containing surrealistic notes in stilted English whose 'preoccupa-
tion with all the sorrowful and vicious conditions and
emotions seemed a despairing thing'.

Scenes like those helped to point up the overall barbarity
of the war and much of Cameron's reporting for *Picture Post*
was less concerned with a military analysis of the situation
and more taken up with the moral issue of the UN's
involvement in the doubtful values of Syngman Rhee's
South Korean 'democracy'.

For already Korea has infected the just and the unjust alike with
the inevitable virus of war; beastliness has begotten beastliness,
and there are some aspects of human behaviour that cannot be
sanctioned by any high-minded principle. Those of us who saw
that battlefield, both in disaster and in victory, are sometimes
impatient at the over-simplifications, the confusions of ends and
means; it is hard to escape the knowledge that the fact of war,
modern war, itself corrupts and debases, and puts a curse on
peace too long delayed.[3]

In trying to assess the feasibility of the war or to question
the justification for the UN intervention, Cameron did not
neglect the course of the war itself. He might not have been
as experienced a war correspondent as Christopher Buckley

who was killed with Ian Morrison of *The Times* in a land-mine accident, but when it came to the bit, Cameron showed that he was capable of covering a large-scale military operation with the best of them. His chance came on 15 September 1950 with the UN landings at Inchon.

The possibility of a seaborne assault behind the North Korean lines was first considered early in July when all the news coming out of Korea spoke of disaster for the United Nations forces. With the bulk of the US forces battling to save the Pusan Perimeter, a counter-attack further north was always going to be an attractive tactical possibility, especially as the Americans had perfected the techniques of amphibious warfare during the Second World War. MacArthur himself had won a solid – and justified – reputation for executing seaborne invasions with great success and it was inevitable that he should want to employ the technique in Korea. As he had discovered in the Pacific theatre, the Japanese had been taken aback by the ability of the Americans to leap-frog islands, using their greater naval strength to land troops behind the main battle-fronts during the liberation of the South-West Pacific in 1944. The tactics helped to speed up offensive operations by sowing confusion in the enemy camp: not only did the Japanese have to divert troops to counter the new and unexpected attacks but they were also demoralized by them. MacArthur could see no reason why the same tactics could not be used in Korea.

As early as July MacArthur was never in any doubt that the eventual target for a seaborne assault should be Seoul, for not only was it South Korea's capital, it was also of prime strategic importance in that it straddled the main north–south lines of communication. The port of Inchon on the west coast provided the key to the door. Although his proposals were taken on board by the United States Joint

Chiefs of Staff, the desperate plight of the UN garrison in the Pusan Perimeter required the bulk of the US forces to fight there. It was not until 12 August that approval was given to his plans and a target date was set for 15 September when the tides at Inchon would be most suited to an attack from the sea. Two divisions, one Marine and the other Infantry, were allotted to the task in addition to a substantial naval force, including elements of the Royal Navy's Far East fleet. They had a bare month to assemble, train and plan for the operation – during the Second World War it had been a generally agreed principle that amphibious operations required at least sixty days to plan and prepare.

At MacArthur's insistence the Joint Chiefs of Staff had settled on Inchon for the landings; but even though the port had much to recommend it, it was a controversial choice. The tidal range was a massive thirty-two feet, one of the highest in the world; sea-walls protected the harbour and the approaches to it were a series of narrow channels with swiftly flowing currents. It was a far cry from the open beaches and even gradients used by the allies during the Second World War from Normandy to Guadalcanal, but MacArthur countered the opposition to his plans by pointing out, *inter alia*, that because the enemy would least expect a landing at Inchon the defences would be minimal and the element of surprise would rest with the UN force. The green light was finally given to MacArthur's plans on 28 August.

Because of the extreme nature of the tides the first assault was planned for dawn on the island of Wolmi-do, which lay across the harbour entrance; the main assault would go in with the evening tide. Both attacks would be preceded by a huge barrage from the Gunfire Support Group which had arrived off Inchon on 13 September with the rest of the invasion fleet. It was the largest task force – 262 ships – which had been assembled since the Second World War. Some of it had come from Japan; one Marine battalion had made a journey from the Mediterranean; others from the USA and the rump from Pusan: amongst their number was the naval auxiliary freighter *Seminole* carrying James Cameron and a number of other reporters. To Cameron, with his memories of climbing in the Scottish Highlands as a young man, the first glimpse of Inchon had all the illusory freshness of the hills of home.

On that evening of haze and filmy rain among the hills it was like an Argyllshire sea-loch, somehow steam-heated and washed with pastel grey. In no respect, and in no circumstances, can Korea be called lovely, nor even likeable; yet at this moment, in the especial doubt of dusk, it came more nearly to being beautiful than I had ever seen before.[1]

His idyll was soon to be shattered. The first rounds from the naval Gunfire Support Group came from six destroyers off Wolmi-do; they were followed by the cruisers which put down an hour-and-a-half-long barrage from their big guns; then came the rocket-ships, while high above the task force Vought Corsairs flew in support of the first landings. The sound and the fury of the bombardment was startling and frightening, louder than Cameron had expected it to be; all this he reported faithfully, yet the keenest insight is in the dying fall of his last sentence, the pacifist's reaction to the reality of battle.

The guns began eventually, an hour or two before H-hour – half-past-five – with a few crumps from the cruisers, an occasional bark of five-inch fire, a tuning up among the harsh orchestra. At what point the laying of the guns merged into the final barrage I do not know; so many things began to take place, a scattered series of related happenings . . . What seemed to be a tank ashore sent some quick resentful fire back but it was soon stopped. Later we found that one ship had tossed a hundred and sixty rounds of ammunition at the tank before it had finished it; the economics of plenty in action.

The naval bombardment described in his report by James Cameron was intensified in the afternoon before the main assault went in – to Red Beach on the northern side of the town and to Blue Beach south of the harbour. The latter target was Cameron's destination: shortly before his wave went in he had noted, somewhat cynically, that the *Seminole* had been 'full of agitated and contending correspondents, all trying to appear insistently determined to land in Wave One, while contriving desperately to be found in Wave Fifty'.

By nightfall Inchon was in UN hands but the victory had not been completed without hiccups to MacArthur's plan. So powerful had been the naval bombardment that Blue Beach was obscured by a pall of smoke which drifted out to sea to meet the advancing invasion fleet. Cameron's landing craft arrived ahead of the main assault and in the confusion he scrambled over the sea-wall into the safety of a trench, 'most happily empty of North Koreans'. Behind him one battalion of Marines had landed in the wrong place and in the ensuing mêlée many of the fighting units had been separated from their tactical support groups. It could have been a disaster but for the paucity of the North Korean defences and the determination of the Marines who got ashore. Inchon had fallen – literally – into the hands of the United Nations forces, but according to Cameron it was not a pretty sight: 'One more unaccountable little city, one more punch-drunk town, one more trifling habitation involved by its betters in the disastrous process of liberation.'

The landings had been a complete success, though, fully justifying MacArthur's faith and determination; the North Koreans were on the run and all at once it seemed possible that the end of the war might be in sight. But as Cameron told readers of the *Picture Post* the battle for Inchon had been won at great cost to the lives of the civilian population and to the generally held belief in the justice of the United Nations' cause.

They [the North Koreans] lost their beachhead, they lost their town, they lost their lives in numbers, and with them the lives of many simple people who shared the common misfortune of many people before them who had the ill-luck to live in places which people in War Rooms decide to smash. It seems clear that they could have hurt us more than they did, but the hammer was too hard.

But there it is, sitting here, one is glad to be alive – a bit ashamed, maybe, but glad.

His words were a far cry from the hysterical praise and hyperbole which greeted the landings in the American press. Hailed as the greatest feat since D-Day – which indeed it was – the news stories added to MacArthur's reputation and reinforced the notion that the United Nations' war in Korea was very much an American affair. Prior to the engagement, MacArthur had housed the four main news agency chiefs on board his command ship, the *Mount McKinley*, which also doubled as a communications ship, thus ensuring that the news of the victory would reach the outside world as quickly as possible. Cameron, too, went back to the *Mount McKinley*, preferring its comfort to the crowded wardrooms of the *Seminole*, but his report was not filed until well after the battle and did not appear in the *Picture Post* until 7 October. One reason for the delay was his reluctance to tell the story of the landings in 300 words of 'cable-ese', another was the increasing evidence of atrocities being committed by the South Koreans on their own people.

It was the job of the ROKs, the South Korean militia, to mop up and secure the town; this they did with violent and furious zeal, rounding up householders, searching them with great toughness, herding them around, ancient crones and toddlers too, with the strange venom of the South Koreans, which is that of the armed adolescent; the hoarded anger of the dispossessed returning.

Cameron had first come across evidence of atrocities in the Pusan Perimeter in the days before the Inchon landings. Outside the station in Pusan he and Hardy had been confronted by a crowd of around 700 political prisoners under the none-too-gentle guard of the South Korean militia. They were not prisoners of war, neither were they convicted criminals on their way to prison: they were simply people who were – or had been accused of being – political opponents of the Syngman Rhee régime. While Cameron was prepared to accept that the Oriental attitude to prisoners was different and that harshness towards opponents had a long-established cultural basis, he was shocked that they should be treated so cruelly in the name of the United Nations. They were filthy and neglected living skeletons on their way to a certain death and Cameron would have none of it.

When he confronted the authorities, though, he met with a dusty response. The International Red Cross agreed that it was 'shameful' but admitted that they were powerless to act and the United Nations Commission blandly told him that it was an internal matter; furthermore, it was unlikely that General MacArthur would involve himself or the US Supreme Command in South Korean politics. Cameron retorted that it was a United Nations affair and as such was the responsibility of all member states, but his arguments met with little sympathy from local officials. To Cameron, their complicity was the ultimate idiocy of a war which he believed to be futile: if this was what the United Nations was fighting for, then it hardly seemed to be worth the effort and the expense of so many young lives.

After the Inchon landings, Cameron wrote up the story of the fate awaiting the political prisoners and along with a selection of Hardy's photographs sent home the package to Tom Hopkinson, the editor of *Picture Post*. When they returned to London the story was checked and double-checked, rewritten and redrafted to make it as matter-of-fact and unsensational as possible. To give Cameron's report a balanced presentation Hopkinson decided to publish a photograph of an American soldier in the captivity of the North Koreans: discovered in a Czechoslovakian magazine, it showed the soldier dressed in a false nose and wearing a swastika. It was also decided to send the dossier to the Secretary-General of the United Nations and to Kenneth Younger, the leader of the British delegation to the UN at the Lake Success peace talks – but this brought no response.

Publication of the story, together with the five carefully chosen photographs, was fixed for 28 October. WE APPEAL TO THE UN was the simple, yet arresting, headline chosen by Hopkinson and the main thrust of Cameron's story was that atrocities of the kind he had witnessed should never have been committed in the name of the United Nations and that the behaviour of the Syngman Rhee régime was a corruption of its values. As Cameron was to admit later in *Point of Departure*, 'it was a journalistic essay of elaborate moderation'.

They [the prisoners] are South Koreans whose crime – or alleged crime, since they have not yet had the formality of a trial – is that

they are possible opponents of the Syngman Rhee régime. They
have for a variety of reasons, and by a variety of people, been
denounced or accused – not necessarily convicted – of being
politically unreliable, 'politically communist'. They have been in
jail now for indeterminate periods – long enough, we can say, for
lack of official information, to have reduced their frames to
skeletons, their sinews to strings, their faces to a translucent,
terrible grey, their spirits to that of cringing dogs.[5]

From the stark reality of the plight facing those crushed
men, Cameron then addressed his main theme.

Barbaric scenes like these are permitted to take place, cynically,
in the most public places possible, under the blue-and-silver olive-
branch banner of the United Nations, with all our supervisors
claiming they are unable (because they haven't tried) to stop the
excesses of a domestic government that is about as democratic
and high-principled as Caligula's Rome.

Cameron went on to underline the fact that the authorities
in South Korea knew what was happening – 'the imprison-
ments without trial, the processing of suspects, the beat-
ings-up, the taping of thumbs to the terminals of field
telephones' – but that they were too busy, or too concerned
with other things, to deal with them.

On Friday 20 October the photo-essay was made up and
shown in paste-up form to the proprietor of *Picture Post*,
Edward Hulton – the usual practice before publication.
Although he offered no comments at that stage, Hulton
obviously used the weekend to brood on the implications of
publishing a story which implicated the United Nations in
South Korean atrocities. At the weekly editorial conference
the following Tuesday, Hopkinson was instructed to
remove Cameron's story from the issue and to replace it
with something else. What followed next was a mixture of
farce and tragedy. Hopkinson met the board of *Picture Post*

and argued that it was the duty of a free press to tell the truth even if, in this instance, the facts were unpalatable to the United Nations and its friends. It was to no avail: the board backed Hulton's right as proprietor to choose what should, or should not, be published in *Picture Post*. Amidst the ensuing dismay and confusion a compromise was reached: to save the magazine Hopkinson would be replaced by his assistant, Ted Castle, and some of the staff would go, including the writer A. L. Lloyd, a Communist who had already come under the suspicion of the proprietor. Hopkinson loyally played a leading role in reaching the agreement which was not finalized until 31 October, a week after Hulton's ultimatum.

Cameron, too, had offered to leave the magazine and the censorship row became a Fleet Street *cause célèbre*. Publications as different as *Public Opinion*, published by the *Daily Mirror* group, and the *New Statesman*, offered their support, the latter claiming in an editorial on 11 November that 'Mr Hulton's action provides unanswerable propaganda to the Communists'. The only winner was the *Daily Worker*: the copy for Cameron's article found its way into their offices and was published on 1 November as a front-page story under the headline, PICTURE POST EDITOR IS SACKED. That same day a bleak announcement, hastily cobbled together by Hulton's board, appeared in *The Times*. It stated that, following a disagreement over the handling of news coverage of the Korean War, 'Mr Edward Hulton . . . has instructed Mr Tom Hopkinson to relinquish the position of editor of *Picture Post*. There is no personal hostility between Mr Hulton and Mr Hopkinson.'

By and by the furore died down and Fleet Street returned to other concerns. Cameron was asked to withdraw his resignation after gaining an admission from the board that the accuracy of his article 'was not now held in question'.

Indeed, they could hardly have done otherwise, for similar stories were by then appearing in other sections of the press. The *Daily Worker*, whose sympathies naturally lay with the North Koreans, had already published a dossier of atrocity photographs in their issue of 5 October. These showed a variety of outrages, including the execution of civilians by South Korean Marines, a dead mother and child and, most terrible of all, a crucified North Korean soldier – all under the headline, DOES BRITAIN STAND FOR THIS?

Both the *Daily Telegraph* and *The Times* had similar stories to tell. Reflecting on the direction of the war in a lengthy article entitled 'Seoul After Victory: Reverse Side to South Korean Rule', *The Times* of 25 October carried a vivid description of the fate awaiting prisoners at the village of Boopyung near Seoul. 290 men, women and children had been crammed into the village police station's six cells, each of which measured a bare eight feet by sixteen feet. Most of them had been incarcerated there for three weeks and the primitive sanitary arrangements plus the overcrowding and the long process of interrogation had left them in a pitiful condition, leaving the writer to argue that scenes of that kind did no good at all to the United Nations and its friends.

Reports of reprisals still come in from all parts of the country. Occasionally they are denied, but this writer has witnessed enough incidents to believe that in South Korea the defence of the local brand of democracy has been no less vicious than have atrocities committed in the name of Communism.

In the final paragraph of his article, Louis Heren, *The Times* Special Correspondent, echoed Cameron's argument that while officials of the United Nations were aware that atrocities were being committed, they were also disinclined to stop them.

An officer of the United Nations investigation team said that reprisals are as numerous as reports of Communist atrocities. Most non-Korean members of the United Nations forces are aware of this, but feel either too helpless to intervene or believe attention drawn to the reprisals would be excellent material for Communist propaganda. Others are of the opinion that their suppression is the responsibility of the South Korean Government, and that as foreigners they cannot interfere in the internal affairs of a sovereign nation.

Given the scale and the nature of the reprisals it was hardly surprising that the British correspondents reported them so fully and in such detail. They were also witnessed by soldiers in the field and after the recapture of Seoul British troops began to take action against any South Korean units they found committing atrocities. On 9 December officers of the 29th British Brigade prevented the mass execution of civilians at Sinmak; to save the situation, one of the brigade's Intelligence Officers, Captain Butler Williams, had to threaten to shoot the local police chief. Two weeks later, *The Times* reported that British troops had again put a stop to executions within their area: 400 men, women and children were about to be mown down in a dry river bed but were rescued at the last minute by the arrival of two British officers. So strong was their revulsion that the commanding officer of the 29th, Brigadier Tom Brodie, issued a statement condemning the South Korean behaviour: 'I am not going to have people executed on my doorstep. My officers will stop executions in my area or in view of my troops.' The incidents were widely reported in the British press and led to a brisk correspondence in *The Times*, condemning both the United Nations and Britain's part in the war. Typical of the protest was a letter from the Archbishop of York arguing that 'if these barbarous executions continue, all sympathy with South Korea will vanish, and instead there will be a general demand that the forces of the United Nations should not be used to protect a government responsible for these atrocities'.[6]

One result of the publication of the atrocity stories was that the executions of women and children came to an end – although the execution of political prisoners was renewed early in 1951 after the United Nations' setbacks in North Korea. Another result was that General MacArthur's headquarters imposed a full military censorship on 21 December 1959. From then until the war's end in 1953, the UN military command operated a strict censorship over all writing, broadcasting and photography; and as the war correspondents depended on the military for all their communications, the censorship was relatively easy to implement. Any attempt to break the rules was met with instant expulsion from the front and 17 correspondents paid that penalty for trying to tell the truth about what had been happening in the aftermath of the Inchon landings.

Far from bringing the war to a successful conclusion by Christmas – as had been forecast by MacArthur – the UN offensive into North Korea had opened a new phase in the fighting. The intervention of the Chinese Army drove the UN forces to a line which wavered along the 38th parallel and the war became a stalemate which was to last a further two years. Soon it became apparent that neither side could defeat the other without sustaining huge losses and the war became increasingly unpopular both in the United Nations countries and in Communist China itself. In the *Picture Post* of 23 June 1951 James Cameron summed up the first year of the war in a statement which spoke only of bleakness and an absence of direction from the leaders of the free world.

To this day there is some confusion and mystery about the exact circumstances of the invasion. To this day doubt and uncertainty cloud the development of the war that was joined that day, the aims and objectives, the plan and the solution. A year has been enough to drive the war stories underground; what news arrives is buried deep in the conscience columns. You cannot blame the news editors; they may try awhile, but they bore easy.

It was Cameron's first report on the war in 1951 and the first to appear since the episode of the atrocity stories. It was also to be his last comment because, thereafter, the *Picture Post* was to pay scant regard to the stalemate in Korea.

Cameron did not stay long with *Picture Post*. In 1952 he joined the *News Chronicle* as a foreign correspondent and remained with that paper until June 1960, a few months before it was closed down. Later, he became more interested in film and television as a means of communication and in 1965 was able to visit Hanoi to report on the 'vile, crude and senseless' war in Vietnam from the North Vietnamese point of view. The story of Cameron's experiences with his colleagues Romano Cagnoni and Malcolm Aird was told in his book *Witness* (1966) but the project can hardly be counted a success. True, the team succeeded in bringing back film from the north, in itself a feat at that stage of the war, but the Americans were suspicious of its admittedly pro-Communist bias. Moreover, the North Vietnamese had not welcomed the visit and had been slow to offer decent facilities to Cameron and his colleagues. As a television correspondent, though, Cameron turned out to be a natural performer and his series for BBC 2, *Cameron's*

Country, was deservedly popular. He received several awards for journalism before his death on 27 January 1985.

Tom Hopkinson also stayed in journalism and became one of the profession's best-respected mentors. He spent eight years in Africa helping to train African journalists and returned in 1966 to develop a scheme of postgraduate training for students wishing to enter British journalism. In 1977 he was knighted for his services to journalism.

As for *Picture Post*, it began its long slide towards eventual closure in 1957. Ted Castle, Hopkinson's successor, lasted six months as editor and was replaced by a long line of journalists who never stayed long in the position and who were unable to realign the magazine's sense of purpose. As it began to lose direction, *Picture Post* spun into a familiar spiral: sales dropped and advertisers became more cautious, trusted contributors fell away, the cover price was increased and revenue dropped again. Although Sir Edward Hulton was to place the blame on the advent of commercial television, both Cameron and Hopkinson remained adamant that the loss of its original editorial character was the real culprit. A further reason for the demise was that Hopkinson was removed from the editorship over an incident which Cameron called the 'punctuation mark' of the magazine's honourable career.

Two considerations emerge from the story of *Picture Post* which have a bearing on the history of war reporting. The first is that censorship can be operated for private reasons outwith the realm of any government dictate: in this case Sir Edward Hulton spiked Cameron's story on his own initiative, not because he had come under any pressure from official sources. The second is the nature of the relationship between editor and publisher and the division of their responsibilities.

It was not as if *Picture Post* was a stranger to controversy:

on several occasions it had led with stories which other newspaper journals found unpalatable and were unwilling to touch. (For example, Robert Kee investigated the problems facing coloured people in Britain in the issue of 3 July 1948.) During the war it had refused to be a placid admirer of Britain's war aims and on one occasion had been banned from the Middle East theatre of operations because it had criticized the mediocre firepower of the British tanks. It had also attracted outspoken writers to its ranks, men like Macdonald Hastings, Maurice Edelmann and Tom Wintringham who had covered the Spanish Civil War for the *Daily Worker*, not because they were controversial, but because they were authoritative. Under Hopkinson's editorship – he had succeeded the founding editor Stefan Lorant in 1940 – a pattern had begun to emerge: *Picture Post* stood left of centre politically and its main editorial concern was with social problems that could be investigated in a discursive yet polished manner. It also provided a lively coverage of the arts, sport and fashion but in its attitude to news and current affairs there was always more than a hint of the crusading spirit about *Picture Post*. Of all the British publications of the period it was best suited to publish Cameron's story.

However, at the very moment that Hopkinson was planning the publication of his plea to the United Nations, his relationship with Hulton was deteriorating. Throughout the war and into the immediate post-war period Hulton had supported Hopkinson's editorial policies. Following the 1950 General Election, though, he had rejoined the Conservative Party and had begun to take an increased interest in the running of the magazine. Hopkinson's reaction was to defend his editorial independence, a task he performed under considerable provocation. More importantly, as far as his immediate future was concerned, he made a private

resolution that he would never be forced to resign, preferring instead to put the onus for his dismissal upon the
proprietor.

In his autobiography, *Of This Our Time*, Hopkinson
explained that while Hulton had been pleased to see the
advent of a Labour Government in 1945 and had rejoiced
that Conservatism had been overthrown, his enthusiasm
was diluted as the years went by. Moreover, he began to
use his column in *Picture Post* to propagate ideas which were
at odds with Hopkinson's editorial line. There were also
other distractions such as the bid made by Hulton's wife to
install herself as fashion editor and constant carping by the
management to go down-market to meet the new demands
of the 1950s. All these difficulties – part and parcel of many
editor/proprietor relationships – Hopkinson might have
countered but for the central problem of editorial control
and by early 1950 it had become obvious that Hulton
wanted to decide the magazine's future editorial policy.
The Korean article provided him with the justification for
making clear his stance both to Hopkinson and to the rest
of the world.

Later, Hulton was to argue that he had instructed the
Cameron story to be withdrawn because he believed it to
be anti-United Nations and pro-Communist in character.
As such, it would be of moral advantage to the enemy were
it published. Had Cameron's exposé been an exclusive
story there might have been some point to Hulton's stance
but by the time of its proposed publication the facts of the
atrocities were well enough known and had been published
in *The Times*. No good reason was served by his decision to
remove the article other than to force a showdown with the
editor of *Picture Post*. If that was his intention, then it
succeeded.

When war comes, the first casualty is truth. Senator

Hiram Johnson's oft-quoted remark, made to the US Senate in 1917, applies equally well in this case. Hulton, the proprietor of *Picture Post*, subverted the truth of Cameron's revelations from the battlefield; in attempting to tell that truth Hopkinson's career as editor was sacrificed.

The Korean War came to a conclusion on 27 July 1953 with an armistice that established a demarcation line between the two countries. The agreement also allowed the exchange of prisoners; there has never been a formal treaty but the armistice, designed to last for three months, has remained in being for over thirty years. It was never a popular war and that may be one reason why it received such a low level of press coverage in its later stages. It also illustrated the difficulty of maintaining a protracted and unspectacular war effort against Communist expansion in a specific area and it highlighted the problems of waging a limited war far from home base. Although the United Nations forces possessed superior weapons and enjoyed the command of the air, they were unable to prevent the Chinese build-up and the lesson had to be learned that greater firepower could not always bring decisive results. Closely related to those military lessons was the political willpower of the allies to stay the course against an unyielding enemy – a test which, by and large, they passed.

The war also posed questions for the war correspondents about the need to tell the truth even if they might be accused of giving aid and support to a Communist enemy. In all those respects, Korea can be seen as a testing ground for other wars in other parts of the world. As James Cameron was to say, Korea was the prep school for Vietnam.

8

The Savage Wars of Peace

In the aftermath of the Second World War peace had no sooner broken out than the first shots were being fired by British servicemen in the long series of counter-insurgency wars, terrorist campaigns and 'aid to the civil power' which characterized British military operations in the post-war years. It is a sorry statistic of the period that between 1945 and the present day (1987) only 1968 stands out as the one year in which there have been no casualties among British soldiers, sailors or airmen. When the Soviet Union published a survey of post-war 'imperialist aggression' in 1976, Britain found herself at the top of their league table of modern 'aggressors'.

To put those figures into perspective, though, many of the incidents in which servicemen were killed were terrorist attacks on personnel and military bases in countries where the British presence was no longer acceptable, former colonies like Cyprus, Kenya, Malaya or Aden. Elsewhere British servicemen had to act as a kind of imperial *gendarmerie*. Within weeks of the war ending in the Far East in 1945 British troops were involved in quelling civil disturbances in Java and Sumatra, they saw action in Indo-China (Vietnam) against Ho Chi Minh's guerrillas and they also confronted Communist Yugoslavs in Trieste. The Greek government was granted military assistance in 1946 in its struggle with anti-Royalist guerrillas and there were major disturbances in India and Pakistan in the period before and after partition and independence. Within the same years of post-war peace British troops also had to cope with civil unrest in Northern Ireland, British Honduras, the Gold Coast and Jamaica as well as guarding the Suez Canal Zone in Egypt and fighting a bloody and protracted terrorist campaign in Palestine.

As so often happened in Britain's imperial history, while the politicians talked, the soldiers endured terrorist attacks, followed by low-level counter-insurgency operations, a facet of warfare in which the British Army began to excel. The worldwide presence of British armed forces, though, was a double-edged sword. On the one hand Britain appeared to have reassumed her habit of imperial rule; on the other the peoples of the colonies were starting to demand independence and to voice their resentment of a foreign military presence in their countries. Even after the loss of India and Pakistan the habit of Empire died hard and throughout the 1950s politicians, a large section of the public and most of the press continued to regard Britain as an imperial power. Trade routes had to be guarded, treaties honoured and colonies defended: all these required a military or naval presence. Later, those same servicemen had to cover the withdrawal from Empire, fighting rearguard actions as one outpost after another struggled its way towards independence and uncertain freedom.

Partly as a consequence of the need to cover the retreat from Empire and partly as a means of maintaining an adequate garrison in West Germany – Britain's contribution to the NATO alliance – the country became a nation in arms. Wartime conscription was continued as post-war National Service and between 1945 and 1960, the year of the last call-up, 2,301,000 men of eighteen or nineteen spent up to two years in the colours of their monarch's armed forces. In addition to providing much-needed manpower, the conscription of some 160,000 young men a year had a profound effect on the way in which the country viewed the armed services: in the eighteen years of National Service, for better or for worse, the people of Britain enjoyed a realistic view of what life was like in the army, navy and air force. During that period of peacetime conscription many National Servicemen fought in the trouble spots of the world and 395 of their number were killed in action. Paradoxically, very little was written in the British press about the National Servicemen's wars – the bush-fire wars being fought in the distant parts of the Empire.

It was not for want of numbers, for after the Second World War the press and other means of communication remained in good fettle. During the 1950s the total readership of British newspapers never fell below 16 million; advertising might have been thin on the ground but sales fully justified the newspaper proprietors' confidence in their product. One noticeable difference with pre-war attitudes, though, was the growing gulf between the 'quality' press – newspapers like *The Times*, *Daily Telegraph*, *Manchester Guardian*, *Observer* and *Sunday Times* – and the popular mass-circulation newspapers like the *Daily Mirror*, *Daily Express*, *Daily Mail* and *News of the World*.

BBC Radio, which had come out of the war with its influence unchallenged, remained a powerful cultural institution; its broadcasts were regarded as the acme of honesty, accuracy, impartiality and good taste. Television, in its infancy before the war, emerged again although it was expensive to purchase a receiver and the programmes were limited in approach. There were less than five million viewers in the first part of the 1950s and even then broadcasts were confined to a few hours a day. The real explosion of television in British society came in 1955 with the establishment of independent television funded by commercial advertising, a move deprecated by many, including Lord Reith, the father of British broadcasting. In the *Observer* of 22 November 1953 he argued that the supporters of independent television were 'trying to promote commercial interests under the guise of Miltonic precepts and at the cost of the country's independence in a vital sphere'.

Although television programmes were carefully supervised – the independent channels were governed by their own public body, the Independent Broadcasting Authority – and in the early days at least there was little to choose between the channels, the new medium had a profound effect on British society. It changed people's leisure habits and altered older forms of entertainment such as the cinema, and by the end of the 1950s it was challenging the newspapers themselves. For example, from the Second World War onwards the public had become used to seeing filmed evidence of dramatic happenings in cinema news-reels such as those supplied by Pathé Pictorial. Although these were always carefully edited and screened long after the event they were at least tangible evidence. As television began to acquire more sophisticated methods of news-gathering, its own news bulletins became more immediate, allowing viewers to have more or less instant access to what was happening elsewhere in the world. These changes were to have a huge impact on war reporting, allowing images of conflict to be shown in people's living rooms either at the time of the fighting or within hours of it coming to an end. By the end of the 1970s this was seen to have become a distinct problem: until then there had been little questioning of the relationship between the new technology and the society it was supposed to serve.

From an editorial point of view most newspapers, the BBC and the independent broadcasting companies continued to regard Britain as a power in the world; their voice was confident, the imagery reflecting success and innovation, and the emphasis was on the nation's historic role as a superpower. The crisis over Egypt's takeover of the Suez Canal and the subsequent Anglo-French invasion in the autumn of 1956 changed all that. The military action was dutifully and widely reported, mainly because the build-up to it had been well advertised but it proved difficult to camouflage the woeful shortcomings of the British military operation. And all the jingoistic words in the world could not paper over the fact that Britain was obliged to disengage from the adventure because pressure had been applied by the USA and the Soviet Union.

The only other major British military operation to receive much press coverage during the 1950s was the EOKA emergency in Cyprus. The bitter guerrilla warfare waged by General Grivas and his fellow terrorists who wanted *enosis*, or union with Greece, was never far away from the public eye. British correspondents were regular visitors to the island and the headline MURDER MILE brought home the reality of modern counter-insurgency war; 105 British servicemen were killed during the campaign which lasted from 1954 until 1959. Many were murdered while shopping in Nicosia, hence the press's introduction of the sinister headline.

The other counter-insurgency wars, such as the long-drawn-out struggle in Malaya between 1948 and 1960, were less easy to report. The country was a long and expensive 22 hours flight away by plane and once there the war correspondent had to encounter a further set of formidable obstacles. Most of the action took place in remote jungle areas necessitating the use of military transport and the only real fighting was witnessed by jungle foot patrols. To accompany one of these on a routine patrol was a gruelling and uncomfortable experience, requiring large reserves of patience and stamina. At the campaign's end it was estimated that every contact made with the enemy required 1,800 man hours of patrol through dense undergrowth where the going was tough and the conditions physically enervating. Even if a correspondent happened to be in the right place at the right time he still had to file his story and in the days before satellite communications that, too, could be a time-consuming and nerve-racking business. Malaya turned out to be the only example of a successful counter-insurgency campaign against Communist guerrilla forces fought in the post-war period but it made little impact on the British public. Most correspondents who covered the war went to Malaya on press facility trips and filed 'colour' pieces about being 'on patrol with the Jocks in the jungle' and such like.

For their part, the military authorities were mildly surprised that the press showed any interest in their activities in such an out-of-the-way campaign. Irritation only crept in when correspondents questioned the Army's 'league table' of kills which was unofficially maintained by the infantry regiments in Malaya. The *Daily Mirror* attacked the practice and after questions were asked in the House of Commons it was forbidden as too barbarous a method of warfare. (The Army continued it anyway.)

At times it was a brutal and bloody war, as any counter-insurgency war is bound to be. The British High Commissioner, Sir Henry Gurney, was murdered by terrorists on the road between Kuala Lumpur and Fraser's Hill in 1951; a year later twelve men of the Royal West Kents met a similar fate in a similar ambush and several hundred white planters in remote areas were murdered by Communist guerrillas. These atrocities caused a good deal of frustration amongst the British forces and led to some unfortunate reprisals: in December 1949 a patrol of the 2nd Bn Scots Guards mowed down 26 innocent villagers as they attempted to escape from a resettlement programme at Batang Kali, north of Kuala Lumpur. An official investigation concluded that no blame should be attached to the guardsmen as they were doing their duty by preventing a break-out of suspected terrorists.

One reason for the apparent lack of press interest in the war was that Malaya was a distant colony, another was the prevailing imperial ethos which saw the war as a police action against an unruly element. Most National Servicemen who served in Malaya have since admitted that they had little clue why they were fighting, or, indeed, who the enemy was. Another guerrilla war, also fought in South-East Asia – the American war in Vietnam – was to have many of the same characteristics. It was also to be the first televised war and in the opinion of many it was to be lost because the public at home began to disapprove of what they were shown in the safety of their own living rooms.

The story of American involvement in Vietnam is a sad history of misguided motives, unnecessary escalation and deception: it cost the USA some 46,000 fatalities plus many more wounded and the financial penalty ran into many billions of dollars. It was also a war like none other the Americans have ever fought – there was no front line as such; the enemy was difficult to identify, being an amalgamation of North Vietnamese regulars and Viet Cong guerrillas; the reasons for American involvement were obscure; and much of the fighting was vicious close-quarter combat or equally vicious war from the air involving the latest military technology. Moreover, after the disastrous Tet offensive of 1968 it became an extremely unpopular war both amongst the public at home and amongst the combat troops in Vietnam. David Parks, a young GI, later wrote that he never felt that he was fighting for any particular cause: 'I killed to stay alive, and I killed to keep from being killed.' And a young Marine told Michael Herr, the war correspondent of *Esquire*: 'We're here to kill gooks. Period.' Given the intense dislike felt for the war and for the American part in it, it is hardly surprising, perhaps, that most memoirs of the period play down any ideological motivation.

The reasons for that disenchantment are not hard to find. For every gung-ho F-4 fighter-bomber pilot who saw the war in Vietnam as a means of stopping the Communist tide from reaching America's West Coast, there were scores of ordinary infantrymen like Parks who regarded the war as an exercise in survival. Men in the latter category, the majority one suspects, were not helped by lessons from the history of their country's involvement in Vietnam – which stretched back to the French defeat in Indo-China in 1954 and to the division of the country into North Vietnam under Ho Chi Minh and South Vietnam under Ngo Dinh Diem. Because US foreign policy at that time tended to see the Cold War as an international ideological struggle and because there was a genuine fear of losing South-East Asia to Communist domination, Diem received American support. To begin with this was restricted to a few hundred military advisers, but by 1963 and the escalation of the Viet Cong guerrilla war it had become 16,000 troops. Two years later saw 75,000 troops in the country as well as massive tactical air and sea support. In 1968 there were half a million US servicemen in Vietnam, fighting a war that had ceased to be a counter-insurgency campaign and that had become instead a mad rearguard action to prop up a gimcrack 'democracy' against the threat of a Communist takeover.

From the outset of the American involvement there was a small press presence in Saigon, the capital of South Vietnam, but it could do little to report the extent of the

growing US commitment to the war. Editors at home
tended to toe the patriotic line, because they felt that it was
not in the country's best interests to divulge the truth.
Correspondents in Vietnam had to tread carefully because
their accreditation came from Diem and transgressions
were punished by expulsion. It was not until the mid-1960s
that it became well-nigh impossible to disguise the real
extent of the American military operation in Vietnam. By
1968 637 correspondents were covering the war, mainly
representing the American, British and French press and
the major US television networks. By then, too, the Americans had put the coverage on a war footing. There was to
be no official censorship but all journalists had to be
accredited by the Joint United States Public Affairs Operation (JUSPAO) to cover 'the operation, advisory and
support activities of the Free World Military Assistance
Forces'. The organization also provided military transpor-
tation and a daily news conference, known as the 'Five
O'Clock Follies', which journalists like Herr treated with a
good deal of caution.

Rounding Le Roi there was a large group of correspondents
coming back from the briefing, standard diurnal informational
freak-o-rama, Five O'Clock Follies, Jive at Five, war stories; at
the corner they broke formation and went to their offices to file,
we watched them, the wasted clocking the wasted.[1]

Because the war was so difficult to digest and because
there was often little to report, JUSPAO officials presented
their bulletins in numerical terms. Thus journalists would
be given statistics of kill ratios, body counts or of villages
friendly to the Free World Military Assistance Forces,
instead of hard information which would chronicle the
progress of the war. While these figures might have provided interesting statistics, in themselves they told the

correspondents nothing about the overall direction of the war. It was one of the failings of the press coverage of the war in Vietnam that few correspondents were ever able to cut through the official version to reach a true understanding of American strategy. Even when correspondents or camera teams did cover combat it was difficult to understand the battle's tactical significance or, indeed, who had won it. Another problem, as Peter Braestrup of the *Washington Post* discovered, was the sheer size of the country and the fragmented nature of the fighting.

... for all media, even prior to Tet, Vietnam coverage required a lot of man-hours per story. For example, to reach a US Marine unit in the field south of the Demilitarized Zone (the DMZ – created by the 1954 Geneva Accords as a buffer area between North and South Vietnam) a Saigon reporter rose before dawn and took a regularly scheduled C-130 flight to Da Nang. Then he usually had to stay overnight at the press center there, catch a dawn plane to the 3rd Marine Division base at Dong Ha, and hope to get out to the unit via a supply helicopter. Getting back to Dong Ha depended on the vagaries of war: it might be by means of a returning supply helicopter or one carrying out wounded. From Dong Ha, the reporter took whatever means he could find back to Da Nang, and dictated his story from there to Saigon by telephone. Getting one story could take seventy-two hours or more. During the Tet offensive, aircraft delays stretched available productive reporting man-hours even thinner. And sheer exhaustion dulled perceptions.[2]

As a result first-hand reports tended to be few and far between and most journalists who covered the fighting had to rely on hitched lifts with the military to get front-line stories. Few remained long with the combat unit they were accompanying and this method of reporting the war came to be known as 'in-and-out' journalism.

The major press presence in Saigon was provided by the wire agencies – Reuters, AP, UPI – which supplied basic

news information but little in the way of analysis. John
Burrowes, who covered the war for the *Sunday Mail*, found
the Reuters' men to be the 'most consistently helpful'
journalists he had met in his reporting career and other
journalists, too, have spoken highly of the professionalism
and integrity displayed by the American and Vietnamese
members of the wire teams.

All the major American newspapers and news magazines
like *Time* and *Newsweek* were represented; and amongst the
British correspondents drawn at one time or another to the
war were John Pilger representing the *Daily Mirror*, Ian
Ward of the *Daily Telegraph* and Nicholas Tomalin of the
Sunday Times (who was later killed covering the war in
Israel). Of these the news magazine reporters had, perhaps,
the rawest deal. Each week they filed around two thousand
words back to head office where the report would be
rewritten by a desk editor who might add other details
gleaned from political sources in Washington. Then it
would be passed to the foreign editor and the senior
executive editors who would cut and rejig the story so that
it could be presented in a clear, colourful and concise house
style. A reporter would be lucky if he recognized ten per
cent of his original work in the final published article.
Newspaper reporters experienced similar problems with
their home bases: their war reports had to compete for
space with major US and world stories and as the war
continued editors became more interested in the peace
initiatives in Paris and elsewhere than in the actual fighting
in Vietnam. They also began to tire of combat stories,
whether they expressed indignation at the waste of war or,
at the other extreme, extolled the virtues of the American
fighting man. It also has to be admitted that in many cases
the journalists' own disenchantment began to creep into
their copy.

They knew that, no matter how honestly they worked, their best work would somehow be lost in the wash of news, all the facts, all the Vietnam stories. Conventional journalism could no more reveal this war than conventional firepower could win it, all it could do was take the most profound event of the American decade and turn it into a communications pudding, taking its most obvious, undeniable history and making it into a secret history. And the very best correspondents knew even more than that.

Michael Herr was not alone amongst the correspondents who came to regard the press coverage of the war as a 'communications pudding' in which the right ingredients were used to create the wrong result. There was no censorship, internal communications were good and by 1972 there was direct telephone dialling to the USA; television companies could rush film to Tokyo for developing and editing and, depending on the importance of its contents, it could be beamed by satellite to Los Angeles for instant transmission to the US networks. (Less spectacular film went by air.) But for all the openness and for all the apparent freedom to report at will, the media coverage of the war was far from complete. There might have been no official censorship but this did not encourage senior officers to divulge information: faced by a reporter asking awkward questions they would refer him to JUSPAO or answer in terms of statistics. Frequently, they had no information to give and were just as much in the dark as the correspondents. Even when they were able to give facts and figures these were often found to be inaccurate or fabricated.

Then there was the problem of overkill. Faced by so much material from Vietnam, editors and producers at home could be selective. This was especially true of the television coverage which offered the most intrusive view of the war in Vietnam. If the majority of the channels were

showing combat footage on prime time news programmes,
for example, then the others had to follow suit. A reporter
for ABC admitted to Peter Braestrup that the most dramatic stories were those involving actual fighting: 'Editors
want combat footage. They will give it a good play.' This
attitude was reinforced by Neil Archer, the Director of
News for ABC: 'A good firefight is going to get in over a
good pacification story.' The trouble was that the violence
escalated and viewers quickly became immune to run-of-
the-mill combat footage; once shown it had to be followed
by more sensational material.

Take one of the most graphic, yet ghastly, images of the
war: the summary execution in Saigon of a Viet Cong
suspect by Police Director Loan. This was caught by a
cameraman and the whole messy business was broadcast
worldwide – the action of the police chief as he raised his
pistol to the prisoner's head and, unbelievably, blew out
his brains. After that piece of film had been shown on news
programmes it became difficult for editors to resist showing
incidents equally or more hideous and in Vietnam there
were plenty from which to choose. There, the cameras had
a field day.

The controlled violence of modern warfare is not only extremely
unpleasant – it is also highly visual. Napalm is the most hideous
weapon I have ever seen used. But aesthetically the initial burst
of the fireball into resplendent tones of red and gold tinged with
black is almost beautiful. Napalm has been shown many times on
television – usually in the distance bursting in an anonymous
jungle. The only time I remember protests coming from the
viewers was in 1972, when in a famous incident a group of
children was burned on a road in Vietnam a short distance in
front of my camera crew. Most of the people who telephoned ITN
protested at the scenes shown as being too horrific. It was one
thing to show the action, quite another to linger in close-up on its
consequences. The Tram Bang incident was an everyday occur-

rence in Vietnam; it was unusual only because it happened on camera.

Christopher Wain, an experienced military correspondent, recorded that personal view for the *Journal of the Royal United Services Institute* in 1974 at a time when the ethics of television reporting of military operations were being questioned both within and without the industry. The Tram Bang incident, like the summary execution, became one of the instant images of the war, frozen in time and recorded for posterity. Both were also destined to become summaries of the war itself, for the simple reason that they had been captured by television cameras and presented to a wide audience. To the outside world Vietnam became a war in which every child running down a road had been attacked by napalm and every Viet Cong prisoner a potential victim of summary execution. Little did it count that the children at Tram Bang had been hidden in a pagoda before the air raid and had wandered out to watch the fighting.

Similarly, footage of jungle firefights or of Huey helicopters swooping into a clearing were only useful in providing images of the fighting; they could not explain strategy or give any indication of the war's progress. In that respect television proved to be a limited means of communication, dependent on the skills of the reporter and the ability of the editors to cut the film into context. In themselves, the pictures of any action told a limited story: the broad panorama could only be seen by placing it within the total concept of the war, and, as we have seen, it was very difficult for correspondents in Vietnam to get a complete understanding. There is also the very human failing of tunnel vision: a camera team caught up in an enemy action will feel that it is much more significant than any other event taking place elsewhere in another neck of the woods.

Not everything, of course, could be shown, and as Christopher Wain found, the careful editing of horrific footage to make it presentable for television audiences breached another ethical code: 'It was censorship for the most laudable of reasons – but what the editor was really doing was to make acceptable something which in reality was quite unacceptable.' (Wain was referring to the editing down of film footage showing a Marine undergoing emergency battlefield surgery without the benefit of anaesthetic.)

Just as the audience at home began to see the war in terms of carefully edited television images, so too were US servicemen affected by the presence of camera teams in Vietnam. In the later stages of the war, especially, young GIs and Marines arriving in Vietnam for the first time admitted that they felt at home there from day one. The Huey and Chinook helicopters and the F-4 jets and C-130 transports were regarded as familiar friends, the jungle clearings seen as half-remembered places like the haunts of childhood, even the language had a ring all of its own. Men weren't killed, they were 'wasted'; the Viet Cong was 'Charlie'; Vietnamese in general were 'ginks'; a machine-gun was never put on automatic, it went on 'rock and roll'. A certain John Wayne-ism crept into the war. Marines wore their uniforms in the careless style made famous by The Duke in *The Sands of Iwo Jima*. Men attacking enemy positions remembered Errol Flynn. A wounded Marine told Michael Herr, 'I *hate* this movie' and Lieutenant William Calley, the perpetrator of the My Lai massacre, admitted that he and his men were in Vietnam to be 'Audie Murphys. *Kick in the door, run in the hooch, give it a good burst –* kill.' Helicopter pilots often flew missions with radios blaring out Jimi Hendrix and admitted later that a similar scene in the film *Apocalypse Now*, showing an air strike to the strains of Wagner's *Ride of the Valkyrie*, was too close to reality for comfort.

Television coverage of the war in Vietnam did not bring it to an end but it did help to make it extremely unpopular at home. Pictures of aerial bombardment, of napalm raids and defoliation, of savage firefights in which young Americans were being killed not only brought the reality of the war into a domestic setting, they also showed what could be happening to fathers, sons and husbands. Families began to understand what their men were going through and as the level of permissible violence on the screen began to escalate, so too were sections of the public alarmed by what they saw.

Of course, there was the question of selective viewing, and some American commentators, like the distinguished critic Michael J. Arlen, have suggested that audiences protected their own sensibilities from the worst violence. In their view many people became immune to the horror and regarded it as just another piece of Hollywood-style entertainment sandwiched between other celluloid dramas. While there is a comforting ring to that reasoning it does gloss over the fact that television is a persuasive medium and that in Vietnam it provided the greater part of the news coverage of the war. In that respect it is difficult to believe that television was not partially responsible for eroding public support for the US policy in South Vietnam. Perhaps that was one reason why the North Vietnamese took little trouble to foster press coverage for their point of view – they may have felt that the standard and level of the American coverage was doing it for them.

Certainly, in 1968, American military leaders were dismayed by the reporting of the Tet offensive as a defeat for the wrong side. On 30 and 31 January units of the North

Vietnamese army and the Viet Cong launched a rash of surprise attacks against the major cities and towns of South Vietnam. The imperial city of Hue was entered and enemy sappers hit the US Embassy in Saigon, thus providing images of cities falling to urban guerrillas and of US troops falling back in disarray, powerless to stop the rot. The media cried doom and disaster and gave the victory to the Communists: by the end of the Tet offensive in March the extent of their mistake was discovered when it was revealed that the US and allied forces had lost some 10,000 casualties and the North Vietnamese and Viet Cong around 58,000.

In a sense, the failure of the media to report the Tet offensive objectively and accurately sums up all that went wrong in the press and television coverage of the war. The correspondents failed to understand US strategy and showed a lack of knowledge about the military operations in Vietnam; in this failing they were not helped by the reluctance of the military to divulge essential information or by JUSPAO's reliance on figures – which often turned out to be inaccurate. Another factor which determined the media's response was the lack of direction from the top: throughout the crisis President Lyndon B. Johnson was indecisive, contradictory and uneasy in his public statements about the direction of the war. The press coverage of Tet may have quickened the nation's desire to get out of Vietnam but it also showed that both the media and the military had a lot to learn about the coverage of modern war and especially about the intrusion of the television camera into the battlefield.

After the American withdrawal from Vietnam in 1973 the media lost interest in the war which by that time had few friends amongst public or politicians. Vietnam became bad news and in the wake of retrenchment and self-questioning the war's victims were forgotten. Vietnam veterans, considered heroes at the height of the fighting in the late 1960s, were badly treated by both the press and television: at best they were regarded as sacrificial victims, at worst as battle-hardened murderers. In *Nam*, his study of the plight facing the veterans in post-war years, Mark Baker provided a sorry picture of their lot. Many had psychological as well as physical scars, they felt like lepers and found it incomprehensible that the public would not tolerate them or understand the necessary part they had had to play in the war. Their problem was not made any easier by the revelation of incidents like My Lai or by the evidence of the long-term effects of Agent Orange, the defoliant which not only laid waste the jungle but also caused genetic defects amongst the native population. And just as the press and television paid scant attention to the after-effects of war amongst Americans, so too did they largely ignore the fate of the 'boat people', the South Vietnamese who tried to escape from their country's Communist rule after 1975, thus reinforcing the view that the US television channels only retained an interest in the war as long as it provided violent and sensational action.

Although the Vietnam war had come to an end by the early 1970s television producers and editors did not have far to look for other conflicts with which to fill their news bulletins. Fighting broke out between Israel and Egypt in 1973 and the Yom Kippur War was widely covered by press and television war correspondents from all over the world. In the opinion of many of their number this turned out to be the first real televised war in that sophisticated news-gathering equipment provided immediate images of the fighting. The Middle East remained the fulcrum of international war reporting with a bloody civil war in Lebanon, involving at various stages the armies of Syria,

Israel and the Palestine Liberation Organization. Reporters and television crews were allowed to cover the war at will and Lebanon became a regular feature in Western news programmes. As had happened in Spain, the vehemence shown by the warring factions found an echo in the response of the international press corps, many of whose members lent their support to the PLO, Druse militia, Maronite Christians, Israelis, or whatever. Their attitudes disgusted Robert Fisk, *The Times* correspondent in Lebanon, who told Phillip Knightley in an interview: 'The fact of the matter is that there are no good guys in Lebanon – they're all bad.' Fisk proved to be the outstanding journalist in the Middle East and was made International Journalist of the Year on four occasions, but his impartiality and professionalism did not win him many friends. As Phillip Knightley pointed out, both the Syrians and the Israelis have accused him – wrongly – of inventing stories or presenting a biased point of view in his reports.[3]

Television coverage of the fighting in Lebanon, which began in 1975, continued where Vietnam had left off. There were close-ups of mangled corpses from the fierce street-fighting and of the victims of the massacres at Sabra and Chatila, for example, and there is evidence to suggest that the presence of a television crew could provoke violence: one of the lasting images of the civil war is of militiamen in heroic pose recklessly firing off rounds of ammunition to please the accompanying camera teams. The best documented example, though, of television helping to change the course of events had happened earlier, during the civil war in Nigeria in 1968.

Nigeria had been granted independence within the British Commonwealth in 1960 and by 1966 a series of military coups had brought General Yakubu Gowon to power as President of the federal republic. Long-standing differences amongst the peoples of Nigeria, however, then led the predominantly Ibo south-east of the country to break away from the republic and to form Biafra; this in turn led to a civil war (1967–1970) which like every other form of internecine strife was a bloody and brutal business. Atrocities were committed by both sides, soldiers lost control and murdered surrendered opponents, old tribal scores were paid off and civilians became the innocent victims of the fiercest fighting. Another grisly feature of the war was that neither side showed much mercy to prisoners, it being considered invidious to capture one's own fellow-countrymen. As had happened in countless other civil wars, little quarter was shown to those who had surrendered.

During the opening rounds of the war the Biafrans had harnessed world opinion to their side, mainly because they had taken care to employ a professional public relations firm, Markpress of Geneva, to handle their press and propaganda campaign. Particular emphasis was given to Nigerian barbarism and it took some time for Gowon's government to wake up to the fact that they were lagging behind in the propaganda war. In 1968, in a belated attempt to convey to the world their 'just and civilized intentions', they arranged for a major press facility trip to the battle-front in the south-east of the country. It was largely made up of British newspaper correspondents and a BBC camera team.

The newsmen arrived in Port Harcourt on 31 August to find an ITN camera team and its reporter, Michael Nicholson, on their way out, having been expelled by the Nigerian military authorities. A few days earlier the British team had witnessed the burning of an Ibo village near Ogwe and the summary execution of a captured prisoner by an army officer called Lieutenant Macaulay Lamurde. The incident had been captured on film by the ITN crew and it had also been witnessed by a French photographer and two other reporters from Norway and the USA, but to add to the horror Nicholson had interviewed the prisoner minutes before he had been shot. No sooner had he assured the man that he would be given fair treatment than Lamurde had trussed him up and shot him as the camera continued rolling. To the incredulous and horrified British television team it seemed possible that Lamurde might have carried out the execution just because they happened to have been there.

Interviewed about the incident a few days later Nicholson told ITN's *News at Ten* programme: 'When he was tied up we thought he was going to be put in the coach. We could not stop it happening, it happened so quickly.' When he was pushed further about Lamurde's reasons and asked if the man would have been killed had the cameras not been there, Nicholson replied: 'This was a question we asked ourselves. Afterwards it occurred to us that we should have attempted to save the man but it happened so quickly.' Although Nicholson and his colleagues had come across other incidents in which prisoners had obviously been shot, on this occasion the Ibos were being rounded up and put in an accompanying coach for future interrogation. The suspicion must remain, therefore, that Lamurde had been so impressed by the presence of the ITN cameras that he decided to shoot the prisoner.

Even if that were not the case, Nicholson had firm evidence of the atrocity; after taking the officer's name he reported the matter to the military authorities at Port Harcourt where the Nigerian commanding officer, Colonel Benjamin Adekunle, was considered to be something of a martinet. This was a telling moment, for an important ingredient in Nigeria's public image was that the only atrocities of the war were being perpetrated by the Ibos themselves. Nicholson's filmed evidence contradicted those claims.

Faced by that overwhelming proof, Adekunle arrested Lamurde, asked Nicholson to identify him and at a field court martial ordered him to be sentenced to death. Furthermore, Nicholson and his colleagues were told to attend the execution; but fearing reprisals they refused and were ordered out of the country. It was left to the incoming press team, of which John Burrowes of the *Sunday Mail* was a member, to witness the death by firing squad of Lieutenant Lamurde. And just as the original incident had been filmed, so too did Adekunle insist that the outcome of Nigeria's justice be recorded for posterity. Lamurde was tied to a tree, blindfolded and a four-man firing squad took aim: then, seconds before the order to fire was given, the BBC camera equipment jammed. The execution was held up for a minute or two to allow reporter David Tindall and his team to rectify the fault; once the cameras were rolling, the sound running, Lamurde met his fate. John Burrowes takes up the story:

The Pressmen exchanged embarrassed looks; the eyes that had seen it all found it hard to take in the scene and little was said as the soldiers from the escort party moved towards the dead prisoner to cut him down from the tree and take the body away. Tindall and his team were having an inquest about what went wrong. It was a sound equipment fault, they discovered. More likely a jangled nerve.[4]

It was not the first time that an execution had been filmed but it was an occasion when the presence of a camera team had influenced the course of events. Had Lamurde not shot the Ibo prisoner in front of the cameras, there would have been no hard evidence of a crime which was obviously fairly widespread during the war. Had the

Nigerians not been so conscious of their public image then the incident might have had another ending. Had the cameras not been present, Lamurde might not have shot the prisoner (given the extent of atrocities involving prisoners, that is debatable) but as Nicholson's evidence could be shown on the world's television screens, then television had also to witness the reprisals. Instead of being an impartial witness to events, television had taken a hand in fashioning them. Adekunle told John Burrowes that Lamurde had been shot in front of the war correspondents because he had committed a crime and because he had given Nigeria a bad name. But as Burrowes cynically pointed out, both incidents gave the world's press an unbeatable story.

What a great story he was going to make for them! A Page One man. And they would resurrect the photo they had shown the week before of him shooting the Ibo, use it alongside the new ones they would take today as he died, and label it 'Black Killer Meets His Fate'. As soon as they could get their copy and processed prints down to the Telecommunications Centre on the Marina at Lagos, the name Lamurde would be chattering out on telex lines round the world . . . the Reuters man would get it on their massive hook-up to the Far East and Australia, to Continental Europe, to New York. Others would want to beat him by getting it to their home offices direct, to the *Mirror*, the *Telegraph*, the *Sunday Mail*, the *Guardian*.

Burrowes's own newspaper, the *Sunday Mail*, gave the incident relatively low-key coverage when the story appeared in its issue of 8 September.

I was one of the journalists who saw a Nigerian soldier die this week. It was in the grounds of a deserted Roman Catholic mission school at Umukoroshe and he stood tall and erect in the shade of a sheki-sheki tree as four soldiers aimed their automatic rifles at him.

The soldier who died was facing the firing squad. And his execution was just one small part of the tragedy of this sad war where soldiers die and babies starve.

By then the story had run its course but as Burrowes had predicted, it had made front-page news during the course of the week. Although both the original murder and the subsequent execution were widely reported the main thrust of most news stories was that both incidents had appeared on television. Lamurde's moment of death was not actually transmitted by the BBC but the neatly edited news story left viewers in little doubt what was about to happen. There was a flurry of public revulsion and *The Times* warned in a leader on 6 September 1968 that 'never should television camera teams film events of this kind which appear in any way to be staged for their benefit, or influenced for the worse by their presence'.

It was a warning which would also apply to a conflict nearer to British television's home base. Within a year of Lamurde's public execution British camera teams were filming the unrest and violence on the streets of Northern Ireland as the Catholic community struck for equal political rights. The escalation of that conflict and the response of the media brought again to the surface all the old shibboleths about the presence of journalists at the scene of any fighting involving the British Army.

To begin with, the military authorities found themselves in an invidious position in Northern Ireland: they were not at war but their soldiers were providing aid to the civil power, in this case within the United Kingdom itself. This meant that the soldiers' every move was under the scrutiny not only of the local population but also of the British journalists and the accompanying camera teams. Most people living in the rest of Britain got their first impression

of the political situation in Northern Ireland from television
news bulletins and it was usually a confused picture of
rioting, murder and mayhem with the British Army and
the Royal Ulster Constabulary frequently appearing as the
aggressor.

In some incidents this view was justified. The Army was
often guilty of using brutality against the local community
– the 'Bloody Sunday' incident in Derry in January 1972
being the most notorious example. But in the early days of
the troubles in Northern Ireland the military authorities
were their own worst enemies when it came to dealing with
the media. For example, if a soldier appeared evasive
during a televised interview his reluctance to speak could
cast doubt on the rest of the Army's evidence. Or if a
reporter met with a dusty 'no comment', the official
response could imply that facts were being withheld. The
IRA was quick to exploit that weakness and proved to be a
master at harnessing the press and television coverage of
the conflict as a propaganda weapon. Discussing their
methods in 1977, the Annan Report commented that:
'Terrorism feeds off publicity; publicity is its main hope of
intimidating government and the public; publicity gives it
a further chance for recruitment.' The claim was not
groundless in Northern Ireland: bomb blasts were timed to
coincide with peak-time news bulletins and the IRA hunger
strikes and deaths in the Maze prison achieved substantial
publicity, especially on the American television networks.

It was not a comfortable position and the Army soon
found itself at odds with the accompanying press corps. In
1976 Robert Fisk disclosed in *The Times* the extent to which
the Army had provided deliberate misinformation about
their activities in Northern Ireland and at the same time a
scandal broke out about the official forging of military press
cards. Both disclosures dented the Army's credibility in the

eyes of the press and led to a higher priority being given to the Army's Public Relations Service.

During this period the media, too, committed silly mistakes, largely because correspondents did not always understand either the situation in Northern Ireland or the reasons for the British presence there. Typical of their errors, as the soldiers saw it, was a tendency to swallow Republican propaganda and to edit statements, especially interviews, to give a story an anti-Army slant. The only solution, suggested by Fisk and others, was for the Army to tell the truth: this did not mean that the media would support the Army at any cost, but that the correspondents would try to support the Army against terrorist outrage. From 1977 onwards the Army made it mandatory for units in Northern Ireland to have a fully trained press officer to deal with the media, partly as a means of improving their relationship with the press and broadcasting representatives and partly to counter IRA propaganda. To help them cope with television interviewing techniques, officers were also sent on acclimatization courses at the Army School of Instructional Technology at Beaconsfield.

By putting its information services on a professional footing in Northern Ireland the Army did much to improve its relationship with the media; unfortunately for all concerned those lessons were not always applied to the later conflict in which Britain unexpectedly found herself engaged – the limited war with Argentina at the beginning of 1982. The flashpoint was the decision of General Leopardo Galtieri's controlling *junta* to reclaim the British possessions of South Georgia and the Falkland Islands through the use of armed force. It was to be a short, sharp war, reminiscent in some respects of Kitchener's Sudanese expedition to defeat the Dervishes; it also demonstrated that the intervening years had done little to lessen the suspicion which traditionally existed between the soldier and the war correspondent.

The first imponderable was that almost everyone in Britain was unprepared for the conflict. There was little public awareness that a crisis was in the offing in the South Atlantic and when units of Argentinian marines attacked Port Stanley, the capital of the Falklands, on 2 April everyone, the press included, was taken by surprise. Even the government and the Ministry of Defence would not at first either confirm or deny that an invasion had taken place and were unable to field questions put to them by British and foreign journalists. The atmosphere of unreality was not dispelled by the news that the Argentinians had indeed taken over the islands and that Britain was to despatch a task force to liberate her far-flung possessions while efforts were made to find a settlement through diplomatic channels. According to Robert Harris, who later wrote *Gotcha! The Media, The Government and the Falklands Crisis* (1983), 3 April turned out to be 'a day of frustration and confusion – a foretaste of the chaos that was to come'.

From the very outset of the crisis the government stood in danger of losing the media as an ally. The Royal Navy, which was to supply the ships and the senior command for the task force, was unimpressed with the suggestion that war correspondents be permitted to accompany the expedition. Echoing the anonymous American military censor of the Second World War who said he wouldn't tell the people anything until the war was over, and then he'd tell them who won, they argued that civilian journalists did not have the necessary training or experience to cope with the conditions and that, in any case, they would only get in the way. Under pressure from the Ministry of Defence they gave way and agreed that six journalists should be allowed to accompany the task force: this was increased later to twelve, to include a camera team and two correspondents representing the BBC and ITN. The decision was met with incredulity in Fleet Street and in the short time available to them, the newspaper editors and proprietors put every kind of argument to the government to make the Royal Navy change its mind. Eventually, it was agreed that fifteen correspondents, photographers, cameramen and sound recordists would accompany the task force and that a further thirteen would travel on other ships like the *Canberra*, a civilian liner which had been pressed into service as a troopship. Some of the journalists had experience of wars in Nigeria, Vietnam and the Middle East but, as Robert Harris pointed out, the Falklands was going to be a very different kind of war.

The armed forces are prepared for war; journalists are not. Most were too young even to have remembered, let alone endured National Service. Yet arguably the Falklands was to require greater physical and mental readiness than any war covered by the media in recent times. The haphazard way in which journalists were selected and sent on their way, in most cases without even the most rudimentary equipment, could easily have proved fatal. As it was, three reporters returned home before the fighting was over, and at least one appeared to be visibly distressed when recalling his experiences.[5]

One of the war correspondents who was prepared was Max Hastings of the *London Standard*. He proved to be something of a latter-day Archibald Forbes, hitching lifts on military helicopters to get to the scene of any action and generally displaying an instinctive ability to get on with the task force's officers. Also, he was as fit as any soldier, a virtue which helped him to scoop the rest of the press corps by being the first correspondent to enter Port Stanley at the conclusion of the hostilities. 'It was simply too good a chance to miss,' he said after walking into the Upland

Goose Hotel on 14 June – the following day the story of his
impulsive mission appeared on the front page of the *Standard*
under the headline 'Max Hastings Leads the Way: THE
FIRST MAN INTO STANLEY'. The feat ensured his
perpetual celebrity, and as *The Spectator* remarked when
Hastings was appointed editor of the *Daily Telegraph* in
March 1986, 'It will now vouch him a welcome among a
readership for whom the first man in Port Stanley has
greater worth than any reporter, however gifted his
despatches.'

(Although the military liked him, Hastings did not
always enjoy the same popularity amongst his colleagues.
Much of the dislike was professional jealousy because
Hastings' reports seemed to receive unrivalled national
exposure, due to the policy of pooled copy being available
to all newspapers, but after the cease-fire he was accused of
the serious charge of failing to deliver another correspondent's copy. The journalist concerned threatened to bayonet him during an angry encounter in the Upland Goose
but was restrained by a colleague with the words: 'This is
neither the time nor the place to kill Max Hastings.')

The second problem facing the media was that the
Falklands are 8,000 miles away from Britain and communications are difficult. All written copy was despatched to
London over the ships' communications systems and was
received by the Defence Communications Centre in the
Ministry of Defence. Spoken reports were also transmitted
by the Navy, in this case from ships fitted with a satellite
communications system known as INMARSAT or MAR-
ISAT. No provision was made for live television coverage.
Although the BBC and ITN tested the feasibility of satellite
transmissions, using systems like SCOT or SKYNET II,
there was a feeling within the industry that the Ministry of
Defence was not particularly interested in providing tele-

vision pictures from the war. Film had to return to London by ship and plane, arriving at least three weeks after it had been shot, and even then it had to survive a viewing by Ministry of Defence censors before it could be edited for transmission. This meant that there were no pictures of the actual fighting on the island, or of the casualties sustained by the task force, until after the final cease-fire.

On one level, the Ministry of Defence's desire to manage the media's coverage of the conflict can be explained by good operational reasons: there were occasions when naval communications had to have priority over press despatches. These restrictions were not always fully explained to the correspondents. There was also a fear amongst some senior officers that explicit stories, especially filmed reports, would be bad for morale at home. (At the back of their minds may have been the American experience in Vietnam.) This led Ministry of Defence censors to ask for pictures of body bags to be removed from film and to hold up footage of damaged ships, like the destroyers *Sheffield* and *Coventry* and the frigate *Antelope*. On another level, the government wanted to maintain a favourable impression of a war that could so easily have ended in disaster: although the British task force did win back the islands it was a close-run thing involving several serious setbacks, including the loss of the warships and the deaths of Welsh Guardsmen during the landings at Bluff Cove. Following the latter incident the BBC was forced to remove the words 'badly burned' from Brian Hanrahan's report on the survivors from the landing ship *Sir Galahad*. His colleague, Michael Nicholson of ITN, wanted the word 'censored' to appear on all filmed reports from the Falklands, but this idea was itself censored.

Similar constraints applied to the press and radio correspondents who had to show their copy to the accompanying Ministry of Defence press officers – or 'minders' as the war correspondents dubbed them – before it could be transmitted back to Britain. Although there was supposed to be no censorship of despatches as such, each journalist being supposed to act in a responsible manner, seemingly arbitrary and unexplained cuts were made to some journalists' copy and this led to a good deal of friction during the voyage south. The war correspondents tended to regard these press officers as civil servants, overburdened by caution and unused to modern journalistic techniques; in turn the 'minders' were suspicious of the media's motives and constantly feared breaches of security. It was not an arrangement designed for mutual trust and tolerance and just as it was said that the television camera need not have been invented as far as the Falklands conflict was concerned, so too did the war correspondents come to believe that the authorities were only interested in 'good news'.

It was the same old story: was the war correspondent to consider himself a propagandist for his own side or was he to be an objective reporter at the cost of criticizing the army he was accompanying? In the report *Handling of Press and Public Information during the Falklands Conflict*, published in 1982, the House of Commons Defence Committee was asked: 'Was it just by chance that the celebrated picture of a San Carlos villager offering a Marine a cup of tea achieved instant currency, whilst others such as the one of HMS *Antelope* exploding suffered considerable delays?' On the available evidence, the answer must be 'No'.

Throughout the conflict newspaper editors remained constrained by the 'D' notices, a set of rules for reporting defence matters agreed upon by the Ministry of Defence and news editors, and by the Official Secrets Act, a wide-ranging though vaguely phrased legislation which basically prevents editors using government information until it has been published or issued in a statement. The media were

further curbed by the suspension of 'off-the-record' briefings, that is the passing to journalists of privileged but
unattributable information under a cloak of confidentiality.
In its place the Ministry of Defence introduced daily
briefings, conducted by Ian McDonald, a civil servant who
was acting head of the Ministry's public relations department. His policy was to keep the press at arm's length and
to provide official, and therefore censored, stories for the
media's use. Because the briefings were frequently televised, he became something of a celebrity, associated in the
public's mind with the news-readers themselves, and
indeed he attempted – unsuccessfully – to copy their style.
Later in the conflict, towards the end of May, off-the-record
briefings were reintroduced and more succinct and up-to-
date hard news stories were made available but by then the
damage had been done to the relationship.

The Ministry of Defence's policy led to mistakes being
committed by both sides and to inevitable recriminations
during and after the conflict. The BBC was accused of
pandering to Argentinian propaganda after its *Panorama*
programme of 10 May 1982 posed the question, 'Can we
avoid war?' Both the BBC's Chairman and the Director-
General designate were summoned to appear before the
Conservatives' backbench media committee to explain their
policies and in the ensuing row Robert Kee, the programme's presenter, first dissociated himself from the programme and then resigned. Much of the anger was
generated by a belief in some government circles that the
BBC's duty was to be 'patriotic' and that it should refuse
to transmit programmes which might appear to be 'defeat-
ist' or 'pro-enemy'. At the other end of the scale, the *Sun*
newspaper displayed an unacceptable level of jingoism in
its issue of 3 May which announced the sinking of the
Argentinian cruiser *Belgrano* with the headline GOTCHA!

In later editions this was changed to DID 1200 ARGIES DROWN? Throughout the conflict, though, the *Sun* maintained a high level of patriotic sentiment, even branding as 'traitors' any opponents of Britain's part in the war.

More seriously, the withholding of information led to supposition, mainly from the so-called 'armchair strategists' – retired service officers, academics and the media's own specialist defence correspondents. In peacetime it is quite usual for newspapers, television and current affairs teams to use experts to provide an objective opinion to a particular problem. During the Falklands conflict the practice was greatly extended and, according to Valerie Adams's recent study, *The Media and the Falklands*, a total of 75 outside commentators provided views of varying accuracy to the media. Sometimes their forecasts of future events could be accurate, such as the speculation surrounding the movements of 5 Infantry Brigade in the final stages of the war. The most common complaint, though, was that the armchair strategists created speculation which in some cases could lead to breaches of security. This was especially true of the taking of Goose Green.

On 27 May the BBC World Service announced that the 2nd Parachute Regiment was advancing on Darwin while 45 Commando and the 3rd Parachute Regiment were moving towards Douglas Settlement and Teal Inlet Settlement respectively. Lt-Col 'H' Jones of 3 Para was furious as he believed that the BBC's announcement would divulge British plans to the enemy: some days after the battle this seemed to be confirmed when a prisoner claimed that the Argentinians had diverted their mobile reserve into the Goose Green area after hearing the news bulletin. Jones was killed during the action but what he and his men could not have known was that journalists had been briefed about the operation a few days earlier and that in London speculation had been rife about when it would take place. The World Service had not been alone in forecasting the action but theirs was the bulletin heard by the task force. At the same time Argentinian commanders must have noted the British movements in the area and reinforced Goose Green to meet any possible attack; so a question-mark must remain over the effectiveness of the broadcast in influencing Argentinian tactics.

In retrospect, it can be seen that the main failure of the Ministry of Defence's management of the news coverage was that, all too often, it refused to take the media into its confidence, thereby creating an atmosphere of suspicion. The suspension of off-the-record briefings removed a vital source of information both about the complexities of the conflict and of the British political and military response to it, and in general the Ministry did little to explain the problems of fighting a war so far removed from home base. A further failing was the inability of the civil servants to understand the role that the media could have played in countering Argentinian propaganda with realistic and trustworthy stories about what was happening in the South Atlantic. This was exposed at the outset of the conflict: because the British media had to rely on Argentinian sources for their reports of the fall of Port Stanley, the picture they painted was one of non-reaction and surrender. Only when the small company of Royal Marines were repatriated did it become clear that they had held their ground before giving in to the superior Argentinian forces.

Even when the Ministry of Defence did issue hard news stories with categorical statements these were often found to be inaccurate, a glaring example being a report on 9 May that the Argentinian spyship *Narwhal* had been attacked and captured without loss. Later, the story was found to be untrue: the boarding party had sustained fourteen casualties. The planting of disinformation was also used for military purposes. Following the reintroduction of off-the-record briefings, the Ministry of Defence was able to convince the media on 20 May that there would be no 'D-Day' style landings and that for the time being the task force would only engage in hit-and-run raids. The following morning at 0400 local time the first landings were made north of San Carlos; by mid-day the task force had established a beachhead covering some ten square miles.

On the Falklands themselves the war correspondents had to face their own share of personal difficulties both from the indifference and suspicion shown by many of the senior officers and from the terrain itself. War correspondents were assigned to pre-selected units and much depended on the attitude taken by the commanding officer. Most were given suitable equipment and fared well; others were less lucky and were given the lowest priority for clothing, rations and communications. The outstanding war correspondent was Max Hastings who showed an intuitive grasp of the fighting and who actually seemed to enjoy the experience. Of the barren bog-ridden uplands over which the soldiers had to fight he waxed lyrical, comparing the moment to fishing in a Hampshire chalk stream. He was also able to relate his eye-witness accounts to professional judgements about the British commanders: he was especially acute in his estimation of Brigadier Julian Thompson, commander of 3 Commando Brigade, who was dubbed 'man of the match' by the land force commander, Maj.-Gen. Jeremy Moore. Although the reporting of the war was often suffused by an old-fashioned brand of enthusiastic patriotism no one was prepared to gloss over the carnage caused by the fighting in June which brought the war to an end. Despite the censorship, both Brian Hanrahan and Michael Nicholson provided sombrely realistic accounts of the fighting at Goose Green and the landings at San Carlos, and the radio reports supplied by Robert Fox of the BBC and Kim Sabido of Independent Radio News were models of their kind – concise, informative and vividly expressed.

Because the dominant trend in the country was to support the government, most of the correspondents brought a fair degree of optimism to their reports and tended to respond to the notion that the public was only interested in 'victories'. Once the war was over those who felt that their stories had been overblown expressed disquiet about their role, feeling that they had accepted official communiqués too readily or that they had succumbed to the Gotcha! mentality. Their unease was probably exacerbated by the shortness of the war and by the media's inability to change its response according to the circumstances. The very haste with which the war correspondents had been selected and the air of unreality which accompanied the departure of the task force made it difficult for editors to fashion their attitudes and once the fighting happened it was all over very quickly.

On the whole, the servicemen in the task force remained unimpressed by the reporting of the war. Lieutenant David Tinker, who was killed on HMS *Glamorgan* three days before the end of the fighting, noted in his diary that he despaired of the press coverage of the war because the war correspondents saw it as a 'real life War Mag' full of grandiose and entirely imaginary happenings.

The BBC were on board and grandiosed everything out of all proportion (Antarctic wind, force nine gales, terrific disruption done, disrupted entire Argentinian war effort, etc). Mostly, they sat drinking the wardroom beer and were sick in their heads: the weather was in fact quite good.[6]

He could have been Kitchener or Haig complaining about the press corps during the march to Omdurman in 1898.

One of the more depressing lessons learned from the Falklands War was that very little had changed in the relationship between the war correspondents and the armed forces. As had happened in just about every earlier campaign, a *modus operandi* had to be established as the war progressed. Generally speaking, the military units, with the British Army's experience of Northern Ireland, were more open in their dealings with the war correspondents while the Royal Navy remained fairly obdurate throughout the conflict. Added to the Ministry of Defence's inconsistencies and discrepancies in providing accurate information it made the reporting of the war a tetchy and difficult business, resented by both sides of the relationship. In the self-questioning that followed, the government-inspired Beach Report came down on the side of providing 'an improved advisory service for journalists' in the event of a future war. It also recommended the introduction of some form of censorship even though it would be difficult to operate, given the scale and complexity of modern means of communication.

While it is unlikely that there will be another war like the Falklands campaign of 1982, it is equally unlikely that the media will allow themselves to be talked out of providing television coverage of any future conflict. The wider availability of satellite delivery systems means that, in theory, the television companies could establish their own communications network and beam back pictures of the fighting as it is taking place. Those who protest that the public would not stand for such a practice will take little comfort from history. Until the 19th century spectators regularly viewed battles from the safety of surrounding vantage points, regarding the whole experience as a massive and not-to-be-missed entertainment.

Finally, the Falklands War demonstrated that the public had lost none of its fascination for war. Just as the American public had become hooked on news bulletins from Vietnam, so too had the British on war stories from the South Atlantic. In May 1982 sales of the *Guardian* went up by 50,000 copies following the re-taking of South Georgia, ITN *News at Ten* attracted an audience of 17.5 million viewers, twenty per cent higher than average. And that interest continues to be fed from the conflicts of the mid-1980s, from Central America, the Middle East, Afghanistan . . . wherever man is taking up arms against his fellow men there will always be other men and women on hand to describe the action. In a moment of self-pity, William Howard Russell described himself as 'the miserable parent of a luckless tribe'; one hundred years later, there seems to be no shortage of his progeny.

Notes

In an attempt to keep notes and references to a minimum, the source of quotations has been placed, wherever possible, in the text.

Chapter One: The Newly Invented Curse to Armies

1 Russell's reports to *The Times* have been collected in Caroline Chapman, *Russell of The Times* (London: Bell & Hyman, 1984).
2 Wood's obituary was published in the *Fortnightly Review*, February 1907.
3 Frederick Villiers, *Five Decades of Adventure* (London: Harper, 1921).
4 Alexander's comments are quoted from J. V. McConnah, 'The Army and The Press in War', *Journal of the Royal United Services Institute*, vol. 98, 1953.

Chapter Two: George Warrington Steevens and the Sudan

1 Steevens's reports to the *Daily Mail* were collected in his volume, *With Kitchener to Khartoum* (Edinburgh and London: William Blackwood, 1898).
2 H. W. Nevinson, *Ladysmith: The Diary of a Siege* (London: Methuen, 1900), p. 240.

Chapter Three: Edgar Wallace and The Great Boer War

1 W. S. Churchill, *London to Ladysmith via Pretoria* (London: Longman, 1900), pp. 204–205.

2 Wallace's reports to the *Daily Mail* were collected in his volume, *Unofficial Dispatches* (London: Hutchinson, 1901).

3 Quoted in Reginald Pound and Geoffrey Harmsworth, *Northcliffe* (London: Cassell, 1959), p. 850.

Chapter Four: Charles à Court Repington and the First World War

1 Bennet Burleigh, *Empire of the East* (London: Chapman and Hall, 1905), pp. 258–259.

2 Charles à Court Repington, *Vestigia* (London: Constable, 1919), p. 253.

3 Charles à Court Repington, *The First World War*, vol. I (London: Constable, 1921), p. 21.

4 E. D. Swinton, *Eyewitness* (London: Hodder and Stoughton, 1932), p. 39.

5 Philip Gibbs, *Realities of War* (London: Heinemann, 1920), pp. 7–8.

6 Northcliffe's letter to French is quoted from Paul Ferris, *The House of Northcliffe: The Harmsworths of Fleet Street* (London: Weidenfeld and Nicolson, 1972), p. 197.

7 Haig's letter to FitzGerald is quoted from Trevor Royle, *The Kitchener Enigma* (London: Michael Joseph, 1985), p. 294.

Chapter Five: Claud Cockburn and the Spanish Civil War

1 George Orwell, 'Looking Back on the Spanish Civil War', *Collected Essays* (London: Mercury Books, 1961), p. 211.

2 Claud Cockburn's writings on Spain were collected in

Cockburn Sums Up (London: Quartet Books, 1981). See
Selected Bibliography for further volumes.
3 Patricia Cockburn, *The Years of The Week* (London: Macdonald, 1968), p. 203.
4 Phillip Knightley, *The First Casualty: The War Correspondent as Hero, Propagandist, and Myth Maker* (London: André
Deutsch, 1975), p. 197.

Chapter Six: Chester Wilmot and the Second World War

1 Alan Moorehead, *A Late Education: Episodes in a Life*
(London: Hamish Hamilton, 1970), p. 133.
2 Quoted from McConnah, 'The Army and The Press in
War', loc cit.
3 From notes in the possession of Mrs Edith Wilmot. The
assessments and memories of Boyd, Sarney, Gilliam and
Horrocks were collected by Alan Wood for a projected
biography of Wilmot. Wood's death prevented the book
from being completed.
4 Barton Maughan, *Australia in the War of 1939–1945, Series
One, Army, Vol. III, Tobruk and El Alamein* (Canberra:
Australian War Memorial, 1966), pp. 148–150.
5 Desmond Hawkins (ed.), *War Report: D-Day to VE Day*
(London: Ariel Books, 1985, rev. ed.), p. 62.

Chapter Seven: James Cameron and the Korean War

1 *Picture Post*, 28 October 1950.
2 James Cameron, *Point of Departure* (London: Grafton
Books, 1986), pp. 74–75.
3 *Picture Post*, 23 June 1951.
4 *Picture Post*, 7 October 1950. Much of this material was
used later in *Point of Departure*.

5 *Daily Worker*, 1 November 1950.
6 *The Times*, 20 December 1950.

Chapter Eight: The Savage Wars of Peace

1 Michael Herr, *Dispatches* (London: Picador, 1978), p. 37.
2 Peter Braestrup, *Big Story* (Princeton: Yale University Press, 1983, rev. ed.), p. 21.
3 Phillip Knightley, 'Our Men Out There', in *The Times: Past Present and Future* (London: *The Times*, 1985).
4 John Burrowes, *Frontline Report* (Edinburgh: Mainstream, 1980), pp. 107–108.
5 Robert Harris, *Gotcha! The Media, The Government and the Falkland Crisis* (London: Faber, 1983), p. 16.
6 David Tinker's letters home were published as *Message from The Falklands* (London: Junction Books, 1982), p. 182.

Select Bibliography

Adams, Valerie, *The Media and the Falklands Campaign*, London: Macmillan, 1986.

Bennett, E. N., *The Downfall of the Dervishes*, London: Methuen, 1899.

Braestrup, Peter, *Big Story*, Princeton: Yale UP, 1983.

Bullard, F. Lauriston, *Famous War Correspondents*, Bath: Putnam, 1912.

Burleigh, Bennet, *Khartoum Campaign*, London: Chapman & Hall, 1899; *Empire of the East*, London: Chapman & Hall, 1905.

Burrowes, John, *Frontline Report*, Edinburgh: Mainstream, 1980.

Cameron, James, *Point of Departure*, London: Grafton Books, 1986.

Chapman, Caroline, *Russell of The Times*, London: Bell & Hyman, 1984.

Churchill, Winston S., *The River War*, vols I and II, London: Longmans Green, 1899; *London to Ladysmith via Pretoria*, London: Longmans Green, 1900; *My Early Life*, London: Butterworth, 1930.

Cockburn, Claud, *In Time of Trouble*, London: Hart Davis, 1956; *Crossing the Line*, London: MacGibbon & Kee, 1958; *View from the West*, London: MacGibbon & Kee, 1961; *I Claud*, London: Penguin Books, 1967; *Cockburn Sums Up*, London: Quartet Books, 1981.

Cockburn, Patricia, *The Years of The Week*, London: Macdonald, 1968.

Cook, Sir Edward, *The Press in Time of War*, London: Macmillan, 1920.

Cutforth, Rene, *Korean Reporter*, London: Allan Wingate, 1952.

Forbes, Archibald, *Memories and Studies of War and Peace*, London: Cassell, 1896.

Fox, Robert, *Eyewitness Falklands*, London: Methuen, 1982.

Furneaux, R., *News of War*, London: Parrish, 1964.

Gibbs, Philip, *Realities of War*, London: Heinemann, 1920; *Adventures in Journalism*, London: Heinemann, 1923.

Glasgow University Media Group, *War and Peace News*, Milton Keynes: Open University Press, 1985.

Greenburg, Susan, *Rejoice! Media Freedom and the Falklands*, London: Campaign for Press and Broadcasting Freedom, 1983.

Hanrahan, Brian, and Fox, Robert, *I counted them all out and I counted them all back*, London: BBC, 1982.

Harris, Robert, *Gotcha! The Media, The Government and the Falklands Crisis*, London: Faber, 1983.

Hastings, Max, and Jenkins, Simon, *The Battle for the Falklands*, London: Michael Joseph, 1983.

Hawkins, Desmond (ed.), *War Report: D-Day to VE Day*, London: Ariel Books, 1985 (rev. ed.).

Herr, Michael, *Dispatches*, London: Picador Books, 1978.

Higgins, Marguerite, *War in Korea*, New York: Doubleday, 1951.

Hooper, Alan, *The Media and The Military*, Aldershot: Gower, 1982.

Hopkinson, Tom, *Of This Our Time*, London: Hutchinson, 1984.

House of Commons Defence Committee First Report 1982–1983, *The Handling of Press and Public Information During the Falklands Conflict*, vols I and II, 1982.

Knightley, Phillip, *The First Casualty*, London: Quartet Books, 1982 (rev. ed.).

Lytton, Neville, *The Press and the General Staff*, London: Collins, 1921.

Monks, Noel, *Eye Witness*, London: Muller, 1956.

Moorehead, Alan, *A Late Education: Episodes in a Life*, London: Hamish Hamilton, 1970.

Nevinson, H. W., *Ladysmith: The Diary of a Siege*, London: Methuen, 1900.

Oberdorfer, Don, *Tet*, New York: Doubleday, 1971.

Orwell, George, *Homage to Catalonia*, London: Secker & Warburg, 1938.

Repington, Charles à Court, *The War in The East*, London: Constable, 1905; *Vestigia*, London: Constable, 1919; *The First World War*, vols I and II, London: Constable, 1921.

Report of the Committee on the Future of Broadcasting (The Annan Report), Cmnd 6753, 1977.

Russell, William Howard, *The British Expedition to the Crimea*, London: Routledge, 1877; *My Diary North and South*, vols I and II, London: Bradbury, 1863; *The Great War With Russia*, London: Routledge, 1895.

Steevens, G. W., *With Kitchener to Khartoum*, Edinburgh and London: William Blackwood, 1898; *From Cape Town to Ladysmith*, Edinburgh and London, William Blackwood, 1900.

Swinton, Ernest D., *Eyewitness*, London: Hodder & Stoughton, 1932.

Terraine, John, *Images of War, 1914 and 1918*, London: Hutchinson, 1970.

Thompson, George P., *Blue Pencil Admiral*, London: Sampson, Low and Marston, 1947.

Thompson, Reginald, *Cry Korea*, London: Macdonald, 1951.

Wallace, Edgar, *Unofficial Dispatches*, London: Hutchinson, 1901.

Williams, David, *Not in the Public Interest: The Problem of Security in Democracy*, London: Hutchinson, 1965.

Wilmot, Chester, *Tobruk, 1941*, Sydney: Angus & Robertson, 1945; *The Struggle for Europe*, London: Collins, 1952.

Index

Aberdeen, Lord, 28
Acheson, Dean, 225
Adams, Valerie, 282
  The Media and the Falklands, 282
Adenkunle, Col. Benjamin, 270–71, 272
Aird, Malcolm, 245
Alexander, Gen. Sir Harold, 37
Amalgamated Press, 135
American Broadcasting Corporation (ABC), 262
American Civil War, 33, 35–6
Amery, Leo, 84
  Times History of the War in South Africa, 84
Annan Report 1977, 274
Apocalypse Now, 264
Archer, Neil, 262
Arlen, Michael J., 265
Army Public Relations Service, 275
Ashanti War, 34
Asquith, Lord, 122, 129–30, 133
Associated Press, 259
Astor, William Waldorf, 48
Athens – Sparta War 5BC, 9
Atkins, J. B., 86
Atkinson, Tindal, 140
Attlee, Clement, 150, 169
Austin, Alfred, 34
Australian Broadcasting Commission (ABC), 183, 190, 199, 200, 206
Austro-Italian War, 34
Azrak, Osman, 62

Baden-Powell, Lord, 85, 87–9
Baird, Gen. Sir David, 17
Baker, Mark, 267
  Nam, 267
Baring, Sir Evelyn, 40
Barnett, Correlli, 179
Beach Report, 286
Beaverbrook, Lord, 136, 228

Bell, Julian, 148
Bennett, Arnold, 135
Bennett, Ernest, 43, 45, 51
Bennett, Winifred, 127
Berkeley, Stanley, 14
Biograph Company of London, 84
Birkenhead, Lord, see also Smith, F. E.
Black and White, 84
Blackwater River, Battle of, 11
Blackwood, William, 51, 72
Blamey, Gen. Sir Thomas, 189–90, 197–200, 206
Blum, Leon, 157–61, 171
Boer War of 1880, 33, 37, 75, 77, 78, 85, 165
  Majuba Hill, Battle of, 33, 78–9, 85
Boer War, Great, 91–105, 165
  Black Week, 75, 92
  Colenso, Battle of, 75
  Jameson Raid, 34, 79–80
  Kimberley, Siege of, 85–6, 92
  Ladysmith, Siege of, 75–6, 77, 85, 89, 92
  Mafeking, Siege of, 85, 87–9, 92
  Magersfontein, Battle of, 75
  Stormberg, Battle of, 75
  Vereeniging, 101–3
  Vlakfontein, Battle of, 96, 97, 100, 103
Bolin, Louis, 167, 174
Bonaparte, Napoleon, 17
  Campaign along the Elbe, 17
Bonar Law, Andrew, see also Law
Boyd, Donald, 184, 187, 191, 200, 206, 210–12
Boy's Own Paper, 34
Bracken, Brendan, 176
Braestrup, Peter, 259, 262
British Army and colonial unrest, 250–51, 254–6, 273–4, 275, 286

British Broadcasting Corporation (BBC), 184, 190, 191, 200, 201, 202, 206, 208, 209, 210, 215, 226, 228, 245, 252, 253, 269, 271, 273, 277, 279, 281, 282, 285
Panorama, 281
War Report, 191, 200–203, 206, 207, 209–13
World Service, 282–3
Brodie, Brig. Thomas, 243
Brodrick, St John, 96, 99
Brooke, Gen. Sir Alan, 211
Brooke, Jocelyn, 184
Landscape near Tobruk, 184
Brooke, Rupert, 13
Peace, 13
Buchan, John, 130, 135–6
Nelson's History of the War, 136
Buckle, G. E., 46, 114
Buckley, Christopher, 214, 226, 232
Bull, Rene, 84
Buller, Gen. Sir Redvers, 81–4, 90, 113
Burleigh, Bennet, 43, 50–53, 64, 65, 75, 84, 85, 90, 95, 104, 110–12
Burrowes, John, 260, 271–3
Butler, Samuel, 13
Byam, Guy, 206
Byrhtnoth, 11

Cagnoni, Romano, 245
Caldecott, Ivy, 91
Calder, J. I., 89
Calley, Lieut. William, 264
Cameron, James, 226–49
Attitude to war, 226–7, 229, 235–6, 244–5
Cameron's Country (BBC 2), 245–6
Childhood, 228–9
Early journalistic career, 229
Exposure of atrocities, 238–40, 245
Korean War coverage, 230–49
Point of Departure, 227, 239
Vietnam War coverage, 245, 249
Witness (1966), 245
Cameron, Sir D. Y., 135
The Battlefield of Ypres, 135
Campbell, Gen. Sir Colin, 25
Capa, Robert, 14–15
Cape Times, The, 91
Carson, Sir Edward, 129

Castle, Ted, 241, 246
Caudwell, Christopher, 148
Illusion and Reality (1937), 148
Cecil, Lawrence H., 183
Censorship, 19, 50, 85–7, 90, 95–7, 101–5, 114–28, 139–40, 143, 158, 167, 195, 196, 214, 228, 241, 244, 246, 258, 259, 261, 264, 276, 279, 280, 284
Central News Agency, 97
Cesarewitch, 81, 84
Chamberlain, Joseph, 80
Chenery, Thomas, 23, 27, 29
Chicago Times & Herald, 82
Chinese Civil War, 224
Churchill, Randolph, 188
Churchill, Winston, 44, 45–6, 51, 82–3, 129, 165, 180, 188, 190
London to Ladysmith via Pretoria, 82
The River War, 46
Clarke, Basil, 135
Clifford, Alexander, 182, 188, 214
Coalition Cabinet of 1915, 129–30
Cockburn, Claud, 145–77
Childhood and education, 152
Crossing the Line, 160
Early journalistic career, 152–3
Reporter in Spain, 155
Spanish Civil War coverage, 149–72
Tetuan Incident, 158–64, 168, 171–2, 176
The Week, 149, 152–3, 156, 157, 168–70, 172
use of propaganda, 158–64, 171–2, 177
Cockburn, Lord, 152
Cockburn, Patricia, 155, 168
Cohen, Harry Freeman, 103, 105
Cold War, 257
Coleridge, Samuel, 17
Collinson, Col., 52
Comintern, 156, 169, 173
Commons, House of, 75, 97, 104, 118, 129, 156, 255, 280
Defence Committee report, *Handling of the Press and Public Information during the Falklands Conflict 1982*, 280
Communism, 146, 162, 173, 217, 223, 255

expansion of, 224–5, 257
US fear of, 224–5, 228, 257
Communist Party of Great Britain, 146, 147–8, 155, 162, 168, 169, 172
Conan Doyle, Arthur, 34, 90, 141
The Great Boer War, 90
Connaught, Duke of, 131
Conscription and conscripts, 145, 251–2, 256
Conservative Party, 48
Contemporary Review, 75
Cook, Thomas & Sons, 43
Cornford, John, 147
Full Moon at Tierz Before the Storming of Huesca, 147
Corrant out of Italy, Germany &c, 15
Corunna, Battle of, 17
Crane, Stephen, 35
The Red Badge of Courage, 35
Creedy, Herbert, 121
Crimean War, 1854–1856, 19–33, 115
Balaclava, Battle of, 24
Inkerman, Battle of, 24, 25
River Alma, Battle of, 23, 27
Sebastopol, Siege and Fall, 20, 23–4, 25–6, 28
Cromer, Lord, see also Baring, Sir Evelyn
Cross, Henry, 43, 70
Crossman, Richard, 161–2, 165
Crowe, J. A., 23
Curtin, John, 190
Curzon, Lord, 100
Cutforth, Rene, 226, 228
Cyprus, guerrilla war, 254

Daily Chronicle, 76, 85, 89, 93, 121
Daily Express, 135, 150, 154, 182, 228, 229, 252
Daily Mail, 33, 47–50, 55, 57–9, 69, 72–7, 84, 86, 89–92, 94–7, 100, 103–7, 116, 131, 135, 150, 174, 226, 252
Daily Mail,
With the Flag to Pretoria, 84
Daily Mirror, 150, 241, 252, 255, 260
Daily News, 43, 91
Daily Sketch, 150
Daily Telegraph, 21, 32, 43, 80, 84,

104, 143, 145, 150, 188, 226, 227, 242, 252, 260, 278
Daily Worker, 149, 156, 168–72, 174, 176, 226, 241–2, 247
Daniel, Samuel, 12
The Civil Wars between the two houses of York and Lancaster, 12
Davidson, Michael, 226
Davis, Richard Harding, 34, 84, 93
Dawson, Geoffrey, 128, 139
Delane, Thadeus, 20–23, 26, 27, 32
Delmer, Sefton, 154
Desert War, see also Second World War, North African Campaign
Diamond Field Advertiser, 85
Dictionary of National Biography, 113
Dimbleby, Richard, 206
Dinwiddie, William, 81
Disraeli, Sir Benjamin, 40, 41
Dixon, Brig. Gen. H. G., 96, 97
Dönitz, Admiral, 210
Donne, John, 13
Donnelly, Charles, 148
Dreiser, Theodore, 148

Eastern Question, 29
Editor/Proprietor
relationships, 240, 241, 246–9
Edmonds, Col. J. E., 121
The Official History of the Military Operations in France and Flanders, 121
Edmundson, Cpl. J. H., 192
Edward VII, King, 102
Ehrenburg, Ilya, 163
Eisenhower, Gen. Dwight D., 185, 186, 201, 208, 215
Esquire, 257
Evening Times, 106
Ewart, Col. Joe, 213

Falklands Islands Campaign 1982, 15, 59, 275–87
Belgrano Incident, 281
Bluff Cove landings, 279
Goose Green, taking of, 282–3, 285
M.O.D. relations with media, 276, 278–84, 286
Port Stanley, battle for, 276, 278, 283
San Carlos landings, 285

Fascism, 146–7, 148, 164, 169, 175, 229
Ferguson, J. D., 135
   A Damaged Destroyer, 135
First World War, 13, 14, 30, 39, 109–44, 145, 149, 163, 165, 167, 182, 185, 197
   Aubers Ridge, Battle of, 126–30, 133
   British Expeditionary Force, 116, 120, 123, 124, 139
   Cambrai, Battle of, 139
   Eastern Front, 138
   Festubert, Battle of, 126, 133
   Gallipoli, Campaign, 129–30
   Marne, Battle of the, 123
   Mons, Retreat from, 124
   Neuve Chapelle, Battle of, 126
   Palestine Campaigns, 138
   Passchendaele, Battle of, 136, 139
   Somme, Battle of the, 136, 138
   supply problems, 124–32, 137–41
   Western Front, 123, 131, 135, 185, 220
Fischer, Louis, 163
Fisher, Admiral, 129
Fisk, Robert, 268, 274
Fitzgerald, Brinsley, 127
Foch, Marshal, 117, 139
Forbes, Archibald, 35–7, 277
   The Soldier's Pocket Book, 36
Fox, Ralph, 148
Fox, Robert, 285
Franco-Prussian War, 34, 35
Franco, Gen. Francisco, 149, 159–61, 164, 167, 168, 172, 173, 175
Friedland, Battle of, 17
French, Field Marshal Sir John, 113, 121, 123–4, 126–9, 131–2
Friend, The, 90
Fuller, Gen. J. F. C., 145

Galtieri, Gen. Leopardo, 275
Gatacre, Gen., 59, 61
Gibbs, Philip, 121, 134, 135, 137
Gillard, Frank, 206
Gilliam, Laurence, 215
Gladstone, William Ewart, 41, 78
Gordon, Gen. Charles, 41–2, 70–72
Gordon, Maj. W. S., 61
Gort, Field Marshal Viscount, 205

Gowon, Gen. Yakubu, 268–9
Graphic, The, 76
Greenwood, Frederick, 48
Grey, Lord, 122
Grivas, Gen., 254
Guest, Capt. Frederick, 127
Guneison, Charles Lewis, 19–20
Gurney, Sir Henry, 255
Gwynne, H. A., 139, 140

Haig, Field Marshal Earl Douglas, 45, 131, 132, 133, 135, 138–41, 286
Hamilton, Angus, 85, 88
Hamilton, Nigel, 213
Hanrahan, Brian, 279, 284
Hardy, Bert, 226–7, 238
Harmsworth, Alfred, 48–9, 55–6, 58, 77, 96, 104–8, 116, 120, 123, 127–32
Harper's, 81
Harris, Robert, 276, 277
   Gotcha! The Media, The Government and the Falklands Crisis (1982), 276
Hart, Basil Liddell, 145
Hassan, Caliph Mulay, 159
Hastings, Macdonald, 247
Hastings, Max, 277, 278, 284
Hawkins, Desmond, 191, 201
Hazlitt, William, 17
Heads of Several Proceedings In This Present Parliament, 15
Hemingway, Ernest, 154–5, 170
Henderson, Hamish, 184
   End of a Campaign, 184
Hendrix, Jimi, 264
Henley, W. E., 48–9
Henty, G. A., 13, 34
Her Majesty's Stationery Office (HMSO), 16
Herbert, Sidney, 26
Heren, Louis, 242
Herodotus, 9
Herr, Michael, 257, 258, 261, 264
Hetherington, John, 197
Himmler, Heinrich, 212
Hitler, Adolf, 146, 158, 161, 164, 169, 172, 175, 178–9, 210, 216
Homer, 9, 10
   Iliad, 9, 10

Hopkinson, Tom, 239–41, 246–8
  Of This Our Time, 248
Horrocks, Lieut. Gen. Brian, 201,
  205, 208
Howard, Hubert, 44, 50, 51, 70
Hulton, Sir Edward, 228, 240, 241,
  246–9
Hunter, Gen. Archibald, 52, 65, 72

Illustrated London News, 23, 43, 84
Imperial Defence, Committee for,
  115, 116, 120
Independent Broadcasting Authority
  (IBA), 253
Independent Radio News, 285
Independent Television News (ITN),
  262, 269, 270, 277, 278, 287
Indian Mutiny, 32, 33
  Lucknow, Siege of, 33
Inverlochy, Battle of, 11–12
Irish Republican Army (IRA),
  274–5
Irish Times, 172
Izvestia, 163

Jackson, Lieut. Col. Graham, 214
Jameson, Starr, 79–80
Johnson, Lyndon B., 266
Jones, Lieut. Col. H., 282
Joubert, Gen, 82
*Journal of the Royal United Services
  Institute*, 263

Katz, Otto, 156, 158–9, 160, 172, 173
Kee, Robert, 247, 281
Kekewitch, Col., 85–6
Kemp, Gen., 97
Kennington, Eric, 135
  The Kensingtons at Levantie, 135
Kinnear, Alfred, 97
Kipling, Rudyard, 13, 34, 90, 91, 135
Kitchener, Elizabeth, 18
Kitchener, Field Marshal Earl
  Horatio, 17–18, 42–8, 50–56, 59,
  60–61, 63–4, 66–75, 77, 89–92,
  95–102, 105, 113, 117–21,
  123–33, 286
Kitchener, Walter, 47
Knight, J. O., 81–2
Knightley, Phillip, 162, 168, 268
  The First Casualty, 162

Koestler, Arthur, 173–4
  Invisible Writing (1954), 174
  Spanish Testament (1937), 173
Kolstov, Mikhail, 163, 172
Korean War, 1950–1953, 220–49
Korean War, 1950–1953
  Atrocities, 228, 238–43
  Imjin River, Battle of, 225
  Inchon Landings, 225, 233–9
  Maryangsan Ridge, defence of, 226
  Parallel, 38th, 220, 244
  Point 282, 222
  Pusan Perimeter, 221, 225, 226,
    230–35, 238
  Taegu, defence of, 230, 231
  United Nations Force, 220–23,
    226, 228, 230–37, 244, 248
  United States involvement,
    220–24, 228, 231, 237
Kruger, Stephanus Johannes Paulus,
  79–80, 86

Labour Party, 155, 169, 176
Ladysmith Lyre, 76
Lamb, Charles, 17
Lamurde, Lieut. Macaulay, 269–73
Lardner, Jim, 155
Law, Andrew, Bonar, 129
League of Nations, 141
Lebanese Civil War, 267, 268
Lewis, Col., 52
Leyds, Dr., 86, 92
Life Magazine, 15
Linklater, Eric, 221
  Our Men in Korea, 221
Liverpool, Lord, 18
Lloyd, A. L., 241
Lloyd George, David, 122, 127, 129,
  132, 135, 139–41, 145
Loan, Police Director, 262
Lom, Iain, 11–12
London Gazette, 16
Lorant, Stefan, 247

MacArthur, Gen. Douglas, 194, 197,
  221, 224–8, 233–8, 244
Macdonagh, Col., 121, 123
Macdonald, Col. Hector, 52, 61–8
McDonald, Ian, 281
MacFarlane, Bill, 191
Mackell, Lieut. F. A., 192

Mafeking Mail, The, 89
Mahdi, The, (Mohammed Ibn Al-Sayd Abdullah), 41–3, 53, 55, 60–61, 70, 75
Mahmud, Emir, 53, 56
Malayan counter-insurgency wars, 254–6
Maldon, Battle of, 10
Manchester Guardian, 43, 56, 70, 86, 93, 150, 202, 252, 287
Mangada, Gen. Julio, 151, 152, 154
Marchand, Jean Baptiste, 74
Marlowe, Tom, 91, 97
Marshall, Howard, 206
Martin, Col. R. M., 68
Marxism, 148, 174
Masefield, John, 135
Massingham, H. W., 93
Matthews, Herbert, 154, 176
Maude, W. T., 76
Maurice, Gen. F. M., 141
Maxwell, Col., 52, 61
Melbourne Herald, 182
Menzies, Sir Robert, 190
Mercurius Politicus, 15, 16
Mercurius Scoticus, 16
Meredith, George, 34
Methuen, Gen., 91
Milner, Lord, 80, 99–100
Milton, John, 13
Monson, Ronald, 188
Montgomery, Field Marshal, 166, 185, 190, 201, 207–12, 217
Moore, Arthur, 118, 119
Moore, Gen. Sir John, 17
Moore, Maj. Gen. Jeremy, 284
Moorehead, Alan, 182–3, 214, 218
Morning Chronicle, 21
Morning Herald, 23
Morning Leader, 93
Morning Post, The, 19, 34, 44, 82, 114, 139, 150
Morrison, Ian, 228, 233
Morshead, Gen. Leslie, 189, 191
Muddiman, Henry, 16
Muenzenberg, Willi, 156
Muir, Maj. Kenneth, 222
Mussolini, Benito, 146, 181

Napoleon III, 29
Nash, Paul, 135

The Menin Road, 135
National Service, see also Conscription
Nazism, 164
Nedham, Marchamont, 16
Neilly, Emerson, 84, 85, 88–9
Besieged with B. P.: A Full and Complete Record of the Siege, 88
Nevinson, C. R., 135
Harvest of Battle, 135
Nevinson, H. W., 76, 85
New Imperialism, 48–9, 73, 80
New Statesman, 172
New York Herald, 154
New York Times, 154
New York World, 35, 84
Newbolt, Sir Henry, 13
Vitae Lampada, 13
News Chronicle, 150, 162, 173, 226, 245
News of the World, 252
Newspaper Proprietors Association, 115, 121
Newsweek, 260
Nicholas I, Tsar, 27
Nicholson, Michael, 269, 270, 279, 284
Nigerian Civil War, 1967–1970, 268–73
Nightingale, Florence, 27, 29
Non-Intervention Agreement of 1936, 161, 163
North American Newspaper Alliance, 154
North Atlantic Treaty Organisation (NATO) Alliance, 251
Northcliffe, Lord, see also Harmsworth, Alfred
Northern Ireland, Civil Unrest, 250–51, 273, 274–5, 286

Observer, 150, 217, 218, 226, 252, 253
O'Connor, Gen. Sir Richard, 181, 188
Official Secrets Act, 280
Orpern, Sir William, 135
Changing Billets: Picardy, 135
Orwell, George, 151, 155, 166, 174
Otway, Lieut. Col. Terence, 205
Oxford Gazette, 16

Page, Walter, 122
Palestine Liberation Organisation (PLO), 268
Pall Mall Gazette, 48, 84
Palmerston, Lord, 20, 28
Pan-Islamic Revolt, 41
Paris, Treaty of, 29
Parks, David, 256
Parslow, E. G., 89
Pathé Pictorial, 253
Pearson's War News, 84
Peiwar Kotal, Battle of, 81
Percival, Jack, 226
Percy, Capt. Lord, 121
Pétain, Marshal, 139–40
Phillips, Percival, 135
Picture Post, 226, 228, 232, 237, 239–41, 245–9
Pilger, John, 260
Pitcairn, Frank, see also Cockburn, Claud
Plumer, Gen. Sir Hubert, 124
Pollit, Harry, 169
Pope, Alexander, 9–10
Pravda, 163
Press Freedom, 110, 114–15, 133
Price, Ward, 226
Prior, Melton, 84, 110
Pritchard, Lieut., 64
Private Eye, 172
Propaganda, 158–9, 167, 194, 255, 269–75, 283
Public Opinion, 241
Publick Intelligencer, 15
Punch, 81, 172

Radio News Reel, 210
Raglan, Lord, 23, 25, 27, 28
Ralph, Julian, 92
Rand Daily Mail, 106
Reade, Winwood, 35
 The Martyrdom of Man, 35
Red Cross Organisation, 29, 84, 238
Reith, Lord, 252
Repington, Charles à Court, 109–44
 After the War, 113
 Army career, 113
 Battle of the Shells, 125–33
 Childhood and education, 113
 Early journalistic career, 114
 First World War coverage, 117–42

 Relations with Government, 139–40
 Vestigia, The First World War (Vol. I & II), 113
Reuter's News Agency, 35, 84, 87–91, 182, 260
Rhodes, Cecil, 79–80, 85–6
Rhodes, Frank, 50, 70, 85
Richards Polly, 90
Ridgeway, Gen. Matthew, 225
Roberts, Field Marshal Lord, 33, 37, 77, 86, 90, 92, 95, 117
Robertson, Field Marshal Sir William, 140
Robinson, Habbakuk, 18
Robinson, Henry Crabb, 17–20
Robinson, Perry, 135
Rommel, Gen. Erwin, 165, 181, 189
Roosevelt, Franklin, D., 179
Rowell, Lieut. Gen. Sydney, 198, 200
Royal Air Force, 178, 188, 203, 206, 207, 223
Royal Australian Air Force, 194
Royal Australian Navy, 194
Royal Navy, 178, 180, 223, 234, 276, 277, 286
Royalist and Parliamentary Civil War, 1642–1649, 15
Russell, William Howard, 20–25, 26–33, 162, 287
 The Great War with Russia, 30
Russo-German Pact, 172, 175, 176, 178
Russo-Japanese War, 1904–1905, 109–12
 Mukden, Conflict at, 111
 Tsushima Straits, Battle of, 110
Rust, William, 169
 Britons in Spain (1939), 170

Salisbury, Lord, 42
Sassoon, Siegfried, 13
 Memoirs of an Infantry Officer, 13
Scobell, Gen., 113
Scudamore, Frank, 43, 50
Second World War, 15, 37, 165, 172, 175, 176, 178–219, 222, 229, 233, 235, 250–53
 Britain, Battle of, 165, 179
 British Expeditionary Force for Europe, 178

Coral Sea, Battle of, 194
D-Day and European Liberation, 200–213, 215
Dunkirk, retreat from, 182
Eastern Front, 179
Far Eastern campaign, 179, 193–9, 234
France, fall of, 178–9, 181, 182
Kokoda operations, 198
Lend-Lease Agreements, 179
Middle Eastern campaign, 180, 197
Midway, Battle of, 194
'Monty's Double', 166, 177
North African campaigns, 179, 181, 184–93
Pearl Harbor attack, 179, 190
Philippines, defeat of, 194
Poland, fall of, 178
Port Moresby, defence of, 193–8
'The Man who never was', 166, 177
Tobruk, Battle for, 181, 189–93
Sherman, Gen. William, 36
Simpson, Sir James, 28
Smith, F. E., 115, 118, 119, 120, 129
Smith-Dorrien, Gen. Sir Horace, 124
Spanish Civil War, 145–76, 247
Alcazar, siege of, 163
Anarchists, 173
Ebro, Battle of, 155
Guernica, bombing of, 174
International Brigades, 146, 155, 168
Nationalist cause, 147–50, 158, 159, 161, 167, 168, 171, 172, 176
Popular Front, 146, 149, 161–4, 168, 170
Press attitudes to, 150, 173, 175
Republican cause, 146–64, 168–71, 173–6
Stanley, Venetia, 122
Star, The, 93
Stead, W. T., 93–4
Shall I Kill My Brother Boer?, 94
Steevens, George Warrington, 40–77, 85, 89
Boer War coverage, 75–6
Childhood and education, 48
Early journalistic career, 48–9
First foreign assignment, 49–50

Re-conquest of Sudan coverage, 50–75
With Kitchener in Khartoum, 72
Stint, Vere, 84, 85
Strangways, Gen., 25
Sudan, Re-conquest of, 40–74, 113, 275
Atbara, Battle of, 53–6, 59
Khartoum, recapture of, 59, 60, 70, 72
Omdurman, Battle of, 33, 46, 51, 52, 60–70, 73, 75, 81, 82, 286
Suez Canal, 40, 180–81, 251, 254
Swinton, Col. Ernest, 119–21, 134, 182

Television, 252, 256, 261–75
Tennyson, Alfred Lord, 13, 25
Charge of the Light Brigade, 13
Thompson, Brig. Julian, 284
Thucydides, 9
Time, 260
Times, The, 17–23, 26, 27, 32, 34, 44–6, 50, 51, 70, 84–8, 112–15, 117, 118, 119–120, 123, 125, 130, 135, 138, 139, 141, 143, 150, 152, 174, 223, 228, 233, 241, 242, 243, 248, 252, 268, 273
Tindall, David, 271
Tinker, Lieut. David, 285
Tomalin, Nicholas, 260

United Nations, 177, 220–21, 222–5, 226, 232–4, 236–41, 242–3, 247, 248–9
United Press International, 259
United Services Magazine, 115

del Vayo, Alverez, 153
Victoria, Queen, 41, 75
Diamond Jubilee, 50, 57
Vidali, Vittorio, 154
Vietnam War, 245, 249, 250, 256, 267, 287
Vietnam War
Boat people, 267
Free World Military Assistance Force, 258
JUSPAO, 258, 261, 266
My Lai massacre, 264, 267
Tet offensive, 256, 259, 265, 266

Tram Bang incident, 259
U.S. involvement, 256–67
Veterans, 267
Villiers, Frederick, 35, 43, 50, 53, 84

Wain, Christopher, 263, 264
Walker, Gen. Walton H., 230, 231
Wallace, Edgar, 77, 89–108
  Army service, 91
  Boer War coverage, 91–105
  Career as an editor, 105–6
  Career as a journalist, 91–108
  Career as a novelist, 106–8
  Childhood, 90
  King Kong (film script), 106
  Relations with military, 95, 96–8,
    105
  Sanders of the River, 106
  The Four Just Men, 106
Walter, John, 17
War correspondents, 17, 214, 215,
  252, 260, 261, 287
  Effects of reports, 25, 26–30, 73,
    131, 136–8, 206, 213, 240, 244,
    249, 256, 261–8, 282–5, 287
  Relations with the military, 28–9,
    30–31, 36–8, 44–6, 53, 83–5, 95,
    119–20, 123, 131–4, 137–8, 167,
    185, 186, 195, 197–203, 208,
    227–8, 237, 238, 244, 258, 261,
    265–6, 274–87
  see also individual correspondents
War Office, 59, 68, 96, 105, 115–16,
  120, 121, 123, 125, 131, 138,
  140, 185, 200
War Press Bureau, 115–18, 121, 182
Ward, Ian, 260
Warwick Trading Company, 84
Washington Post, 259
Wauchope, Gen., 66
Waugh, Evelyn, 152
Wavell, Field Marshal Earl, 181
Wayne, John, 264
  The Sands of Iwo Jima, 264

Week, The, 149, 152, 153, 156, 157,
  168–70
Weekly News, 229
Wellesley, Sir Arthur, 18
Westminster Gazette, 43, 94, 114
White, Gen. Sir George, 80, 85
White, Osmar, 195
Wilhelm II, Kaiser, 114
Wilkinson, Elizabeth, 169
Williams, Capt. Butler, 243
Wilmot, Chester, 180–219
  Early career in broadcasting, 183
  Education, 183
  European Liberation coverage,
    200, 204–15
  Far East assignment, 196–9
  Middle East assignment, 183
  Military career, 183
  North African assignment, 184,
    187–93
  Relations with the military, 185–8,
    194, 196–211, 213
  Sons of the Anzacs (Film), 199
  The Struggle for Europe, 180, 207–8,
    215–17
  Tobruk, 199, 208
Wingate, Maj. Reginald, 46, 50, 61,
  70, 113
Winnington, Alan, 226
Wintringham, Tom, 169, 247
Wolseley, Gen. Sir Garnet, 34, 36–7
Wood, Field Marshal Sir Evelyn, 29
Woods, Nicholas, 23
Woodward, David, 202, 205
Wordsworth, William, 17

Yakub, 64–6
Yeates, V. M., 13
  Winged Victory, 13
Yom Kippur War, 267
York, Archbishop of, 244
Young, Filson, 86
Younger, Kenneth, 239

Zulu, War of 1879, 32